# Two Views of Virtue

**Recent Titles in**
**Contributions in Philosophy**

Asian and Jungian Views of Ethics
*Carl B. Becker, editor*

Platonic Errors: Plato, a Kind of Poet
*Gene Fendt and David Rozema*

The Last Choice: Preemptive Suicide in Advanced Age, Second Edition
*C. G. Prado*

Self-Construction and the Formation of Human Values: Truth, Language, and Desire
*Teodros Kiros*

Diogenes of Sinope: The Man in the Tub
*Luis E. Navia*

Simone de Beauvoir Writing the Self: Philosophy Becomes Autobiography
*Jo-Ann Pilardi*

Stalking Nietzsche
*Raymond Angelo Belliotti*

The Transient and the Absolute: An Interpretation of the Human Condition and of Human Endeavor
*Mordecai Roshwald*

The Adventure of Philosophy
*Luis E. Navia*

Intentionalist Interpretation: A Philosophical Explanation and Defense
*William Irwin*

Natural Law Ethics
*Philip E. Devine*

Anglo-American Idealism, 1865–1927
*W. J. Mander, editor*

# TWO VIEWS OF VIRTUE

## ABSOLUTE RELATIVISM AND RELATIVE ABSOLUTISM

*F. F. Centore*

Contributions in Philosophy, Number 76

Greenwood Press
Westport, Connecticut • London

**Library of Congress Cataloging-in-Publication Data**

Centore, F. F., 1938–
Two views of virtue : absolute relativism and relative absolutism / F. F. Centore.
p. cm.—(Contributions in philosophy, ISSN 0084–926X ; no. 76)
Includes bibliographical references (p. ) and index.
ISBN 0–313–31412–8 (alk. paper)
1. Ethical absolutism. 2. Ethical relativism. 3. Religious ethics. 4. Virtue.
I. Title. II. Series.
BJ1031.C46 2000
171—dc21 99–056461

British Library Cataloguing in Publication Data is available.



Library of Congress Catalog Card Number: 99–056461
ISBN: 0–313–31412–8
ISSN: 0084–926X

First published in 2000

Greenwood Press, 88 Post Road West, Westport, CT 06881
An imprint of Greenwood Publishing Group, Inc.
www.greenwood.com

Printed in the United States of America

The paper used in this book complies with the Permanent Paper Standard issued by the National Information Standards Organization (Z39.48–1984).

10 9 8 7 6 5 4 3 2 1

**To my wife, Helen Angela,**
**and our children, Helen, Paul Matthew, and Laura**

It is always simple to fall; there are an infinity of angles at which one falls, only one at which one stands.

—G. K. Chesterton, *Orthodoxy*, p. 186.

In the first place, philosophers are free to lay down their own sets of principles, but once this is done, they no longer think as they wish—they think as they can. In the second place, . . . any attempt on the part of a philosopher to shun the consequences of his own position is doomed to failure.

—E. Gilson, *The Unity of Philosophical Experience*, pp. 301–302.

# Contents

# Preface

Many things are not what they appear to be at first glance. We know that there is no lead in lead pencils, that abbreviation is a long word while long is a short word, that motion pictures do not move, that the people of the frozen north invented sunglasses while those of the sunny south did not, and that heavy cream weighs less than light cream. Now we will see that, of the four theories of ethics under discussion, all claiming to be humanistic and two claiming to be more moderate than the first and fourth theories, only one out of the four really is both humanistic and moderate.

Another way of discussing this topic is to cast it in the language of human virtue. Questions about virtue fall within the area of ethics or practical knowledge, that is, knowledge aimed at action and doing. Consequently, this study is about being practical, not in the sense of building a better mousetrap or a taller building, but in the really fundamental sense of leading a good life in a good society. In philosophy, making good decisions is called being prudent, and what constitutes prudence depends upon your model of morality.[1]

In this book I am concerned with morals rather than manners. I am not concerned with matters of etiquette and protocol that lie between what is morally right and morally wrong, such as tactlessly wearing an old T-shirt to a performance at the Royal Opera House in London, or with acts that are normally morally neutral, such as buttering your bread on one side rather than on the other. Moreover, my emphasis is on the central idea of each of the different positions and not on the minute variations and disagreements that are sure to occur within each paradigm.

On the level of basic moral models, we can discern at least four possible ethical prototypes: Absolute Relativism One, Two, and Three, and Relative Absolutism. The first theory spells nihilism. Theories two and three are attempts to escape this nihilism. Theory two is the first variation on theory one, and theory three is the second variation. However, the escape mechanisms do not work. In other words, theories two and three reduce to theory one.

According to Absolute Relativism One, virtue hangs on the will of the individual, and would include anyone who substitutes his will for an intellect incapable of knowing reality. In the case of Immanuel Kant, for instance, his claim to having an absolutely universal moral principle is a charade. Kant locks himself in a room, places the key in his pocket, and then claims to be bound by a moral imperative. In fact, all he is really bound by is his own will, something he can change at any time.

All four theories agree that it is impossible to live without meaning in life. The debate is not over the existence of meaning, but the source of the meaning. Where does our purpose in life come from? The issue is not the lack of something claimed to be true and good, but its content. In the first theory the solitary will is the measure of what is good. You set your own goals and generate your own moral criteria, inventing your own definitions of everything, whether it is a fair wage, justifiable homicide, or marriage. You need not, unless you feel like it, take into account the views of your government or religion. This is often referred to as the "liberal" position in moral matters because it allows you to do anything you feel like doing. Ultimately, the first paradigm must maintain that all moral choices are on a par; any lifestyle is as good as any other. The only important issue is whether it works *for you*.

Being a Mother Teresa of Calcutta is on a par with being a Simone de Beauvoir of Paris or a Demi Moore of Hollywood. Being the comic book artist Andy Warhol is on a par with being a Mahatma Gandhi. The only real immorality is thinking that something is immoral independently of your will. If your deeds are illegal, you run the risk of being punished, but that is a chance you may have to take in order to be your own person. Under certain circumstances, being a dissenter can be dangerous. Consequently, for those committed to Absolute Relativism One, it pays to live in a country where as little as possible is illegal.

Whether or not you contribute money to the poor, blow up a government building, or force yourself sexually on your neighbor is your own business. If you are a member of a jury you can vote any way you feel like, ignoring both the evidence and the law. Not harming others is itself a rule that you may or may not freely follow. You can accept the Golden Rule because you will it, or you can reject it. Moreover, if you do accept it, you can do so cafeteria style. You can be selective with respect to those whom you choose to harm or help.

In April 1999, for instance, two suicidal teenagers thought for themselves and did their own thing in Littleton, Colorado. Nobody was going to gain power over them by making them feel guilty or ashamed about killing off some selected classmates. Subjugation was the dirtiest word in their vocabulary. Celebrating some diversity is fine. Clearly, though, moral diversity can be deadly. Nonetheless, many today continue to tout moral diversity for its own sake as the greatest thing since shoelaces.

The fact that you may freely choose not to exercise your absolute right to think and do whatever you please does not change in the least the paradigm's theoretical status. Having a hunting license does not mean that you must be shooting deer all the time. Even though you may choose not to hit your mother over the head with an axe, someone else may do so to his mother—or to yours. Your choices are in no way binding on anyone else. This is an extreme view in the sense that all moral precepts are entirely inner-directed; no outside authority can tell you how to think and act.

Not surprisingly, this view is endorsed by the megamedia moguls and Hollywood types. How could it be any other way? If they were to adopt a responsible approach to the content of their programming the first act they would have to clean up would be their own. If the industry leaders were to endorse, for instance, the fourth view, they would have to drastically alter most of their shows. This would then lead, they think, to a great reduction in profits, and so the mere suggestion that they give up their Absolute Relativism One bias is rejected with ridicule.

As you might anticipate, the second model sees the first model as too antisocial. From the viewpoint of the second paradigm, the first one is merely a way of making mistakes without ever having to pay for them, justified by asserting that there is no such thing as a mistake in the first place. This is a sure prescription for social destruction. As a consequence, we must seek out some objective standard of virtue, which is the society of which the person is a part. Objectivity is thus redefined as intersubjectivity. The second view, therefore, calls upon the will of the populace to tell everyone what is right and good. In effect this means that the representatives of the people rule, and that our highest virtue is civic virtue.

This is also an extreme position because now virtue is entirely outer-directed. We are told what is right and good by a small group of lawmakers and judges. Nevertheless, it is a widely accepted view, especially, as one might expect, among politicians. What is moral is decided by the state, and, as a loyal citizen, you must live by the laws of the land. Legally speaking, under group-think there is prosecution, never persecution. By definition, whatever the group decides is just *is* just and thus no one is ever persecuted.

Group-think, however, is just as arbitrary as individual-think. Can 90 percent of the people vote to make slaves of the remainder? Is a large lynch mob always right and the lone victim always wrong? Is it right for a majority of workers in a factory to coerce the minority into paying union dues under threat of being fired? Can racism, or hate literature (in the form of pornography, for instance), coexist with law and order? Can the state declare Jews to be nonpersons or one male to be the spouse of another male? In general, can one part of the population get away with mugging another part of the population?

Easily, because in the second theory all legal decisions are arbitrary. This is no surprise. In fact it is exactly what you would expect when democracy is misdefined as collective impulse, majority rule, and elected representatives. If the only rights you possess are those conferred upon you by explicit legislation, the state can do whatever it wants with you. If your basic human rights do not pre-exist the man-made laws, there are no inalienable rights. Can we say, in the second view, that the state cannot legislate morality because man-made law must conform to what is morally right? No, because in group-think there is no independently existing basis for inalienable rights.

Another way of understanding the second view is to see it as a state religion. Instead of scripture coming first, followed by civil law, in the case of a secular theocracy civil law comes first, followed by the state religion. Community means unity, and the most fundamental kind of unity is religious unity. Speaking practically, asking what good is religion to society is like asking what good is the mortar between the bricks in a building. So important is the role of religion that, when social divisions deepen, the state itself creates secular sacred dogmas. What usually happens, first of all, is that the state preaches that all lifestyles are of equal value. In time this becomes a dogma of faith that must be adhered to by all loyal citizens.

In the second place, since the dogma of infinite indifference leads to social chaos, the chaos must then be offset by civil laws dictating what is right. In such a system, whatever the civil lawmakers and judges decide is right and just automatically is right and just. If, for instance, you are in business and someone holding moral views approved by the state but obnoxious to you comes to you demanding service, you must suppress your moral convictions and oblige. Toleration is not good enough. The state demands that you accept its views as good and wholesome. We then have what amounts to a secular theocracy, a national state religion superseding all other religions. Very conveniently, then, whether it is cutting off the hand of a thief or the condemnation of a whole subsection of society, as in legalized abortion, the state can do no wrong. This, though, is obviously a dictatorship, and thus whatever advantage is obtained by rejecting the first view is canceled out by adopting the second view.

Being dissatisfied with the group-think approach, the third model proposes that virtue be established on the basis of our interpretation of the will of a supreme being. Both the individual and the group must be bound by something that supersedes both of them. This could be a theocracy, but it could also be a form of religious ethics that places its primary emphasis upon a godly compassion for the problems of the decisionmaker. It attempts a compromise between too much private (individual, inner-directed) power and too much public (government, church, outer-directed) power.

Along with rejecting the first two theories, the third way also rejects the fourth model. With respect to this latter divergence, rather than insisting that certain categories of acts are always and everywhere wrong, disciples of the third way judge each particular act on the basis of the overall situation at the time, the greater good of everyone concerned, and the needs of the decisionmaker in the long run. As a result of balancing one effect of an action against another effect, and after sufficiently long soul searching, you need never feel guilty or ashamed about your action. This rules out in advance any worry about being accused of using an evil means in order to achieve a good end.

Nevertheless, here too problems arise. The defenders of the third way defile their own nest by being too broad-minded. Is God a he, she, it, or they? How much leeway does God give us? On Judgment Day, will God be as sharp of tongue and severe in sentencing as Judge Judy? If there is a variety of interpretations of God's will, how are we any better off in the third camp than we were in the second? Can all religious beliefs be law at the same time? Is it possible, for instance, for a man or a woman to have multiple spouses at the same time? Too much diversity means disorder, which may then be overcome by a state dictatorship, which puts us back into the second camp.

Along with the second view, the third model is also widely accepted today, especially by those priding themselves on being both religious and democratic at the same time. Although really embodying a fake democracy, the third view, as with the second, is typified by a prochoice attitude on a wide variety of issues. As one would expect, the third model is also embraced by many social scientists and politicians because it allows them to disapprove of something in theory, often on religious grounds, while at the same time approving of exactly the same thing in practice. It is comparable to changing from a more demanding religion to a less demanding religion in order to justify one's immoral actions.

Despite its good intentions, the third view does not balance the inner- and outer-directed extremes. Because it does not provide objective precepts of right and wrong, it is useless. Judging an act by its consequences is comparable to a bank of the future with unlimited funds, money enough to pay off any moral debt, no matter how large. In the long run, on the basis of the greater good, any act can be justified. It could be argued, for instance, that the Holocaust was good for the Jews in the long run, thus leading to the conclusion that Hitler is a Jewish war hero.

Figuratively speaking, the third theory grants everyone the right to print his own money. Although this may appear compassionate, in fact it is a very cruel trick to play on people. In opposition to what it thinks of as a harsh morality, namely, one that insists that certain acts, such as sex outside of marriage, are always and everywhere wrong, the third view wants something more flexible. Yet, giving everyone the right to pick and choose what is or is not pleasing to God, which is comparable to granting individuals the right to print money, is a sure prescription for social, political, and economic poverty. Sooner or later people will realize that they are being hoodwinked into taking a sugar-coated poison pill, that instead of getting an egg to relieve their hunger they are being handed a poisonous spider. The result is a move to the fourth theory.

The fourth view remedies the defects of Absolute Relativism Three by supplying those seeking a viable ethics with a route that does away with promiscuity while simultaneously contributing warmhearted compassion to each person's situation. Although not ensuring an easy life, it does, by bringing together both inner- and outer-directed ethics at the same time, allow for balancing the needs of the individual with the needs of society.

Taking an overview, one of the more interesting things about the four theories is that they really boil down to only two positions. Because all subjectivism is nihilism, the first three views stand together. In practical terms, the second and third camps end up being the same as the first. This, though, is not their intention. By and large, those in the first three camps are sincerely concerned about the health and prosperity of individuals and the human race. They worry about the welfare of the family and what is best for children. What they cannot do, though, is provide a solid foundation for such concerns.

For those inclined toward atheism, the second position is the ideal compromise between a divinely inspired ethics and an exclusively inner-directed ethics. For those inclined toward theism, the third theory represents the ideal compromise between atheism and a religion of hard sayings. In fact, however, both models fail to construct a theoretical framework capable of sustaining morality on a plane higher than that of the first theory.

This means in effect that there are really only two basic positions possible in the realm of virtue ethics, the anthropocentric (exclusively man-centered) Absolute Relativism One prototype and its opposite, the theocentric (God and man) Relative Absolutism paradigm—the first two models are openly anthropocentric, the third surreptitiously so, but only the fourth paradigm is genuinely theocentric. Expressed another way, the first three theories differ from each other only in degree; the fourth differs from all the others in kind.

The backsliding of theories two and three can be illustrated by imagining a series of Hollywood actresses, each claiming that she is a good person because she only goes as far as she wants to go. One actress uses obscene language, declaring that her doing so is just an imitation of what the individual she is portraying really does. Another does nude scenes, a third performs actual sex acts, and a fourth actually kills people on camera. Are the first three more moral than the last one? Can all four claim to be imitating reality? Whether in shock schlock or in Shakespeare, why should the foul talk and sex acts be real while the bullets and blood be fake? Come to think of it, why not make a business out of showing in public videos made by real criminals as they really rape, mutilate, kill, and chop up their victims?

In every case, stopping at one point rather than another is an arbitrary act of the will. On the nihilistic highway, every stop sign is arbitrarily placed. The fact that the first actress chooses to draw the line on the other side of talking dirty, and the latter on the other side of killing people, does not make either decision any less despotic. So also in the first three paradigms: the autonomous will is always the last word on what is virtuous.

Moreover, in comparison with the others, the fourth model is the only one capable of sustaining real inalienable rights, the basis for a real liberal democracy. Democracy as a form of government (voting, representatives) should not be confused with democracy as a way of life (inalienable rights). An inalienable right is one that does not depend for its existence upon the will either of one citizen or of all citizens taken together, and can only be found in a truly theocentric moral context.

# Acknowledgments

I want to thank all those who have helped me by their encouragement and thoughtful evaluations. This group must include Richard W. Rousseau, who acted as a prime stimulus for this work, and Crystal Dunne, who helped me with proofreading and the clarification of some parts of the work. In my primary role in life, that of a teacher, I am always learning, and, if the truth be told, writing a book is often more of an attempt to educate myself than an attempt to educate others.

# CHAPTER 1

# *Absolute Relativism One: Individual-Think Is the Measure*

> Of all things the measure is man, of the things that are, that they are, and of the things that are not, that they are not.[1]

## INTRODUCTION

### Who Is in Charge?

Whether large or small, all human societies embody some authority structure. Whether it is the minimum family unit or a whole nation, someone has to be in charge. Every college has its president, business its CEO, movie its director, nation its PM. Someone has the right to sign contracts and others do not, and so forth. Consequently, the contrast among political philosophies cannot be based on the use of authority. True enough, someone in authority may become authoritarian, meaning that power is exercised in a crude and unjust way. This, though, does not diminish the fact that in every human organization there is a distinction between leaders and followers. This does not mean that the followers are inferior as human beings; it means that there is never an equal sharing of power in practice.

Furthermore, in real life there is no contradictory opposition between human freedom and authority, either human or divine. As any traffic cop knows, only someone with the power of free choice can responsibly obey a command. We all know that a scientist who tries ordering about a missile is not going to keep her job for very long. A metallic missile can be controlled, but it cannot be ordered about. Neither can a missile be condemned or praised for its actions. In moral terms, human freedom does not mean doing whatever you please. It means that you can be justly held accountable for what you do. Freedom is about responsibility.

## Different Strokes for Different Folks

If you cast aside social structure, if you hold that each individual possesses the ultimate power to decide right and wrong, you are endorsing the Absolute Relativism One model of moral virtue. In modern times this is the extreme right-wing (do your own thing) position on the political spectrum. Although usually displayed by disagreeing with one another, someone refusing to pay taxes, the nonunion worker objecting to paying union dues, the nun ignoring the pope, the parent opposing all public school education, the high school dropout showing his or her dislike for the Feds by blowing up a government building, or the politician desiring to dissolve the United Nations, all have at least one thing in common, namely, they do not want to be bossed around.

In money matters the right-winger demands the right to make and keep as much money as possible. The taxi driver who works overtime should not have to pay a higher percentage of the extra income he or she earns than someone who does not put in the extra work. The person who invests wisely should not have to pay a higher percentage of his or her income when compared to someone who invests unwisely. Indeed, the best thing is not to have any income tax at all.

In contrast, whereas the constant theme of the extreme right wing is personal license, the constant concern of the extreme left wing (go with the flow) is ensuring control by the state. If you maintain that the power to decide right and wrong resides with a large group, or with a small group representing the large group, rather than with the single individual, then you are bivouacking with the Absolute Relativism Two camp. This view wants to see money and power concentrated in a centralized government. For the left winger, group-think holds the key to human salvation. The group decides who is a full human being with human rights, who is a spouse, what is taught in the schools, and whether or not your body parts can be harvested for use elsewhere. In effect, the state is the main teacher of morals; if it is legal or an embedded part of the culture, it is moral. When consensus is reached, all good citizens must follow the will of the people. Civic virtue is the highest possible virtue.

Nazism is an example of this. Recall that nazi is short for national socialism. Recall also that, for a short time toward the end of World War II, Hitler installed Mussolini as the ruler of the Italian Socialist Republic in northern Italy. Another example is fascism, in which the state is the supreme reality, owning all the major means of production and distribution. The most extreme left-wing position is communism, a system in which all aspects of life, including who gets what and how much, who works where and when, who associates with whom, all culture, art, literature, recreation, and real estate, are strictly controlled by the central planners. In general, even though political tyrannies are often at war with each other over which group is the supreme group, all political dictatorships are left wing.

I will now examine the extreme right-wing theory, beginning with the ancient Greeks. I will then move ahead to more modern times. The thinkers to be considered are Protagoras of Abdera (485–410 B.C.), Ralph Waldo Emerson (1803–82), Walter Whitman (1819–92), Friedrich Wilhelm Nietzsche (1844–1900), Albert Camus (1913–60), and Jean-Paul Sartre (1905–80). As you can see from the dates of the characters in this play of ideas, the modern European nihilists are actually later in time than the American ones, a case of ideas flowing in a direction opposite to that of the flow of immigrants. The exposition of Absolute Relativism One will be followed by a brief critique of it.

## GREEK NIHILISM

### Grandfather Parmenides

Most ancient philosophy is a series of footnotes to Parmenides.[2] For him, pure reason alone must decide the truth about reality, and pure reason deduces that there is in fact no change whatsoever in the world. Using the language of earlier Greek thinkers (oracles, opposites, justice, etc.), he deduces the fact that change of any kind is impossible. Thought and being are the same thing, he insists.[3] Do not be schizophrenic; you must accept as true either the appearances of the senses or the rational conclusions of pure thought. He sees this as a contradictory situation, one part of which must be accepted and the other rejected. He reasons in the following way.

What could possibly account for change? It will either come from what is (being) or from what is not (nonbeing). These two alternatives exhaust all possibilities. If we consider being, we see that change is impossible. It is crystal clear that something cannot become what it already is. It makes no sense, for example, to tell someone who is already sitting down to sit down. If someone is seated and someone else is standing, there is a difference between them, but the difference is not shared. Hence the question, if differences keep things apart, what keeps them together? It must be something common to them. But it is also crystal clear that things do not differ by what is common to them. Now, what is it that is common to everything that exists? Being. Hence, since the world already IS, it cannot become anything at all. Thus, reason tells us that there is absolutely no change.

The only way change can occur is if there were nonbeing, thus allowing something to become what it is not by entering upon nothingness. But this is impossible, says Parmenides. Not only is nonbeing nonexistent, it is so repugnant to reason that we cannot even think it. Not only can it not exist outside the mind, it cannot exist even inside the mind. Nonbeing, therefore, can neither produce anything nor account for anything. Hence, on the basis of either being or nonbeing, there can be no change.

Expressed otherwise, there cannot be any explanation for change within being. Any explanation must come from outside of being. But there is nothing outside of being. As a result, all of reality is only one unchanging being, which we can call God. This is thus a pantheistic (all-goddism) doctrine. Later thinkers, such as Georg Hegel (1770–1831), accepted nonbeing and changed Parmenides' unchanging being into a constant becoming, so that the only reality is constant change.

### Man Is the Measure

Among the Greeks, everyone tried to circumvent Parmenides' dilemma. The atomists, for instance, asserted the existence of that which is not, the void, nonbeing, empty space. The one being was transmuted into the countless little beings (atoms) moving about in the void. Each tiny being possessed the same properties (unchanging, no internal differences, unsensed, etc.) of the one being.[4] Because of its irrationality (claiming that what is not, is), this solution was not accepted by the more thoughtful Greeks. Some other thinkers gave up completely and decided to take the situation as it was. If everything we experience by means of the senses is a deception, then we must learn to live with it. Parmenides' One Reality may have its ways, but man must have his. So said the Greek sophists such as Protagoras of Abdera and Gorgias of Leontini (483–376 B.C.).[5]

Protagoras, for example, sees that Parmenides' doctrine has unavoidable moral consequences. If nonbeing is needed to account for change in the world, it is also needed to account for falsehood in human speech. A false statement says what is not. If, when it's raining, I say the sun is shining, I am invoking the nothing. But this is impossible. It follows that it is impossible to make a false statement. In reality there is no difference between the true and the false, and so the truth can be anything I want it to be. Hence, all individual perspectives are on a par. There is no way to tell the difference between just and unjust police action, proper and improper business practices, decency and pornography, legitimate sex and rape or incest, and so forth. Everything is only a matter of private taste and opinion. Each individual, therefore, becomes the measure of what is virtuous and not virtuous.[6]

This doctrine is not something lost in the distant past. It can crop up anytime and anywhere. It has in fact shown up in more modern times as the identification of nature and man with God (pantheism, everything is divine), or as associated with the desire for absolute freedom, rather than with the failure to solve the problem of change in a rational way. Wherever pantheism or the demand for freedom as an end in itself appears, we can be sure that Absolute Relativism One will also appear.

## AMERICAN NIHILISM

### Terminal Optimism

The New World Emerson was the contemporary of the Old World Charles Darwin and Karl Marx. Overflowing with the American optimism of the nineteenth century, he was the spokesman for the age to come. As far as Emerson could see, the American future held nothing but endless growth. America was a sleeping giant that would soon wake up. He was convinced that America, with its great wealth of both natural and human resources, would soon become the greatest nation in the world. What, though, would be its virtue?

According to what he says in his essay "Compensation," Emerson conceives of God as the one and only real being. Following Hegel's spiritual pantheism, beneath the ebb and flow of the world there lies God, who is the real whole. God is the vast affirmative, the whole, swallowing up within itself all relations, parts, and time. What we call rocks, trees, water, animal life, and so on are all aspects of the one vast reality that Emerson calls God. Sooner or later everything balances out. This is as true of morals as it is of the water cycle. Whatever we put out into the world comes back to us. No criminal ever gets away with anything, and every virtuous person is rewarded.[7]

By gaining rectitude we do not lose anything. The virtuous do not suffer any penalty. Vice, falsehood, and nothingness are all quite useless. They produce nothing of any great consequence or value. Virtue, on the other hand, does add something to being. It is a positive force in the world that augments the reality of God. Evil is nature working at cross purposes, a disharmony; vice is a departure from the balance of nature, the absence of the harmony that should exist between the part and the whole. Virtue, on the other hand, redresses that imbalance and restores the harmony of the natural flow of things. Virtue pushes back darkness and chaos, waters the deserts of negativity, and adds value to changing being. Everything is ultimately one, so that there can be no tax, no cost or charge, for cooperating with the eternal process of compensation. From the divine viewpoint, optimism must always reign supreme.

Emerson continues the same theme in his essay "Spiritual Laws." There is a higher will governing the lives of men. To be strong in our actions we need only be easy, simple, spontaneous, and sincere expressions of ourselves. God is the great soul at the center of nature. In keeping with his pantheism, but contrary to what environmentalists are telling us today, Emerson says that no one can ever wrong the universe. There is a kind of necessity in the world. By placing yourself in the main flood of the divine force that is flowing through the world you can be impelled to truth, right, and perfect contentment without effort. By being one with the great richness of nature (God) you become the measure of truth, right, and beauty. So go with your feelings and you will always be right.

## Do Your Thing!

To Emerson's way of thinking, this is how you become a true hero, comparable to anything found in the fiction of Homer or the religious literatures of the world. The true man cannot be concealed. He will as easily stand out from the crowd as the vicious man fades into the herd. To be a real man one must really be a son of nature. Near the end of "Spiritual Laws" he says: "Virtue is the adherence in action to the nature of things, and the nature of things makes it prevalent. It consists in a perpetual substitution of being for seeming, and with sublime propriety God is described as saying, I AM." To Emerson's way of viewing the world, the content of what is being said is not as important as the magnetic character and force of the speaker.

This supports what Emerson says in his pivotal essay "Self-Reliance." A real man does not conform to the ordinary activities of the typical human society. Instead of conforming to society, do your thing, recommends Emerson, and he (Emerson) will know that you are a true son of the universe, that is, of God. How trite it sounds today telling someone to do his thing, or, to do his own thing, but to Emerson it meant something new and different, namely, that going with God is the way to be virtuous; and virtue always provides its own reward to the honest seeker after truth and goodness.

What, though, is the content of God's teaching? Is there some unbending code of ethics to which everyone must adhere? Generally speaking, Emerson believed in generosity, goodwill, and the evil of slavery. But on what basis? Is his morality supported by his philosophy? No. If it appears that some aspects of Christian morality are right for Emerson, this appearance will have to be attributed more to his personal religious background than to a deduction from his philosophical principles.

In Emerson's key essay "Self-Reliance," he defines genius as believing that what is true for you in your own private heart is true for all mankind. We must live according to our inner light and assume that everyone else will agree with us. Imagine yourself to be the voice of God in the world. To be effective in the world you must accept the place God has provided for you in the world. He urges: "Trust thyself: every heart vibrates to that iron string." If this program is followed, it is sure to have a disconcerting effect on both the individual and his or her surroundings. Emerson says that society is like a business in which, in order to share in the profits, the individual member must surrender his or her liberty. The security of the individual demands conformity to the herd.

This, though, is unsuitable to the real man. The true man is a nonconformist. "Whoso would be a man must be a nonconformist," declares Emerson. If he is, he will immediately face two problems. One will be the misunderstanding of him by other people. Under this heading we have the criticisms of the social leaders and of the ordinary person on the street. The easiest criticism to resist is that of the politicians and academics. This is because the cultivated classes are by and large an effeminate group, with little or no real courage. After all, if they were real men would they be politicians and teachers? Later, George Bernard Shaw will remark that "those who can, do; and that those who can't, teach." Not so easy to resist, however, is popular opinion, the criticism of the ordinary person, and the censure of one's social associates. This sort of reproach, being so personal and close to us, is very hard to ignore. Nevertheless, this sort of pressure must be overcome, and the real man will overcome it.

The other main problem is the nonconformist's own reluctance to change himself. It is hard being your own boss. Here Emerson warns us against the deadening influence of our past and the bookish adherence to the principle of noncontradiction. What I have done in the past can act like a monstrous corpse tied to my present life, holding me back and cutting off every new initiative. Do I contradict myself? So what! Instead of trusting your intellect, urges Emerson, trust your emotions. Do not worry about being predictable. Do not worry about disappointing your family, friends, and associates. In a word, do not worry about consistency. We read in "Self-Reliance" that, "A foolish consistency is the hobgoblin of little minds, adored by little statesmen and philosophers and divines. With consistency a great soul has simply nothing to do. He may as well concern himself with his shadow on the wall." Every great soul has been misunderstood in his time: Consider Pythagoras, Socrates, Jesus, Luther, Copernicus, Galileo, and Newton. To be great is to be misunderstood, declares Emerson in "Self-Reliance."

So let's hear no more of conformity and consistency. The great man is the measure of all things. If this self-confidence is implemented and extended, it becomes an institution in society. A social institution is only the lengthened shadow of one man. The only history of any great significance is the history of human actions. Emerson insists that all history easily resolves itself into the biographies of a few stout and earnest people. The future can be like that for you too, if you are brave enough. There have been many virtuous men in the past; did they wear out virtue? To be virtuous we must give ourselves over to spontaneity and instinct, the driving forces of the great spirit. If a real man does not like something, he expects the whole world to change in order to accommodate him, and acts accordingly.

To those with a raised consciousness, continues Emerson in "Self-Reliance," the relationship between the divine spirit and the human spirit is so pure that there is no need for intermediaries. We do not need governments, churches, mystical seances, priests, or ministers to stand in for us. It would be the height of profanity to think that God says the same thing to everyone. All things are new all the time. All things are sacred. All things are present. All of creation is one continuous miracle. Everyone is his own priest. The worship of the past is the greatest evil. To the progressive person history is an insult. To be truly virtuous you must be prepared to assert yourself, to say "I think this" or "I am this," and not merely quote some sage or saint. You must certainly not appeal to some Old World government or church. Such organizations are the dead hand of the past.

All real virtue lies in the present, the actual doing here and now. He who has more soul will be the more powerful person and will act as a magnet attracting others to his side. "Who has more soul than I, masters me, though he should not raise his finger." What Emerson wants to say is that the action need not be a physical movement. True virtue is a being-there of the great soul. Activities such as undergoing hardships, husbandry, hunting, whaling, war, eloquence, personal weight, and so forth are only signs of the soul's presence. An even surer sign, though, is the strength to be noble according to one's own standards, to stand out from the crowd without being fearful and apologetic. The true man cannot sell his liberty and power in order to save the sensibilities of his associates. "The populace think that your rejection of popular standards is a rejection of all standards, and mere anti-nomianism [lawlessness]; and the bold sensualist will use the name of philosophy to gild his crimes. But the law of consciousness abides." So do not invent excuses; boldly forge ahead instead.

Asserting yourself is no easy task. To absolve myself, to forgive my own sins, and to decide for myself what are my duties are very difficult things to do. To run against the current, to dispense myself from the popular code of morality, to live within my own circle of rewards require that I be so intimate with God that I must almost leave the human race. In "Self-Reliance" we read, "And truly it demands something godlike in him who has cast off the common motives of humanity, and has ventured to trust himself for a task-master." Anyone who thinks that this does not require great self-control should try it for a day and see what happens. Most people would quickly fall back into the routine of everyday life, which is marked by a constant fear of truth, fortune, death, and even of other people. We are now (1841) a nation of wimps, laments Emerson, in which our arts, occupations, marriages, religions, and so on have been chosen for us by society. This is not the way to succeed. We must put off the old and put on the new.

Once we realize the divinity of mankind we also realize that traditional religion is no longer of any use to us. In the new religion, prayer becomes the contemplation of life from the highest perspective. Sounding like something out of a Unitarian hymnal, Emerson says that the new mode of prayer is a soliloquy, not a dialogue. It is me in praise of myself. Prayer as a dialogue, especially when we ask God for something, is evil. He states in "Self-Reliance," "But prayer as a means to effect a private end, is theft and meanness. It supposes dualism and not unity in nature and consciousness." To those enlightened souls who have passed beyond the religious prejudices of popular life, everything is prayer. All work is prayer. Regardless of how commonplace the activity, any communing with nature is prayer.

### The Father of Self-Help Psychology

The true man is the self-made man. Self-confidence breeds confidence in others. Everyone cherishes the strong-willed person who scorns our disapproval and sticks to his or her self-appointed course. Because the masters of social conformity hate him, the gods love him. Emerson quotes Zoroaster as saying that the gods are quick to shower their blessings on the persevering mortal. So away with all conformity and creeds. He asserts in "Self-Reliance" that, "As men's prayers are a disease of the will, so are their creeds a disease of the intellect." Emerson has no use for religious creeds and doctrinal formulas.

Emerson even applies this to traveling. What need does the true man have for the grand tour of Europe? God is everywhere. The soul has no need for travel in order to be itself. There is nothing greater to be found away from home than can be found in your own backyard. After all, what can we learn from the ancient world except imitation and duplication? Let the American artist, for instance, take America as his or her model. Put America first. At a time when rich Americans and the American government were building their stately homes and official monuments modeled after Greek temples, Emerson tells his readers to let the Old World keep what it has, which is undoubtedly beautiful and inspiring, but let us in Boston and New York not imagine that there can be nothing better. It is only because we lack self-esteem that we make idols out of Egypt, Greece, Italy, and England.

Never imitate, instructs Emerson. Every great person is unique. Also, never expect continuous improvement and constant advancement in society. Even though we have made technological and mathematical advances, such as the pocket watch, pencils, paper money, clothing, crutches, nautical almanacs, life insurance tables, machinery, and so forth, in terms of soul we are not guaranteed any advance over our ancestors. Did Socrates, Hudson, Behring, Franklin, Columbus, and Napoleon require such external supports as are supplied by the latest technology? Did they rely on their possessions, or did they put at risk their property and worldly goods in exchange for greater knowledge, adventure, and self-expression? Clearly the latter, and so we should do likewise.

In good scientific terms, Emerson explains in "Self-Reliance" that, "Society is a wave. The wave moves onward, but the water of which it is composed, does not." Society is composed of individuals who live and die. There is no personal immortality for anyone. All you have is the here and now. Instead of using your time to accumulate material goods, use it to better express the one spirit (God) in your own unique way. Forget your political activism, stock market stratagems, and social maneuvers; concentrate instead on moving with the great will. In "Self-Reliance" we are told, "In the Will work and acquire, and thou hast chained the wheel of Chance, and shalt always drag her after thee." Do not be dependent upon external politics, money, medicine, and friends, but only on yourself. In the same essay we are told that, "Nothing can bring you peace but yourself. Nothing can bring you peace but the triumph of principles." The reward for having done something is having done it; virtue is its own reward. It is foolish to expect some reward after you die.

Emerson was very optimistic and strongly tinged with American chauvinism. His first series of essays (1841), containing his central essay "Self-Reliance," was published well before anyone had heard of the progressive philosophies of Karl Marx and Charles Darwin. Not surprisingly, then, we hear him state in "Self-Reliance" that, "Not in time is the race progressive." He is telling his readers that it is not the necessary force of nature that is going to propel human society to higher levels of perfection, but only the efforts of great-souled individuals. If the wave of culture is to crest at new heights, it can only be caused by the efforts of the great-souled individual acting as an innovator in discovery, politics, commerce, and religion.

There is no doubt that action is important, but according to which moral principles? Even later in life, against his own advice against traveling, but apparently in conformity with his own advice about being inconsistent, after traveling widely in Europe, he was never very clear about what moral standards should govern the worldly activities of the new man in the New World. We can only assume that each man must decide for himself what is real and unreal, right and wrong, true and false. Thus, Protagoras is Americanized.

Is this, though, the road to glory or the road to destruction? If God is no longer the supreme being of Judeo-Christianity, and if man is no longer made in the image of such a God, then what, if anything, can we have in the way of morals? If God is simply another name for Mother Nature, and man is only a fleeting aspect of his mom, does anyone have any right continuing to talk about God and man at all? Truly, the corruption of man is followed by the corruption of language.

### Self-Worship

Emerson and Whitman were great friends, at least for a while. Both men, although they lived and died in an age still dominated by Judeo-Christian values, were also prophets of the century to come. In 1859, the same year in which Darwin's *Origin of Species* was published, John Brown was hanged after leading an unsuccessful rebellion at Harper's Ferry, Virginia, which aimed to free the slaves by the use of violence and bloodshed. Yet, only a few years later, after a bloody Civil War, slavery was officially abolished in the United States. It turned out that John Brown, although quite a miserable character in his personal life and family relationships, was also a prophet in his own way.

The most widely accepted reason for ending slavery was that it violated the Christian law of love. The great Frederick Douglass (1817–95) saw the long fight against slavery as a war between Christianity and paganism. In his mind, by 1865 another big step had been taken in recognizing that all human beings are equal before the throne of God. The role of God is essential. Human dignity cannot be based only on the possession of reason and willpower. If this were the case we would be back with Plato and Aristotle, both of whom found it very easy to justify slavery. This is because IQ is variable. The more you have of it the more fit you are to live and rule; the less you have the less fit you are to live and rule. If everyone is indeed equal it must be founded on something more basic than IQ.

By the end of the century, though, public policy was already changing. Although Emerson and Darwin retained enough of their religious background to be absolutely opposed to slavery, their worldview was decidedly anti-Christian, and in time would come to dominate the century that lay ahead. The result would be various renewed forms of slavery, more terrible than the world had ever seen before. Whitman's writings also contributed to this change. Although not really a poem, his *Leaves of Grass* (1855), augmented and revised right up until the day he died, gives us a preview of twentieth-century thought. This prose work, with the sentences broken up into short phrases imitating poetry, is an invitation to worship nature, and especially to worship one's self as a part of nature.[8]

Whitman is constantly referring to himself as an object of worship. He celebrates himself, and sings of himself. What he assumes to be true, he assumes others will also assume to be true. My atoms and your atoms are the same, he says. He dotes on himself. He regards himself as luscious, and as all the good fortune he needs in life. At the end of his life he said that the whole purpose of writing *Leaves of Grass* was to describe himself to others. It was never meant to be a great literary work, only a form of self-expression.

The only thing that really satisfies Whitman is to be able to walk about freely, and to have no one superior to himself. Nothing is greater to himself than himself, not even God. The only qualities worth anything are one's personal qualities. The self reigns above all else. Long before anyone ever heard of the "me generation," Whitman was leading the way. This shows itself in his own lifetime, during which he was downright paranoid about maintaining a good public reputation for himself.

God, for the Long Islander, is not the existentially separate supreme being who freely creates the world. For Whitman, God *is* the world. This view is called *pantheism* and has always been rejected by Judeo-Christian thinkers. Whitman, however, wholeheartedly embraces it. He sees himself and the world as one. He is especially in love with animals. He appreciates the stoicism of the natural world. Animals and trees confront all events with the same indifferent attitude. Night, storms, hunger, ridicule, anger, and accidents are all the same to the trees and the deer. He wishes he could be as unperturbed as they are. Animals do not complain, they do not lie awake at night weeping for their sins, they do not waste time discussing their duty to God, they are never dissatisfied, they never kneel to each other, they do not worship their ancestors, and they are not driven by a mania to possess material things.

### Life Without Fear

Neither do animals fret over death. Whitman regards death as sane and sacred. If anyone should think that he or she is lucky to be born, Whitman is there to say that he or she is just as lucky to die. Nothing is more beautiful than death. This is simply a reflection of nature. Death is a part of life and life is a part of death. When man dies he will return to the soil to be used again for some other purpose. This is how things are in the natural world. The world is full of contradictions: light and dark, feast and famine, life and death, are all together in the world. Everything comes and goes, only nature as a whole remains. So if human beings contradict themselves, why should this be of any great concern to anyone? He, like the world, is large; he contains multitudes. Therefore, the combination of life and death and the mixing together of good and evil are just normal parts of reality.

Whitman's underlying message is anti-intellectual. Sentiments, feelings, instincts, and emotions, not science and logical thinking, are what count the most. Human life, after all, is only a small part of the whole vast universe, a universe that goes on regardless of what happens to us. This view is expressed very clearly in that part of *Leaves of Grass* entitled "By the Roadside." In a subsection called "When I heard the learn'd astronomer," Whitman tells us how he became tired of all of the scientific aspects of astronomy, preferring instead to rise from his schoolroom seat and glide outside into the mystical moist midnight air where he could gaze up at the stars in silence.

Now, there is nothing wrong with viewing the wonders of the heavens. According to Aristotle, philosophy began with just such wonderment. That, though, is the whole point: we begin with sense knowledge and wonderment; we do not end there. Even while not denigrating the senses, we must go beyond the senses to the scientific and philosophical levels of learning. Whitman, though, would have us go backward, thus undoing the work of reason, and finally endorsing irrationalism. We are once again back with Protagoras. Is it possible, then, for me to call myself a good Christian and still blow up government buildings or attack people with poison gas? Of course it is. But, you say, that is contradictory. But, I say, so what? Do I contradict myself? Very well, then, I contradict myself. I am large; I contain multitudes! So sings Walt Whitman in his song of himself.

## EUROPEAN NIHILISM

### The Unbearable Heaviness of Being

Nietzsche must be praised for being an honest atheist. During his formative years he was very much impressed by Emerson's emphasis upon the autonomous self as the source of all virtue. Nietzsche, however, differs from his predecessor in that he is much more aware of the actual moral consequences of such a view. Like the ancients, he rightly locates the most fundamental philosophical issue in the area of being, which has two basic aspects. One is theoretical, namely, how can something be both fixed and in flux at the same time? The other aspect is concerned with the practical meaning of life, namely, how should I behave, how do I get along with other people and the environment? As it turns out, the answer given to the second question is very much dependent upon the answer given to the first question.

For Nietzsche, metaphysics is the study of being, but being, he thinks, must mean what it meant for the ancient Greeks, to wit, that which is absolutely unchanging. This sort of thing can only be something supernatural, beyond the realm of nature, and above anything earthly. We may as well call it God or the divine, for that is what most people would recognize as the eternally immutable. Yet this is precisely where the main difficulty arises, for it certainly seems obvious that the world is not like that at all. Yes, apparently we can think the permanent, otherwise we could not explain the existence of Parmenides, Plato, Aristotle, and others who advocated immutable Greek Being. Nonetheless, the world as we experience it through the senses shows us nothing but change. Should we not, therefore, take impermanence to be the only true reality?

On the basis of sense experience, therefore, Nietzsche decides that there is nothing permanent in reality. There is no timelessness with respect to any one thing. The existence of the universe, though, is eternal when considered as a whole. It has simply just always existed and will continue to go on existing forever; it is simply a brute fact. Although infinite in duration, it is finite in extension and resources. It is also a jumble of inner contradictions, which shows up most pointedly in human life. All matter and force and power are conserved, so that there is never any increase or decrease in their total amounts. If there were an increase we would have to explain where it came from, which would get us back into the religious doctrine of creation, something to be avoided at all costs. In this one world there is no infinite progress, no purpose, and no far off divine event to which the whole creation moves. There is also nothing immaterial in nature. Neither is there any real freedom in human beings. Nietzsche insists that, although there may be constant change and growth in some sectors of the world, there is no automatic advancement in species as taught by Darwin.

### The Enemies of Progress

There is one inherent drive to expand and overpower on the part of anything that is capable of doing so. The world is really one vast will to life and power. The will to life is the will to power in the sense of constantly trying to dominate. Nevertheless, the inferior parts of nature still continue to rule. Nietzsche attributes this to some inner resistance things have to achieving greater heights of power. He seems to think that this holding back is the result of thinking too much. The enemies of progress are the rudimentary forms of knowledge in lesser things, and the intellect in man. This anti-intellectualism comes out strongly when he tries to explain why, if reality is what he says it is, it has not achieved by now the maximum of power and life.

Nietzsche says in his *Twilight of the Idols* (Part X, sec. 14) that species do not grow in perfection. It is the weak that prevail over the strong, and that are always in the great majority. The weak also have more intellect, exactly in proportion as they lack instinct and will. Darwin, he says, forgot that intellect holds back progress. The weak have more intellect because they need it in order to make up for their lack of instinctual power.

By intellect Nietzsche means care, patience, cunning, simulation, self-control, and mimicry, as well as reasoning about things.

Intellect is identified most strongly with females, for whom he has very little respect, precisely because of their constant crying, whining, modesty, subterfuge, trickery, scheming, and lying in order to get their own way. Women are generally known as being more virtuous than men, but this is to their discredit because what passes for female virtue is really only the feeble morality of the lackluster shopkeeper carried to a high level of sickening mediocrity. In *Beyond Good and Evil* (sec. 144) Nietzsche even goes so far as to say that any woman interested in philosophy has something wrong with her womb. (A few years later Nietzsche found out that he had something wrong with his brain.)

In *The Will to Power* (sec. 506–30) Nietzsche emphasizes the opposition that exists between human knowledge and the changing world. Pure becoming is inherently unintelligible. Yet we constantly talk about the world. This is possible because our ideas are simply the collecting together of many sense images and then applying some arbitrarily chosen label to the collection. This doctrine is called *nominalism*. Any thought we may have of the basic principle of reasoning, that is, the principle of noncontradiction (something cannot both be and not be at the same time and under the same circumstances), is only a subjective rule invented by ourselves. It cannot be an expression of something actually in the world because the world is really only an amorphous mass of becoming. Consequently, knowledge, which deals with essences, structured things, definitions that fix things in place, and so forth, must have its origin in something other than the world of nature.

Herein resides a major problem for Nietzsche. If nature is homogeneous throughout, and if there is no such thing as Original Sin, why should the one reality work against itself? It must therefore be the case, figures Nietzsche, that we ourselves are creating the intellectual entities that are falsifying reality. We deliberately create deceptions. We invent things that are not there. These things then prevent us from realizing our own true nature and the true nature of the universe. We are our own worst enemies. Intellect, the very thing that Aristotle and Aquinas hold up as the greatest glory of mankind, is in fact the greatest obstacle to understanding the real world.

To the ordinary "cattle" of society, the greater the intellect of a person the greater the admiration for that person. To the rationalists, Galileo and Newton were much greater than the average person. What a strange reversal, thinks Nietzsche. In Nietzsche's topsy-turvy world, the greater the intellect the greater the capacity to falsify reality. The greater the ability to think logically, to formulate scientific formulas, and to think great ideas about God, the greater the falsity. What we should be praising instead is the power of the will; the ability to take control, first of ourselves, and then of others and the world.

Nietzsche justifies his position by appealing to reality itself. All of reality is a jumble of absurdities; all lies, if you will. And man is a part of it. So it follows logically that what is true of the universal, the genus, the whole, is true of the particular part. As a part of nature, man is naturally a liar, or, to express it more politely, an artist, a maker of images and illusions. Art is the polite form of lying. All of metaphysics, religion, morality, science, and so on are the figments of the human imagination. We read in *The Will to Power* (sec. 853): "This ability itself, thanks to which he violates reality by means of lies, this artistic ability of man *par excellence*—he has it in common with everything that is. He himself is, after all, a piece of reality, truth, nature: how should he not also be a piece of *genius in lying*!"

## Nietzsche's Virtue

Virtue is important, but how do we define it? Certainly it is not a means to an end, because, objectively speaking, there are no fixed goals to be achieved. So it must be an end in itself. Perhaps the best way to understand virtue is to draw a contrast between the virtuous man and the vicious man. We would then use the example of the virtuous man as our model, just as Aristotle had done many years before. With this in mind, Nietzsche gives us the superman, someone who rises above the petty morality of the ordinary member of society. It is he who will forge a new world out of the destruction of the old, thus canceling chaos and revitalizing world order according to his new plan.

In summary, Nietzsche teaches that ordinary people, especially females, are weak and deficient. They exalt in the slave mentality. Members of the herd need society. They want survival, safety, security, peace, and harmony. They crave compromise and fair play, and believe there is safety in numbers. They are the shopkeepers of the world, those directed by society, public opinion, and religion, people who suppress their passions and instincts, prize self-control, and are constantly making excuses for what they do. They use reason, but only to justify their lack of autonomy. They are sentimental and feminine; they love their priests and rabbis; they believe in democracy, which is based on the absurd notion that all souls are equal before God.

Named after Apollo, the old Greek god of light, music, justice, health, healing, art, poetry, and youthfulness, their outlook is Apollonian, that is, sunny, optimistic, and content with the way things are in their peaceful civic life. As individuals, they are afraid to act, and hence the need for strong leaders to show them the way. Basically, they are antilife. Their middle name is mediocrity. In themselves they are worthless. Their only real value is to provide an arena in which the superman can work out his own destiny. In contrast to their sunny reasonableness, the superman is all guts and impulse. He is not the product of extensive education or elevated social class.

### The Dark Side

God is dead, and now the only thing worth pursuing is the production of the superman. In sharp contrast to the members of the herd, the superman stands head and shoulders above the worthless shopkeepers and ordinary people who want nothing but mediocrity, peace, and security. The superman is the supreme odd ball in comparison to the middle-class members of society. Even while being a person of panache, he joyously accepts the terrible, ugly, dirty, and destructive aspects of life, especially as he finds them in himself. He combines the ruthlessness of Julius Caesar with the compassion of Jesus Christ, the cruelty of the natural world with an appreciation of sublime art and music.

The superman rejoices in his own inner strength. He accepts the urge to unify the sensual and the cruel, which is, Nietzsche says in *The Will to Power* (sec. 1050), the "great pantheistic sharing of joy and sorrow that sanctifies and calls good even the most terrible and questionable qualities of life." Creation and destruction are necessarily united, and the art of destruction is as much a fine quality as is the art of creation. Nature red in tooth and claw is on a par with the singing birds and the gurgling brook. The ruthless warrior who enjoys going to the opera is the true nobleman of nature. When one gets beyond good and evil, instead of being mutually exclusive, good and evil blend together.

For Nietzsche, the superman is the tragic man, the Dionysian man, named after Dionysus, the Greek god of fertility and wine, and also known as Osiris, Liber, and Bacchus. But with birth comes death, and with wine the hangover. In a way, his whole life is a tragedy because, regardless of how successful he may be in his chosen field, in the end he faces death, which means to be absorbed back into the impersonal world of nature that is completely indifferent to both his sufferings and triumphs. He is allowed to bow out (commit suicide) at the right time and place, these being decided by himself. He will, though, as a part of the eternal recurrence of all things, come back to suffer again and again.

Later in life, Nietzsche came to talk of the superman more as part of a super race rather than as an isolated individual. The supermen are to be the masters of the world, beginning in Europe. Over time, eugenics will be needed in order to produce and purify the members of the superior class. Instead of letting nature take its slow course, some artificial selection will have to be employed. In time, the supermen may form a new species as far above present men as we are above the monkeys. Most of the time he talks in such a way as not to restrict membership in the super race to those of any one nationality or skin color. Thus, his own form of racism upset the usual forms of racism at the time.

This, then, is the meaning of virtue for Nietzsche. As he makes clear in *The Will to Power* (sec. 258, 292, 552), he expects the superman to fight against mediocrity in order to form his own morality. All morality is a matter of perspective, of interpretation; it must be a human creation. Man is a moral blank working to complete himself. Natural phenomena are neither moral nor immoral; they are perfectly neutral. No action, either in nature or in man, is good or evil in itself. Nature, and actions taken in themselves, are absolutely devoid of value. Morality is a strictly human invention.

No wonder, then, that human beings are in a moral daze. Since morality is only a matter of perspective, and the world is full of different perspectives, provided by numerous sources, the individual is sure to exist in a confused state. This is Nietzsche's explanation for the suffering state of human life. As far as he is concerned, there is no need to appeal to some religious doctrine, such as Original Sin, in order to account for man's confused condition. Unlike animals, human beings can embrace many different valuations. This, though, is not necessarily a bad thing for mankind. As he says in his *The Will to Power* (sec. 259), "The wisest man would be the one richest in contradictions."

With no outside authority to impose a task upon him, man becomes his own taskmaster. As Emerson had pointed out, this is no easy task. It takes a great deal of fortitude and single-mindedness. Not many men possess such traits. Those who do possess them, however, should be encouraged to use them, and to use them to the fullest. Whatever you do, do boldly and fearlessly, with great conviction and devotion. By their sincerity and concentration you shall know them. They are sure to stand out from the crowd. Moreover, they will be respected and honored, at least by kindred spirits. During his own lifetime, Nietzsche thought of the privileged ones as forming a sort of secret society and encouraged what few budding supermen there were at the time to reveal themselves to one another if they wished. Overall, though, he was looking ahead to the future, which was not long in coming.

## The Anti-Christ

In moral matters the concept of an anti-Christ was something more radical than Emerson ever thought of. In his *Twilight of the Idols* (Part X, sec. 13) Nietzsche reports that Thomas Carlyle (1795–1881), although a close friend of Emerson's, nevertheless said of Emerson's philosophy that it does not give us enough to chew on. Nietzsche thought that this might be true, but that it was no bad reflection on Emerson. What else can we expect from a pantheistic doctrine? It yields no definite set of moral principles at all. Did not Emerson himself say that we have to forge ahead on our own, inventing our own new projects?

If Emerson was backward in any way it was on account of his reluctance to completely throw over the old moral principles of love your neighbor, blessed are the peacemakers, and turn the other cheek. In this regard Emerson shared much in common with Carlyle, and also with John Stuart Mill. Carlyle, who also shared with Emerson his great-man theory of history, was very much concerned about the plight of the British working man, whose life was one of drudgery. Emerson, living in America where, unlike England, slavery had not yet been outlawed, was active in the abolitionist cause. Mill, for his part, advocated much greater voting and property rights for both men and women.

Nietzsche, however, had no such qualms about poverty and justice. As Albert Camus would later say of him in *The Rebel*, with Nietzsche the will to justice was replaced with the will to power.[9] For those atheistic optimists of the nineteenth century such as Marx, notes Camus, the main problem was to figure out how to live on earth without divine grace. Their answer was to emphasize social justice. To the socialist's mind, there is something blocking man's path to earthly happiness; remove it and we will return to a Garden of Eden on earth. For the Marxist, it is capitalism; for the feminist, it is paternalism. The great problem of the twentieth century, though, is how to live without either divine grace or social justice. The only answer that can be given today, says Camus, is to emphasize the autonomous self.

Nietzsche openly recommends that the new masters of the future freely use the herd society as scaffolding on which to climb to their rightful position. According to *Beyond Good and Evil* (sec. 195, 261), no member of the herd has a right to life, or to anything else, relative to the superman, while in *The Will to Power* (sec. 464, 727–28, 859) Nietzsche teaches that the superman has a right to attack, to make slaves of others, to form a higher species, and to use other human beings as a means to his own ends. The superman has a right to create his own values even if it means stepping on other people. For Nietzsche, since there is no God, there cannot be any traditional morality. All that the old morality is doing now is holding back the future emergence of the super race. Judeo-Christian morality is thwarting the advent of the superman. It is, therefore, according to *Beyond Good and Evil* (sec. 62) and *The Will to Power* (sec. 400), the most evil thing imaginable in the world today. The sooner we get rid of this miserable religion the better.

Nietzsche realizes that, without the support provided by the Judeo-Christian law of love, the whole set of moral principles that is based upon the idea of mutual love and respect among human beings (love your neighbor as yourself) is destroyed. He takes the continued belief in traditional morality, after the foundation for that belief has been removed, as the very definition of naïveté. We learn the meaning of moral naïveté from *The Will to Power* (sec. 253): "Naïveté: as if morality could survive when the God who sanctions it is missing! The 'beyond' is absolutely necessary if faith in morality is to be maintained." By "the beyond" he means the supernatural. The same thought is expressed in his *Twilight of the Idols* (Part X, sec. 5), where he points out that Judeo-Christianity forms a whole system of doctrine and action. If any basic part is removed, the whole edifice collapses, including all of its moral principles. It must be emphasized over and over again, he insists, that Judeo-Christian morality is not self-evident. It depends upon a certain worldview, which is now destroyed.

## Moral Meltdown

To have a moral meltdown means, then, that not only is the traditional morality gone, but that we have an obligation to invent our own new morality. Nietzsche's rejection of God coerces him to maintain, as we can see from the whole of Book II of his *The Will to Power* (especially sec. 266), that adhering to the old morality is itself immoral. We can call this Nietzsche's Reversal. Realizing that traditional morality without God is impossible, he logically rejects traditional values. Anything else would be dishonest. Henceforth, virtue is its own end and its own reward. Your reward for acting virtuously is the satisfaction you receive here and now. As with Emerson, your reward for doing is having done.

But there is more to the story than this. Those who fully understand Absolute Relativism One know that those who follow alternate lifestyles are not on a par with the members of the herd; they are above the herd. They are the higher people. Acting according to the old morality of divinely instituted purposes, and the old idea that all human beings are essentially equal before God, is a sign of inferiority. For those who take the first theory seriously, the outsider, the one who spits in the eye of the cowardly crowd, the cyberpunk living in cyberspace having cybergasms, is superior to the herd and should have more rights than the members of the herd.

Here we see the full meaning of Nietzsche's Reversal. The oddball who does his or her own thing deserves to be treated with more respect than the routine run of men. While those who attend church are the inferior ones, the bizarre talk-show host, the writer of strange stuff, the far-out artist, the master of the egregious act, the religious dissident and heretic, the bold CEO who throws thousands out of work, and the like, are the true aristocrats of the world, and as such they deserve to be exalted far above the nondescript throngs and mediocre masses of ordinary men.

When Nietzsche said that people such as Arthur Schopenhauer (1788–1860) and himself were the first immoralists, he did not mean that they were the first to act immorally. Do not confuse the right to do something with being physically capable of doing it. In Absolute Relativism One you have the right to do whatever you please precisely because there are no objective standards. In a meaningless universe, pretending that there is something objectively true and good is the greatest immorality of all. This is why Nietzsche had such a low opinion of the moral posturing of John Stuart Mill. As he tells us in his *Twilight of the Idols* (Part X, sec. 5), some people, after every little emancipation from religion, feel the urge to become fanatical about how moral they are when compared to traditional believers.

Nietzsche must have been reading Mill's *Autobiography*. Mill learned his atheism while he was still quite young. Nonetheless, he remained a closet atheist for many years. He did not consider his irreligion to be any great obstacle to leading a decent moral life. In his *Autobiography* he goes out of his way to emphasize the fact that his lack of religion did not detract from his upright morality. Indeed, he considered himself to be more moral than many openly religious people. There are many varieties of unbelievers, Mill said, most of them unknown by believers because they do not associate with them. However, those who do know them will learn that they are more genuinely religious than those who exclusively take for themselves the title of being religious.[10]

Nietzsche cannot understand how anybody can think this way. Isn't it obvious to anyone who thinks at all that without God there is no reason to worry about being true to the old morality, and that such loyalty is itself the greatest form of immorality? Mill's piety is the enemy of human progress. Mill, claims the German, is still tied up with English notions of being a gentleman, keeping a stiff upper lip, helping your neighbor, and all that sort of thing. Nietzsche, though, thinks in terms of how man must rebel against the powerful forces of mediocrity and natural inertia that are forever trying to overwhelm the sprouting superman. The punishment for failing to exert our own consciousness against the forces that are out to conquer us is to lose our uniqueness; to become just one more cog in the impersonal machinery of the world, just one more meaningless cell in the faceless lump of society. Whether it is showing respect for God or for government, piety is the worst of all virtues.

## The Triumph of the Will

There is a close connection between what Nietzsche preached in the nineteenth century and what actually happened in the twentieth. Although in his own lifetime Nietzsche did not actually practice cruelty and torture, and instead chose to live the life of an isolated anti-Prussian critic, there is nothing in his doctrine requiring others to do likewise. Although one superman need not use his claws, there is nothing forbidding others from doing so. Certainly, Nietzsche's own peculiar lifestyle is not a model to which everyone else must conform.

This was indeed the attitude of someone such as Adolf Hitler, who saw himself as a bold, sincere, lonely, lucid, hardworking, faithful servant figure, in love with beauty, especially in architecture, answering the call of his noble destiny. In science, many outstanding intellectuals came to his side, including Philipp Lenard and Johannes Stark, both of whom were Nobel Prize winners in physics, in 1905 and 1919, respectively. And, if we are to believe Mark Walker in his *Nazi Science* (1995), even the renowned physicist Werner Karl Heisenberg (1901–76) was strongly attracted to Hitler's doctrine.In philosophy, Martin Heidegger (1889–1976) responded with enthusiasm to the great leader's view of things.

Another person strongly attracted to Hitler's worldview was Nietzsche's sister, Elisabeth, who is sometimes blamed for deliberately distorting her brother's writings so as to make them useful to the nazis. It was Elisabeth, and her strongly anti-Jewish husband, Bernhard Förster, who led a group of fourteen German families to Paraguay in 1887 in order to establish a pure Aryan colony called New Germany. The colony failed, but the descendants of the original colonists are still there. Bernhard committed suicide in 1889, and Elisabeth returned to Germany in 1893. By then her brother had gone insane and was in no position to produce final editions of his own works. Elisabeth then set about the task of doing so, seeing in his thoughts an irrefutable apologetic for the Aryan cause. The question that keeps coming up today is whether she was justified in doing so. Those who want to keep Nietzsche's nihilism, while rejecting nazism, usually try getting him off the hook by blaming his sister for his protonazism.

From the viewpoint of an objective observer, however, this will not wash. Those who wish to whitewash Nietzsche often claim that the set of notes collected together under the title of *The Will to Power* was drawn from a pile of writings that Nietzsche himself wanted to discard. There are at least two things wrong with this assertion. First, there is no evidence that such was his design. Second, the main ideas contained in the work were already stated in his other works. There is, therefore, no reason to suppose that his *Will to Power* is in any way a distortion of his views. In any event, a philosopher is responsible, not only for what he is willing to state publicly, but also for anything that can be deduced from his principles. Anything a philosopher says can be used against him.[11]

## The Dawning of the Age of Destruction

There is an old riddle asking about the difference between a pessimist and an optimist. The answer is that, while the pessimist is crying that things cannot get any worse, the optimist is assuring everyone that they can. This is supposed to be a joke. In some philosophical circles, however, such a situation is taken seriously.

In the nineteenth century, atheistic philosophy came in two varieties: the optimistic and the pessimistic. Hegel, Marx, and Darwin were the leaders in the optimist camp; Schopenhauer and Nietzsche were the leaders in the pessimist camp. The pessimists, however, were not welcome at the time. The reasons for not accepting Schopenhauer's paradigm were great. For one thing, his description of Christianity as a form of Buddhism was incredible. In a more secular vein, he was running against the tide of the times. In his day defeatism was not tolerated. This was the hour of Darwin and Marx, both of whom were preaching necessary progress into a wonderful future world. Schopenhauer's pessimism did not begin to catch on until 1918, after the Great War.

As we can judge from a popular two-volume textbook in philosophy, *A Beginner's History of Philosophy* (1920), written by Herbert Ernest Cushman, who taught at Tufts, Harvard, and Dartmouth, Schopenhauer was beginning to be read while Nietzsche was still largely unknown.[12] Cushman states that "Schopenhauer's Mysticism consisted in interpreting the Thing-in-Itself as one reality."[13] With him, Immanuel Kant's (1724–1804) thing-in-itself becomes the Great Will. Cushman's main point is that his philosophy is an irrational mysticism. In contrast to the old religion that promised good people heaven, Schopenhauer's oriental mysticism offered no refuge at all. All action is in vain, and our only deliverance is an ultimate nothingness.

In 1920 Nietzsche was given even less attention. Cushman begins his treatment by saying that "It is quite possible that Nietzsche will have a prominent place in the future histories of philosophy on account of the political effect of his teachings upon the Germany of 1914."[14] During the war German soldiers were given a short anthology of Nietzsche's works to carry in their backpacks. In 1920 Cushman is not sure what to make of Nietzsche. Is he a poet, a prophet, or a philosopher? Is the superman an individual hero or the human race as a whole? In any event, Nietzsche's doctrine of the eternal return is certainly more mysticism than rational science or philosophy.

### Albert Camus

There are many heirs to Nietzsche, among them Camus and Sartre. Camus, who was truly a hopeless character, insisted that the death of God means that the universe is eternal and uncaused. It has no explanation, and is therefore irrational. All human endeavors thus become absurd. Now, since the world is not rational, reason (science and philosophy) is not able to know it; and so ethics must reject rational deliberation. Thus, value judgments cannot be based on intellectual knowledge.

All we are left with, then, is a long series of facts, among which is the fact that this decision was made by X at time Y. It is an absurd situation, but that is what living is all about, namely, keeping the absurd alive, which means continuously contemplating it and living within it. The value of human life is its conscious revolt against the antihuman forces of the world, which in practice means struggling on for the sake of struggling on. This is an echo of Nietzsche. In his *Beyond Good and Evil* (sec. 78) Nietzsche states, "He who despises himself still nonetheless respects himself as one who despises." Camus is aware that man is a strange sort of being when compared with the animal world. The fact that man has self-consciousness places him in a special category of being. Indeed, man is so peculiar that the fact he can despise himself is reason enough for him to respect himself, and thus go on living.

The absurd man lives for the now. To the torment of environmentalists and investment bankers, Camus recommends that the absurd man show an indifference toward the future. He should desire to use up everything available to him now. With no afterlife, it is a case of now or never. Camus states in his *Myth of Sisyphus*, in the section on "Absurd Freedom," that "what counts is not the best living but the most living. It is not up to me to wonder if this is vulgar or revolting, elegant or deplorable. Once and for all, value judgments are discarded here in favor of factual judgments."[15]

Since there is no objective right and wrong, there can be no objective difference between morality and immorality, virtue and vice. Thus, man is his own end. Whatever I do is simply another fact of nature. Even though I am self-consciously aware of my actions and I have an obligation to preserve myself, I am in reality just another part of nature. Since man can find no salvation outside of himself, and man himself is finite, there is absolutely no hope. Echoing Schopenhauer, for Camus all human beings are doomed to frustration. This is the real meaning of tragedy. As with Nietzsche, the modern man is a truly tragic figure.

Originally written in 1940 and published in 1942, Camus' *Myth of Sisyphus* is his argument against committing suicide in a meaningless world. Camus was much impressed by one of Dostoevsky's atheistic characters who said that man invented God so as to have a reason for not committing suicide. Aleksei Kirillov, the chief character in Dostoevsky's *The Possessed* (1872), comes to the conclusion that the sincere atheist must either commit suicide or make himself into God in order to justify staying alive. Now, if an individual man is divine, then this divine being should possess the same powers that were previously ascribed to God, including the power of life and death. So Kirillov decides that, by killing himself in a carefully planned way, he would prove that he really is God.[16]

This notion of man-as-God posed a problem for Camus. How can we have both the death of God and the nondeath of man simultaneously? Why is suicide not an honorable thing to recommend to the whole human race? If there really is no God, and if I represent the highest level of perfection in the world, why should I not be able to do anything I please, including removing myself from this absurd world? Camus' answer was to make the preservation of personal self-consciousness an end in itself. The highest virtue is saving my own personal lucid self-consciousness at all costs. Self-consciousness itself is my only reason for preserving myself; self-awareness is its own reward and justification.

However, World War II caused Camus to modify his position. There had to be some concern for the content of one's ethics. The brutality of the nazis (and Marxists) forced him to ponder the heroic acts of those who resisted tyranny. Camus wondered how he could justify such actions in an absurd world. As a result, he became less pessimistic, asserting in his work *The Plague* (1947) that the main problem in life is how to be a saint without God. It is, after all, important to be a saint. Unlike Nietzsche, however, Camus could not accept the doctrine of the superman (an anti-Christ) as the answer.[17]

Nietzsche sometimes compares his superman to Jesus Christ. However, whereas Jesus Christ is the supernatural suffering servant savior leading everyone who accepts him to heaven, Nietzsche's superman is a secular suffering servant savior leading the human species to greater perfection on earth. With the death of God, heaven also dies, and along with it any hope for a supernatural salvation. Nietzsche's superman offers some hope for a way out of an otherwise totally tragic (hopeless) situation. Camus, though, could not accept it, and at the time he died prematurely in an automobile accident (ironically, because, as he himself had said, a premature death is the only fate that could seriously harm the absurd man), he still had not resolved the problem of finding hope in a hopeless world. In the end, Camus proved once again that no atheist can be happy.

### Jean-Paul Sartre

Sartre is cut from the same cloth as Camus. He is just as cynical as Camus, and in fact is so cynical that later in life, after cheering up somewhat, he is still very depressing to read. Even late in life he still could not come up with a consistent ethical theory. For years after his death, scholars searched in vain for some semblance of a manuscript outlining a consistent set of ethical principles. We can see the root of his problem in his failure to produce a position capable of defeating racism.

In both his long work *Being and Nothingness* (1943) and in his short Paris lecture "Existentialism Is a Humanism" (1945) Sartre argues that each individual is completely free. There is nothing that can act as a guide in my moral life except my own will. I am the master of my own lifetime project. My chief goal in life is to create my own self-identity. This is the consequence of taking atheism seriously. Sartre, of course, is not opposed to atheism; what he opposes is a naive, unthinking atheism.

But then, in a later work on the Jews, Sartre negates what he had said in his main works.[18] Even though he continues to talk about the lack of human nature, Sartre wants to do something about solving the problem of Jews living in a non-Jewish society.[19] Sartre says that the word opinion leads us to think that no viewpoint is any better than any other. It is all a matter of taste, about which there can be no dispute. On this basis, the anti-Semite preaches his anti-Jewish message.[20] But no, says Sartre, the anti-Semite is not entitled to such a wrong opinion; he is not morally free to be anti-Semitic.

Sartre emphasizes the fact that there is no such thing as "The Jew," any more than there is any such thing as "The Man." The anti-Semite has created The Jew for his own political, economic, and social reasons. In fact, though, everyone is unique; everyone escapes essential definition. And so, because there is no manness (human essence), there can be no such thing as the rights of man. A fake democracy for the essence-phobic Sartre is one in which all men are created essentially equal. Sartre must reject this fake (American-style) democracy because there is no unified human nature. To use Sartre's own terminology, there are only singular Jews, Protestants, Catholics; Frenchmen, Englishmen, Germans; Blacks, Whites, Yellows. The Jews wish to be integrated into the nation, but as Jews, not as mere specimens of an illusory human nature, and no one would dare reproach them for that.[21]

In contrast to an abstract liberalism, Sartre wants a concrete liberalism. There is no abstract human nature, only a vast collection of different individuals having no nature in common, at least not in any positive sense. The only things individuals share are similar emotions and feelings. As far as citizenship is concerned, as long as we all participate in the work of the nation and contribute to its greatness, we are all entitled to equal rights, even while maintaining our diversity.

Sartre is even willing to use censorship and brainwashing techniques in order to erase racism. To begin with, he insists, the schools must indoctrinate students with antiracism. Furthermore, we should not be afraid to legally prohibit public statements that bring discredit upon any subgroup of Frenchmen, even though such laws are not likely to be effective. Since he conceives of himself as belonging to a mystical society outside the bounds of legality, such laws will never embarrass the true anti-Semite. "We may heap up decrees and interdictions, but they will always come from the legal France, and the anti-Semite pretends that he represents the real France."[22]

The only really final solution to the question of racism, says Sartre, is to change society as a whole. What we need is a socialist revolution that will completely destroy all class differences. Racism is not a function of bad philosophy or theology, but of our social life. For too long we have been a society of elites and the marginalized. Now is the time to level all hierarchies, a theme that was, by the way, later adopted by Simone de Beauvoir and used as the foundation for modern feminism. According to Sartre, the solidarity of socialism will unite everyone in the same economic enterprise. In a nation where the workers are all of one mind there will no longer be any need for racism on the part of those who previously required scapegoats. Under the influence of Marxism, Sartre tells us to change the social structure and the racist will also go out of existence forever.

> Since he [the anti-Semite], like all men, exists as a free agent within a situation, it is his situation that must be modified from top to bottom. In short, if we can change the perspective of choice, then the choice itself will change. Thus we do not attack freedom, but bring it about that the freedom decides on other bases, and in terms of other structures. . . . This means that anti-Semitism is a mythical, bourgeois representation of the class struggle, and that it could not exist in a classless society. . . . In a society whose members feel mutual bonds of solidarity, because they are all engaged in the same enterprise, there would be no place for it.[23]

No doubt Sartre is sincere. Sincerity, however, does not substitute for truth. What is interesting about his antiracism is the utter poverty of his premises. He upholds unfettered freedom, with its corresponding diversity in lifestyles, as the highest human value. But then, in order to justify his desire for a nonracist society, he insists upon the need for a dictatorial government enforcing uniformity. As humans, we *are* freedom, but, like it or not, we must all be comrades. As Henry Ford used to say, you can have any color car you want, as long as it is black.[24]

How, then, can he say that diversity is a wonderful thing, but that social pluralism is evil? Whatever happened to people creating their own lifetime projects? According to Sartre, humans *are* freedom, operating outside of the whole causal order of being. He admits that the means to the goal are determined by the goal, but choosing the goal is up to each person.

And whatever happened to the principle of noncontradiction? Or is it that, as Emerson said, a foolish consistency is the bugbear of little minds? In Sartre's revealing work on anti-Semitism we see that, although we are supposedly 100 percent free, we would be, practically speaking, 100 percent controlled by the state. He even has no qualms about recommending that the central planners of the socialist state employ various forms of brainwashing in order to achieve their goals. But then, perhaps sensing his own inconsistency, as a last resort Sartre makes a desperate appeal to enlightened self-interest:

> The Jew of today [1946] is in full war. What is there to say except that the socialist revolution is necessary to and sufficient for the suppression of the anti-Semite? It is for the Jews *also* that we shall make the revolution. . . . And if we do not respect the person of the Israelite, who will respect us? . . . we must fight for the Jew, no more and no less than for ourselves. . . . Not one Frenchman will be secure so long as a single Jew—in France or *in the world at large*—can fear for his life.[25]

## The True Heart of Sartre

As with Kant, Sartre's personal commitment to the welfare of mankind is completely gratuitous, and in no way binding on anyone else. This is the necessary outcome of his subjectivism. When Sartre, in his *Being and Nothingness*, speaks about the revulsion of nothingness within being so as to produce the nothingness of human nature, he speaks out of necessity. If the world is really nothing but a collection of atoms moving about in space, what possible place could there be for man other than that of being just another lump of atoms? Does an atom of copper know the other atoms in a copper wire? Can a drop of water falling from the sky voluntarily change its course? No.

Yet, within this unknowing and unwilling nature that surrounds us there are special things called human beings. If human nature were something positive it would have to be like a copper atom, and thus unfree. But we are not just another part of impersonal nature. We are beings of liberty; we are ethical beings. Yet how can this be the case? Sartre feels forced into the position of appealing to sheer nothingness for an explanation of what he considers to be the most enigmatic of all philosophical problems, namely, the existence of human freedom in a material world.

What is the result? Where a man's will is isolated from the world and other people, it is thrown loose from its moorings. The situation, as described by Nietzsche, would be like the earth, if the gravitational influence of the sun should fail, being thrown loose in space. Under such circumstances there could not possibly be any such thing as unchanging moral principles for mankind. So, says Sartre in his heyday, man is forlorn and must create himself. Sartre, in contrast to the French secular humanists, who said that the death of God does not matter, insisted that the nazi atrocities proved that the death of God does matter. He, therefore, correctly concluded that everything is permissible if God does not exist.[26]

It is instructive to realize that later on the apostle of absolute freedom, facing the needs of social life, is forced to rapidly backpaddle in a vain attempt to avoid being swept over the Niagara Falls of nihilism. Instead of insisting upon the individual's right to do whatever he or she wants, Sartre has to negotiate with group-think and the need for law and order. He then begins talking about the socialism of abundance and the city of ends. In order to prosper economically and live together in a civilized way (in a city), it is necessary that people develop an integrated humanism. There must be cooperation and mutual respect rather than constant confrontation and the idea that hell is other people. Forgetting that he has eliminated any way of recognizing responsible behavior, he tells people to act responsibly. Although acknowledging the fact that it must exist, Sartre cannot explain how the combination of freedom and responsibility is possible on the basis of his consciousness versus the world theory. Sartre died without ever finding an answer to Hitler's triumph of the will.

We can now be more systematic in our critique of Absolute Relativism One.

## THE LAW OF SYMMETRY

### How Do You Feel About That?

The first theory shows up in Thomas Hobbes' state of nature before being brought under control by the king. It means that anyone can rightfully do whatever one pleases, whether it is drive-by shootings, forced sexual relations, burning down whole cities, genocide, or absconding with the company funds. There are no privileged people. We cannot, for instance, assert that all moral views are on a par, and then exclude the views of the robber, racist, rapist, and the head-chopping Robespierre. If we are going to be nonjudgmental, then we must also accept the actions of Heinrich Himmler and Slobodan Milosevic as morally good.

Expressed otherwise, no one has a right to take offense at anything. If someone says that he or she is offended by what you are saying, you could just as well say that you are offended by the fact that he or she is offended. This would be the case at any time, whether past, present, or future. Does the earth go around the sun or does the sun go around the earth? In matters of science, as well as in matters of morals, is the judgment of one person as good as that of another? Were the cautious cardinals of the Inquisition, who ordered Galileo not to be so dogmatic about the earth's motion, right after all?[27]

The basic rule of personal relations of the first view is the law of symmetry, meaning that whatever you can do to me I can do to you. To elucidate, imagine a man who marries in good faith and who fathers six children, all of whom he claims to love. But then, in middle age, he runs off with a younger woman. Later, the man and the younger woman, now living together in a beautiful new house, suffer a great misfortune. A servant in the house sets fire to the place, killing the man's new lover as well as himself. The man then condemns the servant to hell, claiming that he was a miserable destroyer of goodness and holiness. The man sincerely feels wronged and deprived.

Does such a man really understand his own moral situation? Apparently not. What he fails to see is that the difference between himself and the servant is only a difference of degree, not a difference in kind. Both are nihilists. The man who abandons his wife and family is as much a destroyer as the servant who sets fire to his master's property. Don't both the servant and the master have feelings? Are not the servant's feelings and passions as worthy of respect as the master's?[28]

Or consider the case of a novelist who insults a particular religion and is subsequently marked for death by its leaders. Let's assume that the writer, claiming that there are no objective and absolute moral standards, claims the right to hurl verbal abuse at the religion. Now let's assume further that the leaders of the religion choose to do more than fight with words; they wish to hurl bullets at the novelist. Does he have any grounds for complaint? No. The religious leaders are perfectly free to reject his arbitrary restriction. They are as free to challenge him as he is to challenge them. Likewise, he is free to do to them whatever it is they are trying to do to him, and do it first.[29]

Admittedly, the military might of the religious group far outweighs the strength of the writer, but this is beside the point. If he argues his case on the basis of certain rules protecting his inalienable rights, he would be forgetting his own premise that there are no such rules. Without some transcendental standard, nobody really knows what it means to be fair and just. According to his own doctrine, the age of innocence is gone. No longer can we call upon God for guidance. There is no going back to some objective standard of good and evil. We are now completely on our own. Therefore, the writer has only two options: either run away and hide or stand up and fight (and die). What he cannot do is appeal to some nonexistent set of inalienable rights bestowed upon him by God. Neither can he expect any nation or organization to offer him any support on the basis of such nonexistent rights.

The main point here is that as long as you are willing to take the consequences, you have the moral right to do anything you want. Once the premises are given, there is no way around this conclusion. Any qualms you might have about killing those you do not like, forced sexual intercourse, insider trading, and so on are simply superstitions carried over from some outdated scripture. Moreover, claiming, as with Kant, that this is not so because you can set limits to your own acts will not wash. It simply reaffirms your autonomous will.

A standard rebuttal to the law of symmetry is that, because we are all the same in some ways, people cannot arbitrarily harm or kill one another. Reminiscent of Shakespeare's *The Merchant of Venice* (act 3, scene 1), isn't it true that we all cry, laugh, bleed, suffer frustrations, have problems with our job, family, and friends? However, the attempted rebuttal proves nothing at all about mutual respect. In fact, it is so fallacious that it proves just the opposite. All it shows is that we are constantly in emotional conflict and competition with one another. It really is a case of doing to others what they would do to you—but doing it first! This old joke now becomes the standard of virtue.

## INHUMANITY RUNS AMOK

### No Slippery Slope Here

The pattern for the slippery slope argument against something is to point out that, if certain practices are not curtailed in their early stages, they will escalate until many more areas and people are affected. So, for instance, it might be argued that if we do not stop doctors from killing sick people simply because the sick people desire to die quickly, we will soon find ourselves agreeing to the induced deaths of many other people, for many other reasons. The standard rebuttal to this sort of argument is that there is in fact no reason to suppose that things must develop in such a fashion. With strictly enforced safeguards it is possible to confine such practices to a narrow area.

The rebuttal, however, does not hold with respect to Absolute Relativism One. When you sign a license for yourself to do whatever you want without reproach, you also sign such a license for everyone else. There is, therefore, no slope on which to slip; we all start out as far down as we can go. Nietzsche, for one, sees this very clearly. He says:

> When the Christian crusaders in the East happened upon the invincible Society of Assassins, that order of free spirits *par excellence*, whose lower ranks observed an obedience stricter than that of any monastic order, they must have got some hint of the slogan reserved for the highest ranks, which ran, "Nothing is true; everything is permitted." Here we have real freedom, for the notion of truth itself has been disposed of. Has any Christian freethinker ever dared to follow out the labyrinthine consequences of this slogan? Has any of them ever truly experienced the Minotaur inhabiting that maze? I have my doubts. In fact I know none has.[30]

According to the first theory, all acts are morally permissible. There is no such thing as an unfair labor practice; but then there is also nothing wrong with the police beating protesters to death. Burning down cities is allowed; so is shooting down civil rights marchers. All sexual orientations are on a par, including being oriented toward children. There is nothing wrong with abortion; but then neither is there anything wrong with aborting the abortionist. Girls are free to parade around nude in public; but then men are free to force girls to undergo the procedure of sexual interaction. Blackmailing someone is on a moral par with shooting a blackmailer. Capitalists can charge a hundred dollars for something that cost one dollar to make; but then socialists can take away all of the profits from the capitalists.

It soon becomes obvious that any doctrine attacking unchanging moral standards must end up being antihumanistic. Beginning at the bottom of the hill means that there is no such thing as slander, rape, theft, murder, police brutality, and child abuse. There would, however, still be loneliness, pain, anxiety, sorrow, and anguish, but they would have no moral dimension whatsoever. How can we as human beings live with such a doctrine? We cannot.

A modern example of such inhumanity is the doctrine of the English philosopher Alfred Jules Ayer (1910–89). He claims that any form of objective morality is impossible. This is because even those claiming to have such a thing do not have one. He insists that all morality must be purely subjective. At the end of his work *The Central Questions of Philosophy*, Ayer berates those who claim that they can find moral standards in something outside of their own subjective wills. The only thing that is really objective is science, especially as found in physics, chemistry, and biology.

Typically, says Ayer, people do not regard all moral positions as being on a par. Everyone is sure to prefer one moral system over another. This is simply a fact. In spite of his emphasis on science, therefore, Ayer has to admit that science alone is not enough for the good life in the good society. Earlier in the century, Adler had forced the same admission out of Bertrand Russell. In a debate with Adler, Russell claimed that science was sufficient for civil life, but, under questioning by Adler, Russell had to admit that ethics, which could not be deduced from science, was also needed.[31]

In the same vein, according to Ayer, at no time is any one moral system really any better than any other one. They are all equally subjective. This is because the only extramental reality is physical reality, and within physical reality there is absolutely no foundation for anything other than statements of fact. This means that there is no possible way of getting from the *is* to the *ought*, and so the *ought* must remain forever within the private domain of the subjective thinker.[32]

Hence, whereas science is supposed to be completely rational, ethics is supposed to be completely irrational. Morality is merely a matter of emotions. Virtue is whatever you want it to be. Being virtuous is entirely within your own opinion, without any reference to anything objective, that is, without any possible appeal to anything descriptive of the way things are in the world. Freedom of action must then mean doing whatever you feel like doing.

Obviously, though, Ayer is begging the question here. Claiming that any particular moral system is subjective because all moral systems are subjective is like saying that the mind must be a material thing because everything is material. It is like claiming that you know that each of the many natural laws (e.g., all hydrogen is combustible) is true because all of nature acts in a uniform way, and then claiming that you know that all nature acts in a uniform way because each of the many laws of nature is true.

A rich source of this error is evolutionary theory, for instance, explaining the bright fall foliage of maple trees in terms of human beings who love bright colors, and then explaining our love of bright colors in terms of the survival of maple trees with bright fall foliage. It is comparable to saying that we know that the features possessed by species X have survived because they are useful, and we know that the traits are useful because the traits have survived. Why do we like eating salty potato chips? Because a million years ago our ancestors were short on salt. Why do we have salt in our blood? Because we emerged from the sea. Why do we have iron in our blood? Because we emerged from an iron mine. Why do people today prefer getting around in BMWs rather than on bicycles?

In Ayer's case, the whole point at issue is whether his universal statement concerning moral subjectivity is true. Logically, if the universal (e.g., all men are mortal) is true, its corresponding particular (e.g., some men are mortal) must also be true. But how do we know that the universal is true? Contrary to Ayer's materialistic prejudice, there is plenty of evidence to show that his assertion about all things being physical is untrue. Universal moral relativism is a deduction from his universal materialism. So, once universal materialism is disproved, because of its disagreement with the facts of experience, the rug is pulled out from under his moral relativism.

### The Poison Pill

Nevertheless, someone is sure to ask, how can we have too much freedom? Wouldn't lacking a moral anchor be good for us? Doesn't the existence of a God-given human nature restrict our range of moral choices? We can see this attitude in Nietzsche, who wants to do away with a fixed human nature behind our actions.

> A quantum of strength is equivalent to a quantum of urge, will, activity, and it is only the snare of language (of the arch-fallacies of reason petrified in language), presenting all activity as conditioned by an agent—the "subject"—that blinds us to this fact. For, just as popular superstition divorces the lightning from its brilliance, viewing the latter as an activity whose subject is the lightning, so does popular morality divorce strength from its manifestations, as though there were behind the strong a neutral agent, free to manifest its strength or contain it. But

no such agent exists; there is no "being" behind the doing, acting, becoming; the "doer" has simply been added to the deed by the imagination—the doing is everything.[33]

Why, then, does ordinary language, by means of nouns and verbs, reflect a difference between the doer and the deed? Even worse for Nietzsche is the fact that there is something even more fundamental than the verbal language, which is the level of concepts. This is proven by the fact that translations are possible. When we translate we convey ideas, not mere words. The words are a means to an end. We can do this because words stand for ideas, not directly for things.

What we can imagine is a condition contrary to fact, namely, an inhuman world without a real distinction between a human nature with potentialities to do certain things, and the actual doing of those things. The distinction between potency and act is recognized by ordinary people whenever they talk about what they might do tomorrow and whenever they praise the value of education. Merely possessing native ability is not enough to succeed in life. Even geniuses have to be taught in one way or another. A potential for mathematics or artistic creation must still be nurtured.

The distinction between potency and act is also enshrined in civil law. A simple example will prove the point. When a police officer stops a drunk driver, does the cop immediately shoot him or her through the head? If what Nietzsche says is true, the cop would be perfectly justified in doing so. If the doing of the bad deed is everything, if the human being *is* the evil deed, then the drunk driver is intrinsically evil. He or she is beyond redemption; there is no hope for this person. There would be no distinction between the crime and the criminal, the sin and the sinner. There could be no talk of hating the sin but loving the sinner; so why not just get rid of the sinner immediately?

However, we all know this to be wrong. Indeed, it is a commonplace experience for us to want to be judged by others on the basis of what we could do if given a fair chance, rather than on the basis of what we have actually done so far. This becomes especially important when looking for a job. To get the job requires experience, but to acquire experience requires getting the job. So what is the poor beginner supposed to do? That person must appeal to his or her potency. The full significance of the real distinction between potency and act will become clearer when we discuss the relationship between crime and punishment in the fourth theory.

### Anticipating Relative Absolutism

There is, however, another way of looking at the human condition, which is to regard human beings as made in the image of God, possessing reason and will. Degrading a human being is an insult to God. Human beings remain human beings regardless of what actions they perform. Even criminals have rights. Abortionists cannot be summarily executed, and it is immoral to beat up on prostitutes and fathers who abandon their families. Everyone, insofar as a person is a human being, must be loved and given a chance. This includes the racist, feminist, politician, and village idiot. No one is innately evil. Although fighting for an evil regime, someone can be a brave and loyal soldier. Although an alcoholic, someone can be a great artist, and the like.

This does not mean, however, that all actions must be judged as good. Loving someone does not mean approving of everything done by that person. It means wishing good for that person, which may mean condemning some of his or her actions. Consequently, the individual act is not everything, and to claim that it is would be terribly inhuman. For good or ill, we are always more than our actual deeds. Regardless of our actual deeds, there is always something fixed in the midst of our actions, which is our unchanging human nature, the foundation for any truly human set of immutable moral standards.

## CONCLUSION

Recently, I visited a store advertising a sale on a desktop computer. Part of the advertised deal was a monitor with a fifteen-inch screen. When I arrived at the store I found the computer on display, took out my tape measure, and measured the screen. Instead of fifteen inches it was only thirteen inches. I pointed this out to the salesperson, who responded by saying that the company considered it to be a fifteen-inch screen. I said that was not honest. His response was to repeat his comment about the official position of the company. He even pointed to the code number on the monitor, which clearly contained the number fifteen as the first two digits. Nevertheless, I insisted that the store was trying to sell a smaller screen for the price of a larger one. After all, I explained, if the store could get away with that trick, it could just as well consider the screen to be a twenty-inch screen and charge even more money for it.

This is the sort of thing you get when trying to do business with Absolute Relativism One. In actual practice the theory is useless. It may appear to work for a while, but only as long as people fail to see what is really happening. Sooner or later, however, its practical value always turns out to be a mirage, a trick played on the intellect by the arid conditions of moral poverty. It will always fail when called upon to make the hard decisions on which there cannot be compromise. We can compromise on the rate of taxation, or on how far to open the window, but not on the basic matters of life.

Is it possible for both men and women to have, simultaneously, many spouses? Can a being in the womb of one woman have inalienable rights while one in the womb of another woman does not? What acts as the measure of who is a human being? One's private opinion?

Many people today forge into the world of personal freedom as an end in itself without realizing that such a doctrine must necessarily end in chaos, thus destroying one of the conditions (law and order) essential to the very freedom they claim to prize so highly. The notion that you possess an autonomous will, that you are morally free to do anything you can get away with, is the philosophy of the juvenile delinquent and is always terribly inhuman. It means the end of life and society, and thus there is no arena left in which to carry out one's free actions.

# CHAPTER 2

# *Absolute Relativism Two: Group-Think Is the Measure*

In short, the other teachers were always men of one idea, even when their one idea was universality. They were always especially narrow when their one idea was breadth.[1]

## INTRODUCTION

As a replacement for the first theory, the second view of virtue has many variations, but they are all made of the same fabric. The main emphasis is on group-think: Whatever the group to which you belong says is right *is* right. From the state's viewpoint, if it is legal it is moral. Good government is defined as whatever seems to work at the moment. If the government can get the votes of the lawmakers, judges, and the electorate, then the convenient thing to do is to take a vote. However, if the votes are not available, then the politicians and the special interest groups must switch over to talk about minority rights. The majority cannot be allowed to trample on the rights of the minority, say those in power. In general, as long as the leaders get the laws they want, anything goes. Any argument will do, regardless of how illogical, inconsistent, or out of conformity with the facts it may be. In modern politics, spin doctors are everywhere, outdoing each other in twisting the truth.

Over the centuries various thinkers have attempted to circumvent the first theory minefield by means of group-think. These thinkers would include Thomas Hobbes (1588–1679), Jean-Jacques Rousseau (1712–78), John Stuart Mill (1806–73), Karl Popper (1902–94), Richard

Rorty (1931– ), and Jan Narveson (1936– ). I will now briefly describe each of these variations.

## GODLESS DIVINE RIGHT

### The Government Can Do No Wrong

In Hobbes' time the prevalent scientific doctrine was atomism, a doctrine originally found among the Greeks and later popularized in the Renaissance. According to atomism, the universe is an infinitely large empty area in which a countless number of little specks of 3-D stuff moves around. All atoms are on a par, none better than any other. Each atom is a separately existing thing, having no intimate connection with any other atom. In fact they are constantly colliding with one another. The only way large things can get together is by combining the little things. Hobbes took this view as the last word in science and proceeded to apply it to human affairs.

Hobbes assumes that everyone exists as an isolated individual, yet we are all basically the same in will and intentions. When it comes to being self-governing, we are all on a par. In this original state of nature it is a case of one against another. Everyone is in a perpetual state of conflict with everyone else. For Hobbes, the right to kill is a basic human right. Tradition, because it implies that man is an inherently social being, is gone. As a result, life is sure to be short and brutish. You cannot store up anything for yourself or pass on anything to your children (if any).

Just as someone addicted to chocolate must agree to never eat candy, the only remedy Hobbes can see to the problem of anarchy is to have each individual give up his or her entire liberty to a central power. Then, with all social and political power in his or her hands, whatever the sovereign orders is necessarily just. There is no appeal against the sovereign's decision. Because the king is the law, the king can never be above the law. Thus, in one mighty leap, the ordinary citizen is deprived of both freedom and security.

If, for instance, the monarch decides to have you arrested, tortured, and killed, you have no grounds for criticizing him. As we learn from the *Leviathan*, having surrendered all of your liberty to the central power, you now have to admit that whatever the government does to you, you are really doing to yourself. That is the price you must pay for your social security. The role of the monarchy is to preserve national law and order. If this means sacrificing you, then away you go. The individual must be prepared to die at the whim of the king in order to maintain the collective good of the group.[2]

As an individual, though, you need not die willingly. Thinking like Hobbes means being very legalistic, always figuring out what you can get away with. This is the attitude of the juvenile delinquent, always calculating how many cars he or she can steal without getting caught. For Hobbes, everyone is by nature antisocial, even when operating in a social context. This antisocial nature is never lost. Thus, watching out for number one is the basic law of nature for Hobbes. This means that, although the king can kill you without any injustice, you can, even if you have done something deserving of punishment, do everything in your power to escape punishment without feeling guilty about it. And the king, for his part, cannot hold your evasive action against you. Given the political intrigues of the time, this was a very useful doctrine. This same doctrine is invoked today in the United States whenever anyone uses the Fifth Amendment to avoid testifying, or when a lawyer, knowing his or her client is guilty, tries to get the client off anyway.

If and when you are punished for violating a law handed down by the monarchy it is not because you did anything really bad in any divine sense. Although there is crime, there is no sin. There is no such thing as balancing the scales of justice, because there is no divine standard against which your actions can be judged as good or evil. In such a system, the only reason for punishment that makes sense is deterrence. The lawmaker must make an example of the lawbreaker in order to discourage others from violating the law. This is the basis for the modern argument that certain crimes should not be prosecuted because the punishment does not act as a deterrence to others.

This does not mean that everyone hates Big Brother, or that millions of people are arrested, tortured, and killed. Let's not forget that even in recent times many people have loved their great leader. And even if they do not love him, he can still be useful to them when it comes to making money. Many Parisians, for instance, got along very well with the German invaders during the nazi occupation of northern France in the 1940s and were in fact sorry to see the Germans leave. Even under the most oppressive regime, most people are not arrested, tortured, and killed. Moreover, when all is said and done, we should not forget that dictators still depend upon others in many ways. They may not need lawyers, but they still need policemen, soldiers, doctors, engineers, and others with expert knowledge in order to take care of themselves and their property. They still need the services of numerous workers, cooks, cleaning staff, and so forth. Even tyrants must practice enlightened self-interest.

So we see that the issue is not one of numbers; it is a matter of the principles of power. The key issue is whether the ordinary person is vulnerable to an abuse of power on the part of the government. In a genuine democracy, from natural conception to natural death, no one is vulnerable; in a tyrannical state, everyone, at any time, at any stage of life, is vulnerable. In a dictatorship the central power can be very generous or extremely merciless. In contrast, in a real democracy the government must always treat everyone according to unchanging principles of justice.

For Hobbes, however, there can never be a true democracy. Humans are inherently antisocial. Consequently, government is the enemy of each and every individual. The relationship between the individual and the state is one of perpetual hostility. This is how it must be forever. The only thing you can do is learn to live with it. Thus, every authority figure (cop, soldier, teacher, priest, doctor, etc.) is your enemy. To the extent we follow Hobbes today, this tells us why lawyers are such ambivalent characters. They too are authority figures, but they also help us escape the control of other authority figures. The main job of the lawyer is to help the ordinary citizen find all the loopholes in the law. The main task of the citizen is to get away with as much as he can. And the main job of the central power is to find as many ways as possible to keep the citizen under its thumb.

Another way of viewing Hobbes' doctrine is to see it as a form of the divine right of kings. We see this, for example, in the writings of King James I, who ruled from 1603 to 1625, after whom both the King James translation of the Bible and Jamestown (1607) in the New World were named, and under whom Francis Bacon was Lord Chancellor until his impeachment by the reinstated Parliament of 1621. In addition to being king, James was also an author who wrote on literary theory, poetry, demonology, tobacco, and politics.

In his view, God makes the king and the king makes the laws, to which all citizens must submit whether they like the laws or not. If the king is wrong, or even cruel, it is up to God to punish him, not the people or the Parliament. This view caused a great deal of friction in society. In the end the king lost, but along the way Hobbes was a court favorite. He was so liked, in fact, that he was hired as the tutor to James' second son, Charles, the future Charles I (1625–49), who was also a strong advocate of the divine right doctrine—right up until the time the Puritans chopped off his head.

It is plain that Hobbes is attempting to counterbalance an extreme libertarianism with an extreme authoritarianism. This notwithstanding, he really has not escaped the first theory, even though he says that it now applies to only the king. In fact, though, it still applies to everyone. Every citizen is still free to get away with as much as he or she can. The only real crime is getting caught.[3]

Strangely enough, even though Hobbes' doctrine sounds too tyrannical to be taken seriously by lovers of democracy, we today follow the same thought pattern to a large extent. The typical modern democracy elects representatives, who then make decisions on behalf of the populace. Once a decision is made, those who did not vote for the representative are expected to go along with it. In addition, those who disagree with the decision, even though they did vote for the representative, must also accept it. The difference between the current system and Hobbes' view is that, under the modern system, there is some opportunity to appeal to a higher authority, such as the courts, or to vote the representative out of office at the next election. However, while the representatives are in power, all good citizens must obey the law, the idea being that whatever is done we are doing to ourselves because, some of us at least, voted for that particular set of representatives.

## The People Can Do No Wrong

Hobbes' system of one sovereign power is a tyranny, but just as bad is the tyranny of the majority. According to Rousseau's *The Social Contract* (1762), social unity is due to the existence of a great overpowering general will that manifests itself in society. It is this great will that produces liberty, equality, and fraternity. Along the way, though, there is one great obstacle to be overcome, namely, man-made institutions. Man, says Rousseau, is naturally good, but everywhere he is held in chains by the social, political, and religious conventions of his own creation. These conventions, invented by some in order to control and oppress others, pose the greatest obstacle to human happiness on earth.[4]

As Allan Bloom points out in his study *Love and Friendship*, Rousseau was a very confused person, wanting to have his cake and eat it too. Concerning the influence of Rousseau, who was born in Switzerland, Bloom says, "A Swiss told the French that they did not know how to make love. What is even more astonishing, they believed him and took him as their master in the art of love. The Germans became the apprentices of the French, and in turn instructed the English."[5] Rousseau, though, had some strange notions concerning love. His idea of love was an amorphous mass of sentimentality and feelings. Love for him was basically all sexual energy and emotions, which in turn gave rise to all the social problems experienced by man, such as possessiveness, jealousy, duties, prohibitions, animosities, greed, lust, shame, and guilt. For him, love was the root of all evil.

Rousseau saw this evil everywhere in society. In order to live among other people our emotional energies must be controlled, and they are controlled by some institution or other. In our preinstitutional state of nature, everything was in balance. Every need had an adequate fulfillment, easily attainable by each individual. Women, for instance, as we learn from Rousseau's thoughts on education, existed primarily to serve men, and so, in the original state of nature, men could have all the sex they wanted, without marriage, and without guilty feelings. In the good old days, life was one long porno video. This, though, is no longer the case. Now we have to work hard in order to get a sense of satisfaction. In today's society people are a mess, having a love-hate relationship toward their own institutions, which they both need to prevent chaos and despise because they are controlled by them. In civilized life, we are our own worst enemies.

This situation gives Rousseau endless trouble in social and political matters. For Rousseau, the only good man is the nonpolitical man. As with Hobbes, man is noninstitutional and antisocial in his very nature. Freedom, for Rousseau, can only mean doing whatever you want to do. This, though, if acted upon by each individual without regard to the welfare of others, would produce chaos. He must, therefore, compensate for one extreme by introducing another. In *The Social Contract*, though, we see that for him, unlike Hobbes, the other extreme is not an almighty sovereign but the will of the people.[6] A general consensus is the closest thing we have to the general will of nature working through us. Consequently, a fundamental consensus must be the basis for the laws.[7]

For all practical purposes, the general will must be regarded as infallible. It is a mystical principle making the people into an omniscient deity and consensus into an immutable law. The state can only exist by the consent of the governed. As with Hobbes, obeying the state is the same as obeying myself; the state is an extension of myself. However, contrary to Hobbes, if and when the rulers ignore the will of the people, the citizens are freed of any obligation toward the rulers. They can then replace them with others who are more responsive to the people. By the same token, however, where there is a consensus honored by the rulers, the citizen is bound to obey the state. In this way does Rousseau, the great defender of individual liberty (i.e., the essential right-winger), like Hobbes before him, transmute into a left-winger when faced with the destruction generated by too much individual freedom.[8]

### We, the People

The necessary result is arbitrary centralized government power. In some cases, such as Marxism, the left-wing philosophy is openly expressed. In other cases it is more subtle. For instance, during the CNN show *Crossfire* (21 May 1995), a U.S. senator said that the Christian Coalition should not worry so much about prayer in the public schools. After all, she emphasized, the state allows parents to donate money to the organizations of their choice, does it not? This offhand remark sums up the whole left-wing mind-set. In effect, all wealth belongs to Caesar. Keeping the money you earn is not a right; it is a privilege bestowed upon you by the gracious government. You in turn must be grateful for this privilege, and so there is no justification for right-wingers complaining about the fact they cannot afford to send their kids to the schools of their choice.

A long time before TV commercials, Rousseau claimed that you cannot fool Mother Nature. What nature wants is always right, and the way to apply this in politics is to allow the desires of the people, through whom, once we neutralize the distorting effects of institutions, nature acts in an infallible way. This was his left-wing (the state is God) politics, his romanticism, his casting aside of the intellect in favor of a strong emphasis on group feelings as a way of deciding right and wrong.[9]

Can this godless divine right scheme work? No. If nothing else, it fails the test of psychology. In Judeo-Christian morality, God is always present, always near and aware of our actions. Not so when the state replaces God. Can the police be everywhere all the time? No. Moreover, who is going to police the police? The question then becomes: What can the ordinary citizen get away with when he or she is not being watched by the agents of the state? Well, anything that person can. As a result, unless the average person has internalized the laws of morality, so that morality is operative in the thinking of the person even when there is no government agent observing him, the system of godless divine right breaks down.

Such internalization, though, cannot take place in group-think. The doctrine itself teaches that there is no need for it and, indeed, if there were internalization, the person would be acting in bad faith. The whole point of the second theory is to do away with religious belief as the basis for morality. Under the jurisdiction of Hobbes and Rousseau, you can do whatever you want. Thus, is the godless divine right view doomed to failure? Is any amount of consensus enough to motivate the average godless citizen to rigorously obey the law when it is convenient for him or her not to do so?

## UTILITARIANISM

### Mill's Virtue

John Stuart Mill regarded his book *On Liberty*, begun in 1854 and published in 1859, as one of his best. It was written, Mill explained, because something was needed to counteract the tyranny of the majority, the worst form of dictatorship. Mill's political inspiration came from Joseph Warren (1741–75), an American revolutionary, Johann Wolfgang von Goethe (1749–1832), who taught the duty of self-development, Wilhelm von Humboldt (1767–1835, the brother of Alexander), who taught that individual development promotes originality, and Alexis de Tocqueville (1805–59), a French politician and traveler. Mill's main philosophical inspiration came from the materialists David Hume (1711–76) and Jeremy Bentham (1748–1832), who taught that all intellectual knowledge could be accounted for by refined sensations.

Mill's basic moral principle is that individual liberty is an end in itself; freedom is its own justification for existing. Individuality and development are the same thing. Any restraint insofar as it is a restraint is evil. A man's own plan for his own life is the best plan for him simply because it is his own plan. The principle of the greatest good of the greatest number means nothing unless each man has the freedom to do as he pleases. The life of a poor but free man is better than the life of a fat pig. Mill wants to empower the ordinary man to be creative.[10]

In Mill's hands, however, the ideal is greatly watered down by the introduction of a second principle asserting that the state can impose duties and punishments on people for things that the state regards as necessary for its survival and welfare. By the time he reaches the end of his essay, he has given the state so many powers that one wonders why he wrote it in the first place.

According to Mill, the only reason it is proper to interfere with the right of someone to do as he or she pleases is for self-protection. Assuming that everyone concerned is a rational, civilized adult, preventing harm to yourself or to others is a good reason for interfering with the actions of another, but not to prevent the other person from doing moral or physical harm to him- or herself. This view, Mill claims, is based solely on the permanent practical interests of man, that is, the concrete consequences of actions.

Assuming that we accept this outlook, Mill must overcome one very high hurdle, to wit, finding something that an individual can do that does not affect at least one other person in at least one way. He says in his *Autobiography* that none of his other writings was so carefully composed and corrected as was *On Liberty*, and I would not be surprised to learn that his trying to find an answer to this problem explains why it took so long for the essay to be published. Later in the essay he even tries to overcome the problem by introducing something along the lines of Aquinas' natural moral law and principle of double effect.

The following case illustrates Mill's problem. If, for instance, a society requires a certain number of children to prosper, say three per couple (the couple's fair share), and if one couple has no children, it means that some other couple will have to have six children. Would Mill be willing, in the name of equality, to force some people to have children? If we were to take his approach seriously, it would mean that everything in society (sex, smoking, liquor, driving, fatty foods, etc.) would have to be strictly regulated because, in one way or another, everything affects everything else. In real life there is in fact no sharp division between the private and public spheres of activity.

Mill goes on to say that you can be punished for nonpayment of debts, nonsupport of family, being drunk while on duty, and, in general, in any case where there is definite damage, or even the risk of damage, to others. You can be punished for the mere probability of damage to others, but not for mere inconvenience to society. How, though, can we know the difference? In some cases the state can even protect you against yourself, for example by keeping you from crossing an unsafe bridge, because liberty means doing what you want, and you do not want to fall into a river. Furthermore, Mill justifies things such as forcing civilization on people (colonialism), requiring people to give evidence in court, the military draft, compelling people to participate in joint work required for the good of society, and forcing people to be good samaritans. The more he writes the more the state gains power.[11]

### Compulsory Education

In keeping with his consequentialist view of ethics, we are told that, "On any other subject [other than mathematics and physics] no one's opinions deserve the name of knowledge, except so far as he has either had forced upon him by others, or gone through of himself, the same mental process which would have been required of him in carrying on an active controversy with opponents."[12] This "negative logic," as he calls it, that is, an intense criticism of theory and practice, is indispensable in order to preserve freedom. The freedom not to be educated is a good example of bad freedom. In this regard, husbands have too much power (bad freedom) over their wives and children. Mill says that it is right to force fathers to pay for the education of their children. Mill firmly believes that education is highly important to a democratic society, and so he is willing to force it on everyone.

In general, if we can get the government and public opinion to allow people to be eccentric and do their own thing, the democratic political system is the one best suited to maximize personal freedom. This means maximizing freedom of choice, even in education. In line with this, as long as there are common examinations in subjects such as grammar, mathematics, and science, Mill is willing to allow fathers to send their children to private, even religious, schools.

His reasoning is that a democratic political system, because of the way it encourages creativity and originality, is a good thing, and so it should be preserved. In turn, having an educated population is necessary in order to preserve democracy. If you will the end you must also will the means necessary in order to achieve that end. It is necessary, therefore, that all children be forced to go to school, at least until they learn the basics needed to preserve a democracy.[13]

### The Meaning of Nature

The root of Mill's moral confusion can be found in his confusion about nature. Is the world made up of individual substances, each with its own essence, and arranged in a hierarchy, as commonsense observation tells us? Are there different kinds (species) of things in the world (e.g., petunias, flatworms, deer, chimps)? Or is the world one thing that can assume different configurations at different times? Whether we view nature as an orderly collection of natures (essences) is extremely important in ethics. Mill's whole approach to virtue is not founded on the presence of something, but rather on the lack of something. This absence shows up in his essay "Nature," written in 1855, but not published until after his death. It appeared in 1874 in the collection entitled *Three Essays on Religion: Nature, Utility of Religion, Theism*.

The term "nature" can have only two principal meanings for Mill. Either it stands for all the things in the world along with all of their many properties, or it stands for all of the natural things in the world existing without any human interference. The first meaning is the domain of the natural sciences. The second meaning is the natural realm in contrast to human technology.

On the basis of this analysis of nature it is obvious to Mill that nature offers no foundation for deciding what is good or evil human behavior. Science is neutral with respect to ethics, and, even if it were not, we could not base our ethics on it. The laws of nature are beyond our control. We are subject to them; they are not subject to us. Hence, it is pointless to call upon the laws of nature to guide us in our behavior. Moreover, looking to nature for morals is worse than useless. It would destroy civilized human life. Instead of bringing us solace, raw nature gives us pain and suffering. Mill tells us to observe nature red in tooth and claw, as was also observed by David Hume, Tennyson, and Darwin. If we were to imitate raw nature we would be sunk in a sea of merciless killing and torture.[14]

David Hume, caught in the same dilemma, had wanted to base morality on feelings of pride and guilt, which in turn were based on one's public image. If you think killing your neighbor, for instance, is evil, it is only because it is frowned upon (literally) by those around you. Morality is just a matter of convention. Yet, if your neighbors smile when you kill someone, would that make the killing acceptable? If everyone tells you that you are good, are you really good? Is there not a general principle saying that if something can be arbitrarily invented it can also be arbitrarily eliminated? And what if some neighbors frown while some other neighbors smile while you are killing someone? Which ones do you believe? This aspect of Hume was much too subjective for Mill; some other doctrine was needed.

### Mill's Reversal

Mill's answer was his doctrine of utilitarianism, or the greatest good of the greatest number of people in society over the long haul. However, because he rejects essences (natures) fixed on definite goals, his major problem is that his doctrine fails to define the good in terms of concrete objectives. The best Mill can do is to superficially relate what should be done to what actually is done. But even here he has to avoid the model of cruel nature and take instead the model of an idealized civilized human life.

The question for Mill is, how do we know that something is desirable? In chapter 4 of his work *Utilitarianism* (1861), Mill says that it is by observing that people actually do desire it. Instead of saying that something is desired because it is good, he says that something is good because it is desired, a very significant reversal. An object is visible because people actually see it; audible because people actually hear it, and so on. In parallel fashion, we can speak about happiness as being that which is actually desired first and foremost by people. Hence it follows that each person must regard happiness as being the most desirable thing. This applies to everyone; not only is my own happiness the most desirable thing but so is the happiness of everyone else. Group happiness then becomes the guiding light for all of his ethics. He even states in chapter 2 that the whole of the Ten Commandments and the Sermon on the Mount, without any appeal to scripture, can be derived from his utilitarian doctrine.

### Mill versus Pragmatism

Utilitarianism as the core of Judeo-Christian ethics is very optimistic, but hardly possible. A workable ethics depends upon having a set of goods that are good in and of themselves. There must be absolute goods if we are to make sense out of relative goods. Even assuming that we accept happiness as the ultimate aim of actual human desiring, as someone such as Aquinas would do, we would still want to know about the content of the happiness we all desire. According to Aquinas, the answer would be the fulfilling of our nature. Different sorts of things, with different natures, possess different goals to be attained, and hence have different standards of happiness (contentment for subhuman things). Contentment for a flatworm is not the same as for a lion.

Now, what if there is no nature to be fulfilled? How then can we have future goals? In day-to-day practice we are guided by the actual laws of the land, our past upbringing, and our immediate material needs. However, unless we are planning on doing exactly the same things in the future that we are doing now, these past guides cannot be our future goals. Even though human social history and our own personal past experiences may act as conservative forces in life, there is a theoretical problem concerning the future that utilitarianism cannot solve. In order to act we must have goals. Assuming that we are beings with free choice who can deliberate upon our actions, we have to know where we are going before we go there. Unless we plan on just bouncing around haphazardly, both individually and collectively we must have targets to aim at. If our target is virtue, if we are to love virtue, then what is virtue?

Throughout his works Mill does in fact give the impression that there are things other than freedom that are desirable for their own sake, things such as bodily health, the education of the mind, equal rights for women and the poor, and so forth. How can this be, though, if in fact we have no permanent human nature, if the universe is an essence-less collection of little pieces of matter in motion, if everything is going nowhere in particular? How can we pass judgment on the goodness of an action here and now if we do not know here and now what constitutes goodness?

Something happens, say the hit and run death of a child by a drunk driver; is it good or bad? Who knows? Is human life something to be treasured for its own sake? Is each human life something good in itself, without reference to anything else in the universe? Is each human life sacred? To be useful in ordinary life, an ethical theory must allow us to define good and evil in an uncompromising way. Yet this is something that no utilitarianism can do. This shows up very clearly even if we define utilitarianism as always choosing the lesser of two evils.

## The Inhumanity of Utilitarianism

Is it morally permissible to freely choose the lesser of two evils? If we define an evil act as one that should not be done, then this aspect of utilitarianism will not work. This is because saying that it is permissible to do evil for a good end is to embrace a contradiction. It is tantamount to saying that something forbidden is not forbidden. With respect to the lesser of two evils situation, Mill thinks that he can figure out whether something is right or wrong by examining its consequences. What is the overall, in the long run, all things considered, on balance, effect of the action? Is the action going to produce the greatest good of the greatest number?

But this approach very quickly gets Mill into a destructive dilemma: either he knows what is good before seeing the consequences, in which case he need not wait to see them, or he does not know what is good beforehand, in which case he can never know whether or not the consequences are good. No matter what consequence results, for instance, a prostitute's making money from that sort of business, he would always have to ask of it, is it good? And this would continue on for one effect after another, forever. Put otherwise, the main problem with any consequentialist theory is that it can never say in a definitive way what is really good and evil within the confines of its own theory. Consequently, we fall back into the first camp, in which we can arbitrarily declare anything to be good here and now, or at any time.

Aristotle, for instance, on the basis of a human nature with definite goals to achieve, could say that things such as the ability to know, to see, and being healthy are things good in themselves.[15] Aquinas could appeal to the eternal law of God and the natural moral law founded on an eternally stable human nature for his definition of the good. But what can Mill appeal to? Basing his view of man on a totally materialistic philosophy of nature, he is bound and determined not to have anything to do with essences. How, then, could he ever tell whether the consequences of a certain act are either good or bad? The most he could affirm is that they just are, period.[16]

### The Ten Prisoners

The problem can be clearly seen in the case of the ten prisoners. Assume that you are living in a utilitarian universe. In this world you are a prisoner who can gain freedom for yourself and eight other prisoners by agreeing to pick out any one of the other nine prisoners and killing him. According to the utilitarian principle, the greatest good of the greatest number should prevail, and so, since the lives of the nine add up to more happiness than the life of the one, it would be ethically permissible to kill the one. The choice would be the lesser of two evils (one death versus ten deaths). To make sense of this scenario we have to assume that each person is of finite value, a value that can be reduced to a quantitative measure so that the values can be added up.

However, if the one killed is an innocent human being of infinite value, then the act would be the morally unjustified act of murder, and we are not allowed to commit an immoral act in order to attain a good. If we were allowed to kill the one to save the other nine, why not sacrifice a whole nation to the whims of a brutal dictator in order to save nine other nations from the agonies of war, as happened when the British appeased Hitler before World War II? The proper moral decision in the case of the ten prisoners is to refuse to cooperate with the brutes running the prison, even if it means that all ten will be murdered. In the infinite afterlife all parties will receive proper treatment.

There are many similar cases that would fail to survive the same analysis. Can the state force the redistribution of wealth and the reorganization of the workers?[17] Can we justify throwing overboard some passengers in an overloaded lifeboat? Can we justify deliberately killing off civilians in order to end a war more quickly? Can we justify killing old people in order to give young people more material goods? Politically speaking, can the greater good formula mean anything other than tyranny?[18]

### Begging the Question

In order to say that the results of an act are good, we must know to what extent the results measure up to some standard of good. In his *Autobiography*, Mill emphasizes the point that his father was led to reject the Judeo-Christian religion because the notion of an all-good, all-powerful, all-loving God and the existence of evil in the world are mutually exclusive. What Mill completely overlooks, though, is the problem of good, something not ignored by Nietzsche and Sartre. The problem is knowing what is good, for, without knowing what is good, objective moral judgments are impossible. The same holds in any system in which rightness is judged by consequences. How do we know a good consequence when we see one? If virtue is its own reward, how do we know that we are being rewarded? This simply takes us around full circle, looking for some objective measure whereby to distinguish arbitrary wants from real human needs.[19]

As a theory of ethics, therefore, utilitarianism is so inadequate that it cannot even begin to make sense without some foundation in human needs. Any workable ethics requires something permanent in the real world as its foundation. If major life-and-death decisions were founded solely upon our peculiar and momentary wants rather than upon our universal and eternal needs, any semblance of an agreeable human social life would be impossible. Some thinkers, such as Nietzsche, were aware of this, but urged their disciples to accept such a result joyfully anyway. How much joy, though, can we take in the utilitarian national socialism of the 1930s and 1940s?

## CRITICAL DUALISM

### Darwin and Dewey

In his lengthy work entitled *The Open Society and Its Enemies*, Popper carries on a sustained attack on anyone who maintains any sort of divinely inspired moral value system. Popper's American mentor in this endeavor was John Dewey (1859–1952). One of Dewey's earliest essays was *The Influence of Darwin on Philosophy* (1910). In several later works, such as *Democracy and Education*, *Freedom and Culture*, and *Experience and Nature*, he attempted to apply Darwin's evolutionary theory of common descent with modification to man's social life, but in a way consistent with democracy.

Dewey's central idea is that, in a world without essences, the only reality is change. Hence, teaching fixed doctrines makes no sense; tomorrow they will all be different. The best we can do is to get people ready for the next development around the corner. We must teach scientific methods of research. Technique, not content, is the key thing.

Confusing the end, meaning an ending or full stop, with a goal or purpose, Dewey, at the beginning of chapter 10 of his *Experience and Nature*, denies that the good of something can be identified with its natural end.[20] Natural processes are purposeless; they come and go, rise and fall, change and return, in constant cycles with no fixed termination point. Instead of looking to natural processes for answers to questions about good and evil, we must look to the intelligent working over of our human experiences. In place of objective moral goodness we now have values, meaning the imposition of human appraisals on the environment. Schools can no longer teach morality; the best they can do is hold discussions on values clarification. In this new world of constant flux, the best we can do is to always remain open to change and new experiences. By continuously interacting with our environment, our experience grows and progresses, and, if applied intelligently, so will society. Dewey thinks it very important to always look ahead. The old materialism thought in terms of antecedent causes; the new materialism thinks of future possibilities.

Dewey expects that in the future the individual will always remain important and worthy of great respect, not because he or she is an image of God, but because each individual is a unique material being capable of reasoning and willing. Being different from everyone else bestows upon each person his or her individual rights. Nevertheless, it is also important, insists Dewey, that we form good habits of investigation, and that society be ruled by a consensus of all the people. As important as the individual is, he or she must be a team player, subordinated to the group consensus. This is how we preserve both democracy and orderliness.

### Karl Popper

The same basic themes of science, consensus, progress, the future, and the individual were shared by Popper, and were later (1950) distilled and concentrated into the one volume edition of *The Open Society and Its Enemies*.

Popper was appalled by the rise of national socialism in Germany. What could cause such a thing to happen? By this time in his life he was already a materialist, and so he could not call upon Satan or Original Sin to explain such events. Neither could he call upon Darwin's evolutionary theory for an explanation, because the events of evolutionary development were unique events that could not be subjected to laboratory tests and repeated over and over again for purposes of checking and confirmation. Generally speaking, though, he claimed that science can do no wrong and has never caused any wars. Although the fruits of science have been used for war, Popper could not think of any war waged for a scientific aim or inspired by scientists.[21]

### Protagoras versus Plato

Popper's social and political philosophy is founded on two pillars. One is that there is a great difference between what goes on in nature and the nature of ethical values. The other is the importance of the rational scientist, as opposed to the mythical assertions of supernatural religion. Popper takes Plato as the epitome of the irrational approach to life. Popper's heroes are Socrates (before he was perverted by Plato) and the Greek sophist Protagoras.

It was Protagoras who promoted for the first time the sharp division between the ways of nature and the ways of man. This dichotomy is the critical dualism that Popper himself advocates as the foundation for all rational thinking about morals. The ways of nature are not the ways of man. There are no natural essences against which we might judge good and evil, right and wrong, just and unjust, fair and unfair. Protagoras knew that man is the measure, and Socrates knew that moral decisions are reached by discussion and consensus among men, not by some appeal to the divine. According to Popper, because Bertrand Russell also knows it, in contrast to mystery mongers such as Alfred North Whitehead and Arnold Joseph Toynbee, Russell is the greatest rational moral philosopher.[22]

In opposition to everything scientific stands Plato, whose whole intellectual effort was directed to returning Greek society to the good old days of irrational romanticism. His nostalgic outlook demanded gangsterism, collectivism, tribalism, human servitude, and racism. He lived on fatalism, taboos, magic, prophecy, fortune-telling, and oracles. He thought that history dictates what must happen in the world, that there are laws of history guiding society such that nations have predetermined destinies.[23] Plato did his best to discourage individualism. He denied the fundamental difference between the facts of nature and the human choice of values. His whole attitude toward human life was organic; he thought of society as a sort of body with a soul. Plato was also devoted to certitude in knowledge and authority in politics, with the knowledge class alone having the right to rule.

But why, then, if they really have nothing to offer the serious thinker, have the philosophies of essence managed to survive for so long? Popper's explanation for this strange event is even stranger. He blames religion in general, and the Catholic Church in particular, for keeping alive a worldview that should have died out centuries ago. Comparable to the way modern evolutionists talk about some species of insects and reptiles that have been around through many geological upheavals, implying that the species have no right to have existed for so long a time, Popper claims that, even though the views of Plato and Aristotle have no right to exist, they were artificially kept alive by the authoritarian medieval church. If the early churchmen had been truly rational they would have elevated atomism and the democratic doctrine of the ancient Greek thinker Democritus of Abdera (460–370 B.C.) to the highest level. Instead, the Middle Ages, because of its commitment to mystery mongering, chose to depress the empiricists and elevate the tribalistic collectivists.[24]

Popper's reference to Democritus as a defender of democracy is also strange. For Democritus, a human being is simply an accidental collection of atoms. Each lump of atoms is unique. This fascinates Popper. If it is true that each person is unique, then any sort of tribalism is ruled out. The only political philosophy that can be derived from such a view, thinks Popper, is a democratic system in which each person has an equal vote. It also means that each person is entitled to his or her own freedom of action. Each person can do as he or she pleases; freedom does not mean anything if it does not mean something physical rather than just something internal, like freedom of thought. "Self-analysis is no substitute for those practical actions which are necessary for establishing the democratic institutions which alone can guarantee the freedom of critical thought, and the progress of science."[25]

### Man versus Nature

Popper sees his ethical position as one in which there is a constant tension between nature and man's moral decisions. He says his view is the ideal balance among various extremes. He will not allow a biological form of ethical naturalism. By its confusion of a fact and a norm (the is and the ought), it would produce only beastliness. A sociological approach, in which whatever happens to be the fact of moral behavior in a particular society at a particular time (when in Rome do as the Romans do), is also ruled out because it would be a case of might-makes-right. This, along with a majority vote on everything, can be used as a means for crushing out individuality.

Also, combining a real spiritual nature with the sociological approach must be rejected. The idea that we must derive our moral norms from the spiritual and social nature of man is wrongheaded, first of all, because man has no spiritual nature, and secondly, because talk about the superiority of the soul over the body can be used to justify totalitarianism. What becomes of democracy if our political system is based upon the view that some souls are morally superior to other souls? Would we not end up with a worship of superior soul-power? It would become, as with Plato, a case of the elite pitted against the ignorant masses. In such a case, the superior soul would have the right to rule.

Showing that he does not understand the natural moral law, Popper also scolds Aquinas' modern followers for using the term natural law rather than the term natural right. Popper seems to be laboring under the notion that the natural moral law begins by assuming that the ought is derived from the is. According to this misunderstanding, talking as if moral law had something to do with the course of events in nature can only give the impression that we must imitate nature, including all of nature's cruel behavior. Natural right, on the other hand, conveys the meaning of an equalitarian situation.[26]

After taking natural moral law to mean imitating nature, thinks Popper, it is no wonder that modern Thomists still persist in the view that hierarchy is natural, and that different people are more or less fit for certain roles in life. Popper, though, prefers the great leveling philosophy of Democritus and Protagoras. Everyone is on a par when it comes to morality. Nobody has a privileged view of the truth. Down with hierarchy; up with toleration.

## Popper's Virtue

In the first place, the first virtue is tolerance. There should be the utmost toleration shown toward those who are tolerant. There should, however, be no toleration of the intolerant. This means that the moral decisions of our fellow tolerant human beings should be accepted readily.

In the second place, instead of following Mill's approach of maximizing happiness, we should follow Popper's own maxim of minimizing suffering. This means that no government should force things on people because of the misguided notion that it has an obligation to make people happy.

In the third place, there is no room for the benevolent dictator. Do not trust in the goodwill of men, admonishes Popper. Trust instead in institutionalized means that guarantee that the first and second points will actually be carried out.[27] He insists that any government plan to make people personally happy is evil.[28]

The whole situation can be seen in Plato versus Protagoras. Plato believed in "an inherent natural order of justice in the world, that is, the original or first order in which nature was created. Thus the past is good, and any development leading to new norms is bad."[29] Protagoras, in contrast, advocated the view that nothing is above revision. Facts may be absolute in the sense that they agree with the way the world really is at a particular time and place (Popper calls this the correspondence theory of truth), but facts, situations, and circumstances change, and so must ethical norms.[30]

For Popper, the only way to rationally solve our problems is by applying the scientific method. Each new bridge cannot be crossed until we come to it. But what would happen, wonders Popper, if people were to use their freedom in order to deny their freedom? As Plato was aware (*The Republic*, 562c-565c), there is a paradox concerning democracy, freedom, and tolerance. Am I not free to be intolerant, unfree, and antidemocratic? Cannot the majority decide to let one man rule? Is not the decision to let the majority rule itself an example of dictatorship? Yet, as Popper points out, if we say that only the best and the wisest people should rule, how would we know who they are?[31]

Popper's answer to this paradoxical situation is twofold. One answer is to turn the tables on Plato. Regardless of what theory of sovereignty is hit upon it will always suffer from the objection that it might choose to undo itself, thus bringing about its opposite. Even John Adams' "rule of law, not men" might end up refuting itself if it were the law that one man should rule. The only way out of this problem is to outlaw unitary rule. Certainly the rule of law is better than the rule of men, but this is not good enough unless the law itself is so arranged that it cannot undo itself. The whole mechanism of government must be geared to preventing the rise of tyrants. The great evil is not that government by consensus will make mistakes; very likely it will. The great evil is that we will not be able to correct our mistakes because we have committed the unforgivable sin of allowing a dictator to assume control. He admits that a benevolent dictator may in fact make better decisions than the voters, but that is not the main point. Popper's point is that a despotism would not be self-correcting.

His second answer is to admit that the rational individual is a good in him- or herself. Democracy is a means to an end that is good in itself. Rational thinking is the one virtue that is its own end and its own reward. Popper considers himself to be a democrat; as such he is committed to the preservation of the conditions of freedom. If some day the situation should change in favor of a Hitler or a Stalin, he would still think it right to fight tyranny. "And should we live to see the day when the majority vote destroys the democratic institutions, then this sad experience will tell him only that there does not exist a foolproof method of avoiding tyranny. But it need not weaken his decision to fight tyranny, nor will it expose his theory as inconsistent."[32] In general, says Popper ending his book, we should always do our best to avoid intolerance, unless of course we are dealing with "aims which are worthy in themselves."[33] In the end, it seems, intolerance still has a place.

## Popper's Pipe Dream

Popper accuses Aquinas of saying that loving someone means wanting to make that person happy.[34] In politics, this is the most dangerous of all ideals, for it can be used as an excuse for passing all sorts of restrictive legislation.[35] Communism, fascism, and nazism, for example, wanted to force happiness on people. Nonetheless, despite Popper's wishes, his philosophy leads to just the opposite situation. Allan Bloom pointed this out in his *The Closing of the American Mind* (1987), wherein he makes it clear that merely wishing for democracy is like building castles in the air.

In response, Sidney Hook, in his review of Bloom's book, pointed out that, in a pragmatic context, speculative questions about how we can refute nazism philosophically are usually replaced by questions about how we can keep people like Hitler from obtaining power. Hook, however, like Popper, admitted that he had no firm foundation for refuting nazism. Popper merely asserted that tyranny is evil because it would make the work of scientists very difficult. But why are such people so valuable? Because they are a means to progress. But why is progress so important? Because it just is, that's all. It is an absolute good, and those who promote it are doing something absolutely good.[36]

So one thing leads to another: in circular fashion we have progress, which is the basis for the autonomous individual, which is the basis for toleration, which is the basis for democracy, which is the basis for progress. Around and around we go. One assertion supports the other and the other supports the one. Rationally speaking, though, this is all very unsatisfactory.

Popper also takes some other basic things for granted, such as the existence of human freedom and the unity of the human race. Yet neither of these things is consistent with his basic materialism. Popper makes it clear that he favors Marx's materialism, even if he rejects Marx's collectivism.[37] But he is just as idealistic as Marx with respect to his views on the importance of human unity, freedom of choice, and human progress. Popper's ultimate commitment seems to be to the progress of the whole human race. This is to be achieved by individuals utilizing the broadly defined scientific approach to solving problems in a completely free fashion. But what if there is no freedom and no unified human species? How can there be one human race if each lump of atoms is unique?

Popper has undermined his own utopian dream. Yes, toleration is good, and if we had it on a universal scale there would be no more Hitlers. But this is like saying, I wonder why the rich people seem to have all the money? Admittedly, toleration and nazism are incompatible. If we could get everyone to accept the ideals of democracy, then everyone would have accepted the ideals of democracy, and we would have universal democracy. Now we all know that this is a very big if.

True, the universal acceptance of toleration will prevent a Hitler or a Stalin from rising to power. An equally important question, though, assuming that democracy is what we should aim for, is, how do we get people to accept and work for that great goal? Plato had exactly the same problem thousands of years ago. He knew that people required absolutes to live by; what he failed to do was to get the Athenians to actually accept what they needed.

Finally, it is only reasonable to ask, what constitutes progress for Popper? It is important that people be free so they can exercise their rationality to the highest degree, and so that the rational people of the world can bring about progress. But, what is progress? Popper answers: To move toward an end that is good for us all as human beings. What is that end? Well, says Popper, we must decide that for ourselves. That is fine, but then what sort of goal should we aim for? Obviously, one that is worthy of us. Fine, but who decides what is worthy of us? Popper has no answer. Unlike Popper, Nietzsche at least understood that, if he were to kill God once and for all, he would have to get rid of the notion of progress once and for all; hence Nietzsche's doctrine of the eternal return. Popper, though, does not see this.

Popper cannot have it both ways at once. Supposedly, the society exists to serve the needs of the individual, not vice versa. Yet decisions about public right and wrong belong to the group consensus, not to the individual. How, then, can anyone criticize the group when, in its collective wisdom, it decides to do something that does not favor the scientific interests of the citizen? The only way Popper could circumvent such a situation would be to invoke the existence of some law that supersedes both the individual and the group. Yet this is exactly what his vision of the open society forbids. Regardless of his wishful thinking, therefore, he is back in the clutches of Absolute Relativism One.[38]

## PRAGMATISM

### Rationalized Religion

As Richard Aaron points out, John Locke (1632–1704) considered himself to be very reasonable in matters of civil government and religion. The Englishman wanted a rationalized religion, but in order to get it he had to play down the role of creeds and churches. In Locke's system, doctrine did not count for much. Being religious was not so much a matter of *what* you believed as it was the fact *that* you believed. Attitude is what counts.[39]

In his *Essay Concerning Human Understanding* (1690; 4th edition 1700), Locke addresses the issue of how to overcome the warring religious factions in Europe. In Book IV of the *Essay*, after outlining the limitations of the human mind when it comes to knowing the world outside the mind, and describing the way ideas are formed from sense-data and then organized within the mind so as to give us knowledge, Locke says that the best way to hold down religious conflicts is to approach religion in a rational way, that is, in basically the same way that we approach the world through science.

Reasonable religion should be like mathematical physics, meaning that all beliefs must be supported by good reasons, which means something that we can see for ourselves by means of our senses.[40] All evidence must be weighed so as to provide us with a balanced view of what is more or less probable. All improbable beliefs are to be suppressed, thereby allowing us to reach some sort of lowest common denominator among religious doctrines.

An example of what Locke is talking about can be seen toward the end of his *Essay* (IV, 20, 10; see also I, 4, 12) where he is discussing the sources of erroneous religious thinking. One major source is enthusiasm, meaning the adherence to certain beliefs on the basis of faith alone. He states:

> Take an intelligent *Romanist* that, from the first dawning of any notions in his understanding, has had this principle constantly inculcated, viz. that he must believe as the church (i.e. those of his communion) believes, or that the pope is infallible, and this he never so much as heard questioned, till at forty or fifty years old he met with one of other principles: how is he prepared easily to swallow, not only against all probability, but even the clear evidence of his senses, the doctrine of *transubstantiation*? This principle has such an influence on his mind, that he will believe that to be flesh which he sees to be bread.

On the basis of private intuitions, innate ideas, or sheer faith, anyone can claim anything. How, then, do we separate foolish from reasonable statements? Can we really take the notion of papal infallibility seriously? If whatever the pope binds on earth is bound in heaven, why can't he rewrite the laws of nature? Such a notion, says Locke, is silly. He states (*Essay*, II, 33, 17):

> Let the *idea* of infallibility be inseparably joined to any person, and these two constantly together possess the mind; and then one body in two places at once shall unexamined be swallowed for a certain truth, by an implicit faith, whenever that imagined infallible person dictates and demands assent without inquiry.

Can the body of Christ, as in the Catholic Mass, be in many different places at the same time? As a result, all religious statements must be subjected to a critical analysis on the basis of what we can immediately experience through the senses. Must we then initially reject all statements as false?

Some 160 years after Locke, in some notes he made to himself on 12 January 1860, John Henry Newman (1801–90) remarks that:

> Hitherto a man was allowed to believe till it was logically brought home to him that he ought not to believe, but now it seems overtly to be considered that he has no liberty to believe till it has been brought home to him in a rational form that he has a right to do so.[41]

Newman agrees that we need standards whereby to judge whether some claim is worthy of belief, but why the assumption that you are wrong until proven right by science? Also, is it really reasonable to withhold assent until you know in every detail what something is? Is it reasonable to believe in the reality of heaven even though we do not know exactly what the joys of heaven are? Newman says yes. If it were not rational to take risks we would all have to just sit down and die right now. Life is built largely on faith, not scientific knowledge. In Newman's outlook, whereas secularism subtracts something from what you have, supernaturalism adds something to what you have. Religion is positive; secularism is negative. Newman accentuates the positive.

Is Locke overreacting to the confusion of so many different religious claims? Has Locke really examined his own first principles? True, the onus of proof is on the affirmative, but why must we take a negative attitude toward everything rather than remaining open-minded? The answer, suggests Newman, is because Locke wants to cut off all discussion of faith even before it gets started. Parallel to Descartes' (1596–1650) emptying his basket of all apples so he can then put back in only the good ones, first Locke drives out of his rational house every statement about the extramental world (the blank tablet), and then he allows back in only those statements that meet his arbitrary standards.

But now let's see what happens when we follow Locke out to his logical conclusion. Yes, it means getting rid of transubstantiation, but it also means getting rid of science. For example, do we see the earth move? No. Do we know that the earth moves? Yes. But how? On faith. From our earliest days we have been taught that the earth moves around the sun. However, if we were to go along with Locke, we would have to say that the earth does not move until we see it for ourselves.

Now we all know how foolish it would be to insist upon such eyeball verification in every case. So why not accept transubstantiation on faith? Would such a belief really be any more irrational than believing that the earth moves around the sun? How can Locke take to be moving that which he sees with his own eyes to be unmoving? Locke is only fooling himself if he thinks he sees the earth moving. It is much more reasonable to say: Accept what you see unless you have some good reason not to accept it. This, though, was not Locke's path, and the later course of history went along with him.

### Kant and Newton

About a hundred years after Locke, Kant, in his *Critique of Pure Reason* (1781), outlines a plan for making all real knowledge like Newtonian science. He allows people to keep on talking about traditional philosophical problems, such as the existence and nature of the soul and God, but he declares that they can never come to any true and certain knowledge about such things. All true knowledge is restricted to the interface between the information of the senses and the internal mental categories that the mind impresses upon the sense-data. The result is science.

In contrast, all philosophy is one step removed from all sense-data. Philosophy is a purely mental operation, forever cut off from the outside world. Thus philosophy is doomed to forever circulate round and round within the mind, leading nowhere. In this way Kant explains why philosophers are forever warring with each other, while scientists, in the tradition of the incomparable Newton, are always agreeing.

### Logical Positivism

Still later, a group of thinkers, under the tutelage of A. J. Ayer in the English-speaking world, decided to carry the whole process out to its logical culmination. Wanting to separate foolish (meaningless) statements from meaningful statements, they decided, under the banner of Logical Positivism (or Logical Empiricism), that all traditional philosophy is composed of foolish statements. Only science is significant, meaningful, and worthwhile. In contrast, philosophical issues, such as the existence and nature of the soul and God, are not worthy of being discussed at all. All discussion of such matters must be stopped before it even gets started.

However, as we know today, the effort of this sweeping program to suppress all traditional philosophy was a failure, the reason being that science could not live up to its standard of empirical science. This is because, in fact, there is no such thing as empirical science. The most basic axioms, principles, and laws concerning nature cannot be proven by heaping up sense-data. All science is intellectual knowledge, meaning that it must transcend the senses. Whereas the novelist delights in endlessly describing countless differences and details, the scientist delights in sameness and unity. Science must have universality and necessity, things that cannot be had by the senses. To deny the supraempirical nature of science is to deny the very possibility of science, which is just what Logical Positivism did.

To summarize, then, without realizing the full implications of their own theories, first Locke got rid of religious faith, then Kant rendered philosophy irrelevant to real life, and then the Logical Positivists disposed of science. Thus, by 1960, all of religion, philosophy, and science was gone.

### Skepticism and Politics

Religious skepticism, especially, affects politics. We note, for instance, that the religious right today is much more Protestant than Roman

Catholic. There are historical reasons for this. Thinkers such as John Locke represented the typical Protestant problem of the era. In classical protestantism the tendency was to emphasize diversity and individuality, which can be very helpful in developing a democratic system of government. However, this is true only to a certain extent. Under protestantism the system very quickly moves to the extreme of disintegration. The state must then move in to restore order, which means in effect a secular state religion.

Respect for the intellect was high in the thirteenth century, but disintegrated during the Renaissance. The 1500s were revolutionized by the "back to the Bible" and the "faith alone" formulas. The attempt of Descartes to reestablish confidence in the intellectual realm, although appearing to work for a while, proved to be in vain. By the time Locke arrived on the scene, protestantism was well on its way to compromising on everything. Locke was a Whig, which meant that he hated any sort of dogmatic religion. He favored the toleration of all religions, just as long as they were all forms of protestantism. He did not favor the toleration in civil law of atheists, Jews, Muslims, and Roman Catholics. Locke's basic position was that, in one way or another, all such people were traitors to the state. Atheists could not swear to God that they were loyal, Jews formed a separate society of their own, while Muslims and Catholics owed their allegiance to foreign powers.

Locke's Whig legacy is still with us today. Protestantism emphasized the isolated individual in direct contact with God without any intermediaries. Everything was privatized; there was the private interpretation of the Bible, private conscience, and a private priesthood. Along with the rejection of hierarchical authority, there was little interest in dialogue and mutual understanding. When applied to politics, protestantism ushered in the separation of church (read churches) and state. This then led to the secularization of the state, which interpreted the separation of church and state to mean the separation of the Judeo-Christian religion and the state. The state then turned its attention to suppressing all political forms of Judeo-Christianity so that it could reign supreme in all areas of life. The state, in effect, took over the religious function, and religion became little more than a department of state.

Why is this sure to happen? In protestantism, where there are many competing sects, no one sect can allow any other sect to gain too much political power for fear that the powerful sect will persecute the others. It follows that each church must have its own territory, schools, organizations, and so forth. We see this, for instance, in the arrangement of the original American colonies. As it happens, this mutual fear must sooner or later drive all the sects out of power, thus leaving the secularists in complete control. Now, even though the state may still count among its citizens many religious people, such citizens find themselves cut off from the social agencies and schools that their ancestors had founded in the first place. Hence the modern religious right movement to restore the power the churches possessed in the past. In a word, although at first a political system with very limited central state power may be the child of protestantism, the child soon grows up and kills his parent.

## Grasping at Straws

Fervently believing that we cannot find the truth by means of science, philosophy, or religion, some thinkers grasp at straws in an effort to salvage human morality, and especially the ethical superiority of democracy. Despairing of defending political freedom in any scientific, philosophical, or religious way, Richard Rorty, for instance, adopts a blind faith attitude toward the value of each person and the goodness of liberal democracy. We must, he thinks, substitute group-think for an individual's ability to know the world as it really is. He states:

> This substitution of objectivity-as-intersubjectivity for objectivity-as-accurate-representation is the key Pragmatic move, the one that lets Pragmatists feel that they can have moral seriousness without "realist" seriousness. For moral seriousness is a matter of taking other human beings seriously, and not taking anything else with equal seriousness. It turns out, Pragmatists say, that we can take each other very seriously indeed without taking the intrinsic nature of reality seriously at all.[42]

Can you as an individual know things as they really are? No. A collection of individual wills, however, can concoct a reality, so that what things really are independently of the human will becomes irrelevant. This is how we are supposed to avoid the extreme of skepticism (moral indifference, nihilism, Absolute Relativism One) and the extreme of dogmatism (the third and fourth views). The question is, though: How much of Rorty's claimed ignorance is feigned? Doesn't he know for sure that mankind is merely a mistake of genetic replication? Is the key move of pragmatism a magic wand making basic questions concerning nature, man, and God disappear in a puff of smoke?

If God does not exist, if we lack free choice, and if we are merely accidents of evolution regurgitated up out of the primeval slime, our ethics will certainly change from a God-centered morality to a man-centered morality, regardless of what the pragmatist may wish for. Asserting on the basis of blind faith that, regardless of what we really are, we can still go on pretending that each person is of great value relative to the rest of the universe is a very irresponsible move. Instead of toleration, we get imitations of Hitler and Stalin.

For Rorty, following in the footsteps of Dewey and James, the only acceptable moral theory is Absolute Relativism Two. This stance must be accepted as the super doctrine governing all other doctrines. Modern democracy is a discussion among equals, presupposing no particular set of moral rules. The true view for everyone is that there is no privileged (eternal, dogmatic) set of moral principles binding on everyone. The democratic conversation is an end in itself. The primary purpose of the process can be nothing other than the process itself. It is as if social life were some great gambling casino in which you are allowed to play as much as you like, but, even if you win, you are never allowed to leave the casino. The aim of playing the game is to play the game. Expressed otherwise, the fruits of the tree of democracy are to be freely eaten by everyone, but no one is allowed to examine the kind of soil the tree needs to grow and prosper.

Rorty summarizes his antifoundationalism approach for us in a candid newspaper interview with Martyn Oliver. Rorty insists that there is no human rational nature to which a foundationalism could appeal for support. There is no one thing called mankind, no essence to human nature, no one unified human species, and hence no such thing as natural moral law. It is all a matter of working things out pragmatically, seeing what works and what does not. It all comes down to what you feel, not what you know, unless someone wants to start talking about knowing one's own feelings.[43]

Rorty strenuously objects to the introduction of religion into the public forum. Although the American Founding Fathers may have thought that it was necessary, he states that today religion is unnecessary. It is as if, to use an example not used by Rorty in the *Times* interview, once we had used a ladder to get to the top of a building, we can discard the ladder. It is interesting to note, though, that the people he mentions as leading the way to the higher ground (e.g., Tennyson, the abolitionists, the suffragettes, the civil rights leaders) were all inspired by Judeo-Christian principles of morality. Lest we forget, the only reason the Founding Fathers could say that certain truths about the human condition were self-evident was because the doctrine of essential human equality had been taught to them by many years of Judeo-Christianity.

When asked what is necessary, Rorty says he does not know, but he also says that not knowing is acceptable because democracy does not need a foundation. All it needs is a series of answers to Marxists, fascists, and nazis that point out in a pragmatic way that democracy is better for human growth and development than are other political systems. He thinks of political democracy as a pragmatic arrangement, worked out over the centuries by competing groups, for the preservation of open discussion. All he knows is that, because there is none better, liberal democracy is the best, and that is that. Although he does not think it would ever happen, given the choice between sacrificing philosophy and sacrificing democracy, Rorty would unhesitatingly give up philosophy; that is how emotionally committed he is to the value of democracy; that is how strongly he feels on the subject.

At the same time, though, Rorty says that there is a common vocabulary suitable to democracy. Unlike the religious evangelist who asserts that he rejects something solely and simply because it is opposed to his religion, Rorty demands that everyone leave his or her religion aside when he or she enters the arena of democratic discussion. What is common to the democratic outlook is the negative doctrine that no worldview can be absolutely true. Upon entering a pragmatist saloon, you must always check your religion at the door.

More positively speaking, the language of toleration is the only language we really need. It soon renders all tribalisms and dogmatic worldviews obsolete. Rorty states that he takes religious toleration to mean a willingness on the part of religious groups to discuss matters without dragging religion into it. For example, religious people who hold the view that Jesus Christ is the one and only savior of the world must give up their religion if they would participate in the democratic process. Or, to say the same thing in a different way, all religions are subsidiary to liberal democracy. What Rorty has done, in effect, is to create a new religion, a super doctrine, that must now act as the established state religion. Failure to conform means excommunication.

## Rorty's Betrayal

Why, then, all the rigmarole about the need to accept liberal democracy without any scientific, philosophical, or theological foundation? Certainly, philosophers must go out of their way to examine first principles, especially their own. To leave your own first principles unexamined is a cardinal sin for someone claiming to be rational; it is a gross dereliction of duty. The philosophical mind must not adopt such a negligent attitude. Yet this is exactly what Rorty does.[44]

Contrary to Rorty's blind faith, talking about democracy is not like talking about the principle of noncontradiction (something cannot both be and not be at the same time and under the same circumstances). The basic principles of reasoning cannot themselves be demonstrated by any sort of reasoning process, for attempting to do so would require the use of the very principles that one is attempting to demonstrate. The principles are known intuitively by every normal thinker. But, as Rorty himself admits, there is nothing inevitable about liberal democracy; some nations have it and some do not.

How, then, can any reasonable person claim to be an antifoundationalist in social and political philosophy? It is the same thing as being an anti-intellectual, not only with respect to theology, but also with respect to philosophy and science. It is like pretending that a building can float in air. Does merely declaring the existence of antigravity make it real? Why would an otherwise reasonable person, who knows how to get by in the world, lead a family life, handle financial affairs wisely, and the like, ever propose such an irrational scheme of things? How is it that, when the existence of individual human beings (such as one's mother) can be explained, a society of individuals cannot be accounted for?

I suggest that the reason for this studied neglect is not that a certain basis for liberal democracy does not exist, but that those who disclaim any foundation for it do so because they do not want to admit what that foundation actually is. They are so repulsed by the thought of having to admit the need for a religious foundation that they would rather turn irrational and disclaim all foundations. This prejudice is so strong that those caught in its grip would rather lose democracy than defend religion.

Rorty, for instance, in the *Times* interview, says that there is still a great deal of inequality and suffering in the world's liberal democracies. By saying this, though, he is implying that there is some divine standard that has not yet been met. After all, if there is no transcendental standard against which to measure the degree of goodness in a society, how can anyone know that there is less goodness than there should be? If the highest standard available is not divine, but only a self-created human norm, what prevents someone from declaring that the actual state of social justice at any particular time is in fact the ideal state of social justice for that particular society, thus affirming the present perfection of the society and denying the need for any further change?

Rorty then terminates the interview by saying that he is not optimistic about present-day democracies being able to correct their own shortcomings. If his pessimism is confirmed, the consequences would not be to his liking. Not being able to solve their own problems in their own way means a slide into some form of extremism. Rorty, though, does not see how he can do anything about it. Fatalistically, whatever is going to happen is out of his hands.

### Bearing Witness to One's Self

According to Rorty, democracy must be self-justifying. Logically speaking, though, this begs the question. How do we know that democracy is superior to other forms of rule? Because of its good results. And how do we know the results are good? Because they are produced by a democracy. And what do we mean by democracy? The will of the people. It is a continuous process in which a consensus is reached about what is proper for us at this time in our history. The practical expression of our will is the vote. Yet how can voting ensure justice? Justice for all cannot be merely a matter of numbers. If that were the case it would be possible for 51 percent of the population to vote to make slaves of the other 49 percent of the population. It is easy to see that democracy can no more mean voting on everything than freedom can mean doing whatever you please. If a liberal democracy were to mean the sanctification of the ballot box, the population could very well participate itself out of democracy altogether, as happened in Italy in 1922 and in Germany in 1933.

The notion that I really am X simply because I claim to be X is one of the most naive delusions of our age. Such self-justification is irrational. So how can anyone just assume democracy into existence? Democracies do not grow on trees. Neither do they just spontaneously spring up. Democracy, like faithfulness in marriage, is a rational decision. It is created by design. It demands certain dogmas not contained within the political process itself. We have to know about the divine origin of human rights (thus making human rights truly inalienable), the infinite worth of each human being from conception to natural death, the eternal destiny of every individual, the need for punishing the guilty and rewarding the innocent in appropriate ways (the punishment must fit the crime, no zero tolerance, etc.), the essential equality of all human beings taken individually, and so forth. A clear distinction must be made between the essential nature of man and the many accidental traits of a particular person, such as weight, height, shape, age, sex, skin color, IQ, nationality, athletic ability, shoe size, and so on.

Instead of taking the human tyrant's viewpoint, which regards each person as merely an expendable cog in a great machine, in an authentic democracy everyone is looked upon from the divine point of view. Freedom means having the power to do what is right and just, not whatever you please. The latter would necessarily lead to chaos, thus quickly destroying the democracy. Being liberal does not mean being loose. Quite the contrary, it means being inflexible about what is essentially right and just. Justice must be the main aim of a liberal democracy, not libertarianism. No truly moderate person today, for example, would say that black slavery is acceptable, as long as we do not have too much of it.

To perform well in practice, a democracy has to be like a playing field bounded by definite borders, and upon which everyone must play the game according to a certain set of definite rules. The important point is that the rules must come from some source outside of the political process itself, not from the whims of the referees and judges within the system. The referees and judges are there to see that the rules are applied uniformly and consistently, not to invent the rules as they go along. Denying the need to go outside the political process in order to seek the support for the political process is to have us forever running in circles, resulting in a more and more powerful central government.

The political deficit of extremism, like the financial deficit, is not natural. It is acquired. Just as a democracy must be deliberately created, so an atmosphere of extremism must be deliberately created. The typical method for creating an extreme position at one end of the political spectrum is attempting to maintain an extreme position at the other end. There is a natural tendency on the part of human beings to rest in the middle. When the middle position is denied to them and they are forced to sustain an extreme position for a long period of time, there will always be a reaction back toward the center. Unfortunately, the usual result of a powerful push back to the center is an overreaction propelling people through the center and over to the other extreme. Hence, if we begin with a left-wing extremism, the result is bombings and killings as the right-wingers attempt to change the situation. We thus return to the right-wing inhumanity of Absolute Relativism One.

## ENLIGHTENED SELF-INTEREST

### You Scratch My Back and I'll Scratch Yours

This paradigm begins by naively defining freedom as being unimpeded in doing whatever you wish, while libertarianism means the right to do whatever you wish. Following Hobbes, all human beings have an equal right to get away with whatever they can. As human beings, we have no intrinsic worth, but we may be valuable on an individual basis because of our usefulness to others. The result of this very bad beginning is a gaggle of contradictions. As with old Hobbes, after affirming our right to kill each other as a basic human right, the disciple of this theory must quickly move to cancel it out.

Socially speaking, the total freedom view is totally impractical, and so its advocates must quickly turn tail and run. Jan Narveson, for example, after giving everyone a license to kill, immediately takes it back. According to Narveson, anyone practicing what he preaches, such as by choosing to love fighting for its own sake, must be warned that he or she can be summarily executed in order to ensure the safety of society.

> Those who think that war for its own sake is a good thing are important. Those people, however, have to make another utility calculation, to determine whether what they have to lose from war (which is generally a lot) really is outweighed by what they have to gain from it. And I think we can say a couple of things to those people. First is that luckily there are not very many people like that and the thing for the rest of us to do is kill them—take them up on it and get rid of them. I say that in a spirit of explaining to them what they have to be thinking about if they want to get into this business. And that seems to me to be a very strong argument.[45]

Narveson then goes on to say that, when you do not stop to help an injured person, the person is no worse off; you have not harmed the suffering person in any way. Moreover, neither should anyone attempt to change society for the better, except perhaps by preaching the gospel of freedomism. Nonetheless, charity is a virtue, and we are all better off if we help one another, but on a strictly voluntary basis. We are even told that, parallel to Mill's closing of a defective bridge, regardless of what a person may freely want for himself, he is better off in Europe today than he would have been long ago. There is, it seems, such a thing as progress in morality.

Nevertheless, regardless of Narveson's sincere desires, nobody can eat his cake and have it too. Trying to do so, however, is typical of those who fail to examine their own presuppositions. In this regard, Narveson never does manage to escape his first love, Mill, who likewise never questioned his own first principles. In both cases the basic problem stems from an unquestioned materialism. There are three main points of note here.

The first is that, assuming materialism is true, in such a philosophy of being there cannot be any human freedom at all. Materialism and human liberty are incompatible. This means that there is no human responsibility, which means that there is no point to discussing ethical standards at all. Therefore, talking about any human morality at all is meaningless.

In the second place, within a materialistic context, saying that we are all equally free is meaningless. Think about what it means for people to be equally free to do as they please. I know what it means to say that two plus two equals four: it means that there is the same quantity on both sides of the equals sign. But how can this apply to human beings? Does equality mean that we all have exactly the same number of atoms? Is a 300-pound football player equal to a 100-pound cheerleader? What if the cheerleader weighs 300 pounds? The upshot of this is that qualitative equality cannot be based on quantitative equality.

The same problem shows up at any level of inquiry. No two whole organisms are the same; no two parts of the organisms are the same; no two atoms in the organisms are the same. If there is equal freedom of action it must be based on something spiritual in us, something that makes us all the same, and that frees us from the determinism of matter. Yet this essential foundation for human rights (the real existence of one human nature shared by all human beings) is exactly what we cannot have here. All we have is a collection of different lumps of matter.

The third point is that, even assuming that there is such a thing as human freedom, there would be no basis for distinguishing right from wrong human actions in any objective sense. This means that all moral evaluations, of whatever content, are on an equal footing, which means that, once again, all discussion of ethical standards is meaningless. There is no way anyone could condemn forced sexual relationships, the voluntary degradation of pornography, the extortion of money by means of kidnapping, or the blowing up of government buildings. So, even if it is true that the general feeling of most people is that an individual should not go around killing other individuals and destroying property, we must wonder about special circumstances. Are we now living in normal times, or is this the time for daring, decisive, unconventional action?

This sort of reasoning could easily be used by a Marxist terrorist such as Carlos the Jackal, who, after being captured by the French, referred to himself as just another good family man. Carlos, we discover, is about to blow up the Empire State Building. Should we tell him that there is a general moral rule against doing such things? If we did, it would be perfectly proper for Carlos to respond that he honestly believes in the general rule that arbitrary killing should be avoided, and that in fact he himself faithfully follows the rule.

However, a general rule is not an absolute rule. The definition of murder is not an eternal verity handed down from above. Indeed, as a Marxist he knows that the very idea of an eternal verity is only some sort of anachronistic religious nuisance. The evil of murder is only a generalization based upon what most people seem to want most of the time. It is nothing more than the summation of many individual opinions over a long period of time.

So why can't there be exceptions? I would not dream, affirms Carlos, of going around like a madman, indiscriminately killing people. But in this case, since I am at liberty to choose my own lifestyle, and since what I want to accomplish is so very good for the whole human race, we are dealing with an exception. In the long run, all things considered, in light of the greater good to be achieved, the act is permissible. So I agree, says Carlos, senseless killing is definitely out, but killing for a good purpose is a bullet of a different caliber. Blowing up a building or an airliner is not gratuitous violence; it is *not* violence for its own sake; it is violence for a good cause, and that makes all the difference in the world.

For the extremist, a good end will always make the means, however destructive and bloody, good as well. Within the arena of enlightened self-interest, even though indiscriminate killing is ruled out, carefully considered selective killing is justifiable. A good end and a good motive can justify anything. Other exceptions might be contraception, abortion, infanticide, active euthanasia, dealing in drugs, or the use of extortion in order to raise money for a really good cause. In the case of active euthanasia, for instance, the man who kills his deformed child or old mother does not look upon himself as a murderer. Carlos the Jackal is a murderer, not him. He would not dream of killing anyone other than his deformed child or old mother. He is, he tells himself (and us), a good man.

In the same way, the nazis could claim that they were right. Both sides fighting the terribly destructive Thirty Years' War, which ended indecisively in 1648, could claim exactly the same thing. The communists and fascists could make the same claim. Those living alternate lifestyles could say: Of course, as a general rule, people should get married and have children; but there are exceptions, you know. Should those leading alternate lifestyles be allowed to adopt children? Why not? It is unusual, but, given our present needs, it is just as acceptable. And what about polygamy? Are the rules for males different from the rules for females? Should wives be faithful to their husbands, but not vice versa? Generally speaking, husbands should not beat their wives. Yes, but what about under special circumstances?

### The Wrong Stuff

Another feature of enlightened self-interest shows that it is worse than useless in actual practice. It tears away the very basis that might be useful for reforming bad people. For example, if someone holding to the Ten Commandments, the Sermon on the Mount, the Golden Rule, the laws of the Koran, and the like, should go astray, there is something to which he or she is accountable. For instance, if someone is not honoring his parents with the proper understanding, love, care, and financial support, he or she can be reminded of his or her religious obligations and thus repent. In contrast, anyone believing in enlightened self-interest will have no basis for repentance.

We might try saying to that individual: If you do not take care of your parents, your kids will not take care of you. To which he or she can respond: Children caring for their parents is not written in the heavens. It is a purely pragmatic consideration. It is good only in the sense that mutual aid helps everyone to survive longer and live better. But, if I should decide not to participate in such projects, what appeal can you use to persuade me to do so? In fact, there isn't any.

Maybe I am a deranged environmentalist, loving rat beings more than human beings. Maybe all humans (beginning with others, of course) should be wiped off the face of the earth. As with Schopenhauer, maybe merely existing is the greatest sin. I dare you to prove me wrong. How about: Only if all children take care of their parents will everyone on average be better off? But, if no human being, in any generation, is really worth anything, why bother caring for anybody? What then? Should the demented ecologist and lunatic animal rightist be shot on sight?[46]

In a similar fashion, the standard that I might have used to stop slavery, showing disrespect for others, or a religious war, namely, that such practices are violations of the person's own religious principles, such as the commandments to love one's neighbor as one loves himself and to love one's enemies, is now taken away. Atheism in no way solves this problem. In fact, atheists, such as Hitler and Stalin, are much more likely to go to war with one another than are theists.

The paradox of inconsistency, therefore, can apply to the faith of atheists as well as to the faith of theists. It is the paradox you find when dealing with criticisms of any particular belief system. Even granting the fact, for example, that Christians do not always practice what they preach, it makes no sense for someone to criticize them for their inconsistency unless what they (the Christians) preach is correct. In general, you may note an inconsistency between doctrine and behavior, but you cannot *condemn* the members of a given belief system for acting inconsistently unless you admit that the doctrines are true. This is more than simply tolerating the doctrines. You must accept them as true.[47]

If the critic does not accept the doctrines as objectively true he or she would be in a very awkward situation, comparable to that of a comedian trying to rid him- or herself of something sticking to his or her finger. In the typical comedy skit, the more the comedian tries to throw off the sticky item the more it continues to stick to his or her finger. Similarly, the more the critic condemns the members of religion R for not living up to their own moral doctrines, the more he or she emphasizes the fact that he or she embraces their moral doctrines as right and true. After all, what is evil about the members of R killing off those who disagree with them unless using violence in order to have your own way really is morally wrong? It must be the case that, if R contains a doctrine forbidding such behavior, then R is indeed the true religion.

Typically, those employing enlightened self-interest as a substitute for religion begin with Hobbes' imagined state of nature and end with their own doctrine as the antidote to wanton murder, rape, and so forth. The idea is not to end up, like Hobbes, with a rigid dictatorship, but with a liberal democracy. Unfortunately, however, enlightened self-interest does not outlaw moderate, selective, and temperate forms of murder, rape, and so forth. If by way of rebuttal we say that murder by definition means wrong killing, then we are back where we started, having to define what is wrong in a per se way.

The main point of enlightened self-interest is to have ethics without God, soul, and churches. Under the new regime, however, there would be no reason for the disciple of libertarianism to accept Judeo-Christian doctrine as true, and therefore no reason to free the slaves, stop the war, or care for one's parents. This person's only motivation would be the desire to save his or her own skin. And, if you should run into someone who really preferred war to peace, even though you might threaten him or her with immediate death, I doubt that you would live long enough to finish your sentence.[48]

If the warrior does not care for his own life, or for the lives of others, there is nothing we can say to him. The only recourse is to the centralized sword of the state. So freedomism, it turns out, is merely a gimmick to pull us into political tyranny. Mussolini, Hitler, Stalin, and Mao Tse-tung are prime examples of libertarianism in action. Therefore, freedom as an end in itself (freedomism) is really a trick. It is all part of a sneaky left-wing plot promoting political despotism. However, once we see through the deception, what is left? We will then either advance to one of the next two positions or fall back into Absolute Relativism One.

## CONCLUSION

The main point of group-think is having atheism without nihilism. The main critique of the second view is that there is no way to achieve such a goal. By leaving out God, the second position is the same as the first. All morality is reduced to a welter of conflicting factions, which are held in check by the forces of cultural inheritance, social pressure, popular will transformed into political policy and centralized dictatorship. Then, once an evil is established, it becomes commonplace. Things such as slavery, the Holocaust, infanticide, and bribery become banal and trite. Such things are treated as if they were binding on the moral conscience of each individual. Those who do not go along with the current practices are accused of being intolerant, or unpatriotic, and therefore deserving of a more severe punishment, as, for example, those who block the entrance to an abortion clinic.[49]

When subjected to critical analysis, however, we see that group-think is useless. And when used to support democracy, the second view provides no foundation for democracy at all. It is only our own self-delusion that sustains the value of liberal democracy as a way of life. Consequently, since no intelligent person can accept such deceit, the search goes on for something better.

# CHAPTER 3

# *Absolute Relativism Three: The Good Goal Is the Measure*

> If so, then why should we not do evil so that good may come of it? That is what we are accused of preaching by some of our detractors; and their condemnation of it is just. (Romans 3:8)

> Knowing this we are positioned to develop a judgment of proportion, namely, a judgment as to whether we are causing less harm by performing the action or omitting it. In other words, we are positioned to judge whether the action is describable, all things considered, as an act of beneficence in a conflicting world, or what is the same, whether there is a proportionate reason for performing it even though harm is inevitable.[1]

## INTRODUCTION

Those in the third camp recognize the failings of the first two theories, but still do not want to embrace the fourth model. They believe that the idea of God as a taskmaster must be replaced with a more motherly image. The third theory permits the individual, after serious soul searching, to make up his or her own mind on the morality of an action. There must be some moral system that allows us to claim to believe in moral principles, especially as associated with religion, but that also allows us to work many variations on the moral themes so as to always remain flexible and open to new experiences.

Once we have weighed the different consequences relative to each other and have decided upon some course of action that we think will produce the larger good, then we are free to do the deed. At this point our decision becomes a real moral choice, one that is objectively valid for us. By sincerely attempting to make sure that the end product of the decision is good in proportion to both the effort involved in the actual process of carrying out the decision and with respect to the results obtained, the human decisionmaker can ensure that the decision is moral. In this way, the decisionmaker can also be sure that the choice is pleasing to God. This ethical theory is usually known as proportionalism. It can also be called situation ethics.[2]

## ETHICS AND RELIGION

### The Most Practical Knowledge

Some areas of study (e.g., logic) are independent of a belief in God. Ethics, though, is not an autonomous study. This is because man, in fact, has a supernatural destiny. Consequently, in the practical arena (ethics), any attempt to be self-sufficient is ineffective in guiding human life. In this sense, everyone is a hippie; every generation is a beat generation; everyone is searching for meaning, trying to find the hidden holiness in life. Thus, as we know from history, all efforts to crush out religion have failed. Smart revolutionaries know that it is much wiser to replace an old religion with a new one rather than trying to eliminate religion altogether.

To take an example from ancient times, according to Aristotle's intention, ethics was a practical sort of knowledge; yet in practice it remained theoretical. With regard to the actual aim of life, it was a failure. Aristotle's philosophy did not permeate the concrete reality of man; it did not stir man's hopes or desires. What is infinite in man was disregarded. With Aristotle, man's spiritual status was ignored. Hence, although his ethics was genuinely humanistic, and although he recognized the importance of purposefulness, it was disappointing because it was still very much a secular humanism. There was no divine creation or providence, no personal immortality, and no essential human equality. As far as the individual was concerned, death was the end.

The very best Aristotle could hope for was semihappiness in this life, consisting in one's contemplation of the eternally existing movers of the heavenly spheres, responsible for the eternal motions within the eternal universe. Unable to account for the immortality of the soul, Aristotle logically concluded that perfect happiness was unattainable. For Aristotle, what little happiness one could have always came late in life. It was restricted to the intellectual elite, and only at the expense of having slaves to permit free men leisure time for contemplation. To be semihappy a person must have pleasure, friends, wealth, good looks, bodily health, and long life. How many, though, can attain all this? There is thus a current of pessimism underlying Aristotle's account of the human condition.[3]

This is why the Greeks had real tragedies in their repertoire of plays, whereas none can be found in Judeo-Christian literature. An extensive review of Judeo-Christian works that might be considered tragedies, including Shakespeare's plays, reveals that they really are not comparable to tragedies found in classical pagan literature. According to one such analysis, a tragedy is consummated when a dream of innocence is confronted by the fact of guilt and then followed by an acquiesce in that guilt. A truly tragic world is a world without the possibility of redemption. Nietzsche, coming after Christ, saw this very clearly, and so describes his superman as a classical tragic figure. However, such a person is not possible in the Judeo-Christian view of life. While still on earth, if the faithful one is living a spiritual life, he or she can achieve a large measure of happiness even here and now. Consequently, nothing in literature has yet appeared that is both truly Judeo-Christian and truly tragic at the same time.[4]

## The Tragedy of Absolute Relativism Three

Unfortunately for modern Judeo-Christian morality, the third model is an unsuccessful attempt to import a fuzzy logic into real life situations. In significant moral matters the real world is an either-or affair. The fuzzy-minded people keep wanting to have it all, whereas the clear-minded people know that they cannot. Although in fuzzy logic every effort is made to avoid facing up to the fact, in the real world the principle of noncontradiction always applies in all affairs of human significance. As much as it is nice to dream about having everything at once, if you should ever try actually living such a life, the school of hard knocks is always ready to dump a bucket of cold water on your head. The tragedy of the third view is trying to be both God-centered and exclusively man-centered at the same time.

No doubt the third-model patron has good intentions. He or she wants a balanced position, which is viewed as a system with great flexibility. For example, can a jury acquit a caring doctor in an assisted suicide case? Normally, the jurors think to themselves, doctors should not bring about death, but let's be flexible about this. Members of the jury, intones the defense attorney, let's look at the facts. The poisoned person, as far as we know, is happy to be dead. His relatives, since both his and their suffering has now ended, are happy he is dead. The government is happy because it need no longer support him. Let's face it, concludes the attorney for the defense, some people are better off dead, and the deceased is one of them. Hence the question: Why should anyone be punished when everyone is so happy?

Overlooking the fact that there is such a thing as mutual abuse, the same line of reasoning can be used to justify prostitution. After all, in some cases at least, the independent businessperson is happy and the satisfied customer is happy, so where is the harm? So also in the case of the art dealer who, when arrested for selling forgeries, says to the judge: The artist is happy, the ignorant customer is happy, and I am happy, so where is the crime? This can be seen in other areas as well. If there were no such thing as mutual abuse, then practices such as dueling, gang wars, and animal fighting would be regarded as both moral and legal. What is wrong with two consenting adults freely deciding to fight a duel? What is wrong with the members of one gang scheduling a fight with the members of another gang? Are they not, at least in many cases, all consenting adults?

In fact, since there should be nothing illegal about such an event, why not show it on TV? Cable companies could even list it as a special event, for which they could charge a high fee. Those who died in the fight might even be regarded as heroes, at least in the entertainment industry. In addition, why can't cock fights and dog fights be regarded as just another form of entertainment? The animals are owned by people who freely consent to use them for the purpose of entertainment. What could possibly be wrong with that? As you can see, there is just no end to the number of things that can be done among consenting adults. And such things can also be good for the economy.

Those who follow the third model usually consider themselves to be religious people, but not overly rigid. They believe in God, in the power of love, and in the need for compassion. However, what they ardently wish to discard is the notion that there is only one way to stand upright in the moral sphere. They believe in the existence of moral principles, but reject any sort of fanatical allegiance to them. They prize toleration above orthodoxy, and adaptability above pigheadedness. As with Walt Disney's Jiminy Cricket, the general rule is to always let your conscience be your guide.

What, then, of the infamous mass murderer Pol Pot, who committed suicide in Thailand in April 1998? Between 1975 and 1979 he murdered two million peasants in his effort to enforce the Marxist ideology of collective agriculture in Cambodia. Those who knew him described his personality as being very charming. In the 1950s, after studying in Paris, Pol Pot set up a secret communist party in Cambodia. During this time he worked as a teacher in a private school and was described by his students as exceptionally polite and quiet. After being armed by North Vietnam, he seized power in 1975. A year before his death he described himself to a reporter as a sincere man whose main purpose in life was to help people achieve a better life. He insisted that he was not a savage butcher, his intentions were always honest and pure, and that he would die with a clear conscience. It is clear from such cases that conscience alone cannot tell us what is morally right objectively speaking.

Although claiming to adhere to traditional religious principles, third-camp theorists maintain the mutability of moral norms. As said by Joseph Owens, they hold in common the view that the fear of absolutes is the beginning of wisdom.[5] They also have something else in common, to wit, the rejection of the authentic natural moral law. If nature is spoken of at all it is only in the fashion of Protagoras. Simplifying somewhat: nature has its ways; man has his; and never the twain shall meet—unless I feel like it!

## THE JUSTIFICATION FOR THE THIRD THEORY

### The Is and the Ought

To avoid merely tautological statements, such as saying that wrong killing (murder) is wrong killing, the justification for the third model begins by distinguishing between descriptive and prescriptive statements. This difference is widely recognized and can be found in all of the different ethical theories, including Relative Absolutism. The is-ought contrast did not have to await the arrival of David Hume to be discovered. It was known to the ancients, as we can see from Book I of Plato's *Republic*, as well as to later thinkers, such as Aquinas.[6]

For Aquinas, the first sort of statement deals with the facts of the matter, the way the world is, what is true of the world, or speculative knowledge, beginning with being and handled according to the principle of noncontradiction. The second sort of statement deals with what should be the case, an evaluation of the situation, or practical knowledge, beginning with the principle of do good and avoid evil. In contrast to our knowledge of the world, we do not see evil as we see a rock or a tree; we do not observe crime and sin by means of the senses.

It is true, though, that ethics is not an autonomous subject area. Morality presupposes certain facts about reality and human nature, such as the existence of God and our possession of intellect and free choice. This arrangement, however, should not be interpreted as a reductionism. Being dependent on X is not the same thing as being reduced to X. Even though information from the theoretical side of knowledge is needed to have ethics, ethics is not the same thing as theoretical knowledge. It is the difference between a necessary and a sufficient condition rather than the identification of one thing with something else, such as 50/100 being the same thing as 1/2, or, in materialistic philosophies, as concepts being the same thing as refined sensations. Instead of a reductionistic relationship, the relationship between practical and speculative knowledge is like that between a violinist and his or her violin. One is not the other, and yet the violinist is dependent upon that instrument in order to make music.

Here are some examples of the descriptive use of language: (A) Man walks into room. Man's grandmother is sitting in rocking chair. Man thinks about getting all her money. Man picks up axe. Man raises axe in the air. Man brings axe down on his grandmother's head. His grandmother falls over dead. (B) Three-hundred-pound football player grabs one-hundred-pound cheerleader. He penetrates cheerleader's vagina with his penis. Cheerleader cries out. The large football player hits cheerleader over the head with a rock. Cheerleader's life functions cease.

Here are some examples of the prescriptive use of language: (A) An evil man, acting out a plan to gain his grandmother's great wealth, murders his grandmother in cold blood by hitting her over the head with an axe. (B) A cruel and heartless football player, in a fit of sexual lust (perhaps magnified by watching many hours of pornography), overpowers, rapes, and murders one of the cheerleaders for his own team. (C) Today, two men were sentenced to death in the electric chair for murder. In both cases, the jurors, citing the vicious nature of the crimes perpetrated by the criminals, recommended that no mercy be shown to the savage criminals.

As we see from these examples, there is an important difference between these two ways of speaking. In the first way no moral statement is made. Everything is matter-of-fact. In the second way, however, there is no doubt about the judgmental language. Although killing or sexual intercourse may be morally neutral terms, murder and rape are certainly meant to convey a moral meaning. Whereas a scientist, insofar as he or she is a scientist, can be satisfied with the descriptive usage of language, ordinary people cannot. Indeed, it is the duty of the jury in the cases cited above to pass judgment on the people involved in the cases, judgments that always at least imply some system of morality. Nonetheless, we can still ask the question: At exactly what point in the judgmental process does morality enter the picture?

The third paradigm is based upon the premise that no physical activity is either good or evil in itself. All physical acts, such as the lowering of an axe on someone's head or the penetration of someone's vagina by someone's penis, are morally neutral. There is no such thing as an action that is intrinsically evil, that is, evil in and of itself. When discussing ethical issues, the "object" of one's action is simply the physical action itself; it is what is done by the person with the conscious intention of doing it. There are no evil "objects" in the sense of actions that, by their mere doing, would constitute an evil act. There is always a difference between the physical activity and the moral character of the act. Thus, no action in and of itself can be automatically labeled wrong. No deed in and of itself is per se good or evil.

Of course, once we know an act to be one of rape, murder, torture, or adultery it cannot be done. The second variation on Absolute Relativism

One *does not* aim to justify acts judged to be wrong by the morally responsible agent. How, though, do we know an act to be wrong? The main work of the third theory is supplying a means for figuring out the answer to that question.

And so, at no time can anyone in authority, whether civic or religious, declare that a particular species or kind of act is always and everywhere wrong for everyone all the time. That is to say, no whole class of acts can be declared immoral. If there were such a category of acts (e.g., contraception), nobody, once he or she became aware of the category and its content, could perform the act and be morally good at the same time. However, since there is no such category of acts, the third-theory disciple can never be accused of promoting an evil means to a good end because every possible act is morally neutral until he or she views the overall situation and makes a moral judgment on the act in terms of its overall effect and the balance of harm and healing resulting from the action.

In the third model, acts become good or evil only when all the circumstances, including the mind of the actor, are taken into account. Since any physical behavior when considered alone is in the realm of the premoral, morality does not enter the picture until the mental attitude of the agent and the overall context, including future events and effects, are studied and understood. Advocates of this view of virtue would probably recognize the actions mentioned above concerning the grandmother and the cheerleader as morally evil, just as they would agree that torturing and raping little children is wrong.

The reason for this, however, does not depend upon the nature of the acts themselves. The evil status of the act depends upon the intentions of the actor and the overall set of circumstances (the extended object) surrounding the action in question. In the above examples the total situation shows that the acts are evil because the grandson is out to harm his grandmother in order to gain immediate access to her wealth, and because the big football player must do great harm to the cheerleader in order to satisfy his craving for sexual self-expression.

Under other circumstances, however, the same physical actions might be right. What if the grandson really needs the money more than the grandmother? What if the football player has a real psychological and physical need for sexual intercourse there and then? What if the grandmother wished to die? Then her grandson could not be convicted of murder; it would be a case of euthanasia. What if the cheerleader was happy to have sexual intercourse with the big, strong, handsome football player? Then there was no crime committed. Thus, until we know all the pertinent circumstances surrounding a case we cannot pass judgment on the moral character of the particular action. Because of this, a third-model disciple cannot be accused of willing an immoral action until he or she actually wills to do something in view of all the circumstances. This must be the situation because the deed that the individual is thinking about doing is neither good nor evil when considered in isolation from his or her willing of it. The complete "object" to be judged must include how the agent sees the overall situation.

Aside from making the advocates of proportionalism appear more loving and merciful than their more rigorous Relative Absolutism opponents, the paradigm has another advantage. Those following the third model are usually very much interested in the great social issues that dominate the news of the day: jobs, pollution, overpopulation, war, poverty, crime, the marginalized, welfare, the oppressed, and the alleviation of personal hardship. Their central social theme is the improvement of society as a whole. Furthermore, they want the improvement to take place quickly. They are preoccupied with bringing about revolutions rather than evolutions. For this reason, the greater flexibility of the third model serves their purpose very well.[7]

## REALITY CHECK

### Maudlin Love

A particular sort of act cannot be always immoral and not always immoral at the same time. Within a theistic context, the third approach sounds like a tolerant route to take. Lurking beneath the surface, though, are dangers so deadly that it must be rejected. It is in fact the Absolute Relativism One view in disguise. This occurs for several reasons, such as its maudlin definition of love, the volatile nature of one's emotions, the subjective nature of one's intentions, its susceptibility to fads, the undetermined nature of the future, and because of the hole-in-the-dike effect.

To begin, what is the meaning of love? Today there is the widespread idea that love is just another word for sex, or that any relationship involving a strong emotional feeling is a love relationship. This view represents the common state of mind in which love, sex, and hot feelings are confused with one another. Many people claim to be offended by the very idea that God would condemn any act that is rooted in emotional feelings. This meaning of love, though, is so broad that it includes everything and anything.

Referring to feelings is a very vague way of talking about love, and equally vague talk about the importance of love in human life in no way tells us about the moral value of particular types of human behavior. If this use of the word would cover all forms of interpersonal human activity, including sexual activity, then it is very short on providing a useful view of love. In fact, human morality cannot be based on feelings alone. This fact is often obscured by sloppy language. For example, the expression "making love" is often a euphemism for sex. This is like calling pornography adult entertainment when in fact it hardly rises above adolescent immaturity. In other cases, some claim that marriage is simply a caring relationship with bodily pleasure. This definition is often used to support divorce and remarriage. No love, no marriage—period. It is also often used to defend trial marriages, which are quite useless. In order for a trial marriage to be true-to-life it would have to last fifty years and provide for raising three kids along the way.

According to the maudlin view of love, you can do anything in the name of love. Do you love your city? Is it being overrun by street gangs? Why not round up the gang members, stand them up against a wall, and shoot them? Can you love your country and still give away its military secrets? In a book by Yuri Modin we learn how the old Soviet Union benefited from secrets passed on to him by Anthony Blunt, Guy Burgess, John Cairncross, Donald Maclean, and Harold (Kim) Philby in the 1940s. Modin, a KGB (State Security Committee) agent, was the London handler for the group. According to Modin, all of the spies had a passionate love for England. By their actions they hoped to bring Marxism to England, which was to them an expression of their true love.[8]

In fact, though, love and emotionalism are not the same thing. Strong emotions may follow upon the actions of the intellect and will, but emotions are not a substitute for the intellect and will. Sodomy, for instance, is not forbidden love; it is forbidden sex. Looked at from another angle, it is wrong to say that rape is violence, not sex. Rape obviously is sex; it is not love. There is no essential connection between love and sex. If one were the other, rape would be love, parents would be having sex with their children, teachers with their students, and priests with their parishioners. These examples show the need for a hierarchy of values; some values must take precedence over other values. Yes, for instance, we want a peaceful city, but we also want to preserve the higher value of each human life. Consequently, street gang members cannot be rounded up and shot.

The influence of maudlin love is especially important with respect to marriage. In general, if a legal marriage is only for cementing feelings into place, why can't anyone with feelings get married to anyone else? What about fathers and daughters, grandmothers and grandchildren, aunts and nephews? Moreover, why restrict marriage to couples? Cannot people love in groups? What about five men and ten women tying the knot and getting all the legal benefits? As a result, it is obvious that the candy-store-love claim proves too much.

The same holds for those sentimental Christians who see in the Bible a justification for any and all sorts of sexual relationships. They say that it is absurd to believe that God would condemn any lifestyle rooted in love, that is, the schmaltzy (Yiddish for melted fat) feeling experienced by the lover. However, precisely because the sugar syrup view of love does not allow anyone, whether individual citizens, teachers, social workers, doctors, lawmakers, judges, and so on, to discriminate between good and bad sorts of interpersonal human relationships, using love like a thick molasses to cover up all defects in human sexuality will not work.

Without an anchor in divine destiny, given a certain amount of emotionalism, anything imaginable can become a marriage, with all the attendant legal trappings. Once we break the bond between sex and reproduction it is easy to start using lachrymose love as a substitute for the real basic meaning of marriage, which is an exclusive lifelong commitment of two people to each other for the purpose of creating and caring for children. This destruction of the connection between sex and reproduction is widespread today, with more and more ridiculous results.

If, for example, the purpose of sex were primarily the expression of mature mutual maudlin love, then wherever there is adult mutual love it would be proper to have voluntary sexual relations. Aunts and nephews, uncles and nieces, fathers and daughters, sons and daughters, sons and sons, adults and older boys, cousins and cousins once removed, priests and parishioners, priests and nuns, nuns and bishops, teachers and students, bosses and secretaries, and so on could be having, in good conscience, sexual relations with each other. If we follow this line of reasoning, would God condemn incest that is rooted in love? Of course not. Consequently, the mature mutual love dogma would justify all forms of sex, including incest, fornication, and adultery.

Moreover, the Bible clearly says that I must love my neighbor as I love myself. Notice the lack of any reference to either age or gender. This would mean, then, that I should be having sex with everybody, including young children, and also with myself, which is impossible.

In addition, don't some people have an emotional attachment to their pets and cars? What judge, for instance, would be so cruel and closed-minded as to deny the legality of a marriage between a woman and her beloved dog? Restricting marriage to the human species is unfair discrimination. Such injustice must stop. According to the third-model theology of the loopholes, as outlandish as it may sound, if two males can get married, why can't a woman and her dog, or a man and his car, tie the knot? Why should our animal friends and mechanical companions be denied equality? Under such a regime, declaring a woman and dog relationship to be a legal marriage, with all the accompanying monetary benefits paid out of the public purse, is as reasonable as declaring that two males can be married to each other. After all, don't all people in such cases have loving intentions?[9]

## A GRAND ILLUSION

### Good Intentions

Contraception is a modern example of good intentions gone to the dogs. In the third-model, your intentions play a major role in making an action good or evil. As applied to the technology of sex, this means that the use of contraceptives is permissible on the condition that my attitude is positive and directed toward sooner or later having children. Do I will in a general way that God's plan for the family be fulfilled? Then that is sufficient to keep me moral. As long as I intend to have children sooner or later, then it is fine for me now, due to present problems, to engage in contraception. When my problems are behind me my good intentions will bear fruit. The point is that the proper intention about the future exists now, thus preserving me from immorality.

In contrast, this is precisely what the fourth view cannot allow. Deliberate self-sterilization, even though temporary, is quite different from, say, taking a required medicine that has infertility as an unwanted side effect. It is still true to say that the road to hell is paved with good intentions. To argue in terms of averaging out one's intentions over a whole lifetime, instead of talking in terms of each individual act here and now, is one of the easiest ways in the world to justify anything. As another old saying goes, if you plan on changing what you will be then you must change what you are. If the meaning of good intentions is that in the future I will finally get around to being moral, then it is self-deception to claim that I am really being moral right now because of my intention to be moral in the future. Like overweight people whose diets always start tomorrow, those who think in terms of good intentions alone, to be activated in the future, will never be good.

What happens, though, when we look at good intentions from another angle? If the meaning of good intentions is that one's attitude is the determining factor in one's status as a moral being, then what we are really doing is engaging in a camouflaged version of the end justifying the means approach to morality. We must never forget that no one does evil willingly. Hitler and Stalin thought they were doing good; their intentions were fixed on goals that were, to their minds, wholesome. In the same vein, saying that an individual act of contraception is moral as long as the overall plan is fixed on a socially responsible goal, namely, the creation and care of new members of society, which is to fulfill God's plan for the family, could just as easily justify all sorts of other acts, many of which even those in the third camp would regard as reprehensible.

For instance, a woman, whose intentions are the purest, when married to a husband who refuses to have children, might decide to poison him so that she might marry a better man, that is, one with the right intentions. Is this bad? After all, her overall intention is good. Therefore, would taking the life of her evil (because of his wrong intentions) husband really be a sin, even though it might violate civil law? Not according to the moral managers of the third theory.

Furthermore, Absolute Relativism Three allows us to remedy one violation of the natural moral law by another violation. If, for instance, a woman with children is abandoned by her man, it would be immoral for another man to come along and treat them as if they were his real family. Doing so would only compound the injustice. Yet the third theory allows such a thing. Assuming that the new man is interested in true love, it would certainly be moral for him to care for their material needs, but sexual relations and future children must wait until the woman gets an annulment. However, if the basis for the relationship is anything other than real love, the man could just as well live with a whole series of abandoned women and children.

Two immoralities do not make a morality. This point cannot be emphasized too strongly. We can see this today with respect to the AIDS virus. Some argue that no method for defeating a diabolical disease is diabolical, and so, even if immoral, condoms should be allowed. One wonders, though, if no preventative measure is diabolical, would it be proper to place all those with AIDS in concentration camps, as was done in Cuba? Isolating those suffering from contagious diseases is an acceptable social practice, is it not? Once we admit that the end justifies the means, we could go even further, perhaps to the point of surgically operating on those with AIDS so as to make sure that they cannot engage in sexual activity. Couldn't such operations be called necessary evils or the lesser of two evils? The same thinking can be applied to other situations. Was it moral for many Ukrainians to side with Hitler during the nazi invasion of Russia because Hitler was the lesser of two evils when compared with Stalin?

### Misplaced Proportions

Without a doubt, intentions are of great importance. Intentions, though, cannot be taken in isolation. This is why Aquinas states that the whole goodness of an action cannot depend solely on the goodness of the will. There is also the content of the action to consider. If the act is bad in itself, then, even if the person sincerely wants to do good, the action remains evil. For an action to be wholly good, the rightness of the will must harmonize with the rightness of the act.[10]

Even though in every specifically human act intentionality is always present, dragging intentionality into the nature of the act itself can only serve to confuse the issue. It is like saying that a man, who has been torn apart by a tiger, is not really dead because the tiger is not a free agent. Or it is like saying that an act of murder is not really an act of murder because the killer suffers from a brain tumor. Intentionality, especially if the agent suffers from a mental or physical impairment, bears upon the guilt of the agent, not upon the nature of the act itself. The only time you as an individual can kill is when someone is unjustly attempting to kill you. Yet even then you cannot will the death of the person, either directly or indirectly. As Aquinas states in his *Summa Theologiae* (II-II, 64, 6): "According to man considered in himself, no killing is allowed, because, even though a man is sinful, we must love the nature that God has made, and which is destroyed by killing him."

In the case of self-defense, the distinction between what you want and what you foresee is important. Your desire must be to stop the attack, not to kill the attacker. This is shown by using the minimum amount of force needed to deter the attacker. In Relative Absolutism, the action (cause) is proportioned to the effect. In contrast, in the third view, the concern is with the balance (proportion) of one effect (the good end, saving your life) relative to another effect (the bad end, harming the attacker). Because of this, in theory four, economic, social, or psychological reasons, such as claiming that someone is causing you mental stress and anxiety, cannot be used as an excuse for killing someone.[11]

The fourth moral position in such matters is outlined for us by Aquinas. In his *Summa Theologiae* ("Whether it's lawful to kill a man in self-defense?") Aquinas says that it is, provided that the force used does not exceed the minimum necessary to stop the attack. "Nothing hinders one act from having two effects, only one of which is wanted while the other is not" (II-II, 64, 7). Aquinas views this as commonplace. Applications of the principle of double effect abound.

Examples would be a doctor administering a painkiller to a sufferer, foreseeing that it will shorten the patient's life; a soldier falling on a hand grenade in order to save his buddies; buying a small car rather than a large car, knowing that in an accident your chances of injury are much greater; a company fairly and honestly driving a less efficient company out of business. Other examples would be police officers, firefighters, construction workers, mine workers, stuntmen or -women or others who place their lives in danger while doing their job. We might also include here those who engage in dangerous entertainments, such as mountain climbers and race car drivers. Another example would be the captain's closing of the watertight door on a ship's compartment that has sprung a large leak, foreseeing that any sailors trapped inside will drown. This is not a case of sacrificing a few in order to save the many. It is a case of doing something moral (closing a door) to save the ship, but which also has a simultaneous unwanted effect.

In each case there is an action that is at least neutral in its morality (e.g., riding in a small car) having two effects, one good (getting to work) and the other bad (getting mashed in an accident). What makes the action morally permissible is not the equal weight of the two effects (ends, outcomes); it is the balance between the means (the car used to get to work) and the desired end (working for a living).

So also, if operating so as to remove a part of the body (the action) in order to save the life of a pregnant woman (the wanted effect) is morally permissible, then, if the part is a cancerous womb, the unwanted death of the developing human being is not murder. Such a case is not justified because there is a proportion between the life of the mother and the death of the baby (a life for a life). Neither is it a case of one life (the mother's) as opposed to two deaths (the mother's and the baby's) if the doctor fails to act. According to Aquinas' principle of double effect, the action is moral because there is a proportion between the operation (the action) and the desired good result (saving the mother's life).

If this were not the case it would be moral for IRA members and British soldiers to kill each other as long as they killed each other in equal numbers. Is it acceptable for members of nation A to rape and kill members of nation B as long as the latter rape and kill an equal number of the former? If Moscow is nuked by the United States, are things put right if Washington D.C., is also nuked (a capital city for a capital city)? To think in terms of a balance between the two effects opens the door to every sort of evil imaginable. Unless murder, for instance, is evil per se, and thus never to be freely chosen, it is easy to justify balancing one set of killings with another set, especially if both can be made to occur at the same time. Yet this is exactly the sort of thing allowed by the third theory.

## FEMTHINK

### Religion and Gender

This emphasis on balancing power and weighing outcomes also allows for a close association of the third theory with modern feminism. Male and female rights must be proportioned to each other and equalized as far as possible. This is the way things should be, not just essentially speaking, but in all ways. Any talk of special roles for men and women, roles assigned by God and that cannot be changed one for another, must be discouraged. What should be encouraged is the blending together of the feminine and the masculine, beginning with our understanding of God.

Modern feminism began when Simone de Beauvoir (1908–86) declared that everything womanly is the artificial creation of cultural conditions. Today some women are so extreme that they refuse to indicate on a job application form whether they are male or female. No doubt, even though it is true to say that some things womanly are cultural, the universal claim that there are no significant differences between male and female derived from nature has to be one of the most inaccurate statements ever made. There is also no doubt that some of what modern feminists demand is worthwhile. However, the worthwhile parts are in no way unique to femthink. The good parts can be found in the fourth model of morality and without any extremist assertions. In any event, there is no way the good parts can make up for the destruction caused by the bad parts, the main error being the feminist support of the separation of sex and reproduction. Such a separation makes sex into a mere game, an insignificant pastime, which anyone, of any age, can play with anyone else.[12]

Ironically, this separation has produced just the opposite of what the feminists say they want. It encourages men to look upon women as merely masturbation machines, lumps of flesh with temporarily useful openings at both ends. Thanks to feminism, men no longer think in terms of wife and family. They have no reason to support a woman once the fun is gone. As a result, it is very difficult for a woman to find a decent husband, and even when she thinks she has found one, in a short time he is gone. Under the tutelage of modern feminism, women have become their own worst enemies, allowing themselves to be used and thrown away by men. So where are the promised equally-available options of marriage or career? They do not exist for most women. Whether she likes it or not, the modern woman must satisfy her current male with premarital sex, work outside the home, and so forth. Moreover, the feminist devotion to contraception and abortion leads to depopulation. Consequently, one must wonder, what good is social equality if there is no longer a society in which a woman can be equal?

Furthermore, some feminists claim to be religious, but only on their own terms. Regardless of their religious tradition, femthinkers follow the same pattern. First, change the character of God from being a jealous God, whose will must be done, to a nice woman only interested in allowing human beings to do their own thing. Either that, or make the world into God and God into the world (pantheism), so that worshiping nature becomes the new religion. Either view has the effect of making morality so ambiguous that anything goes. Next, regard all scriptural laws as culture-bound so that they no longer hold in a general way. And then add for good measure that even if such laws still hold in a general way they are not binding on the individual. All laws must be adjusted to what the feminist wants.

Catholic feminists, for example, want to see women as priests and are upset because the pope and bishops continue to insist that a priest must imitate Christ with respect to his male status. In rebuttal, some feminists say that if the priest is to imitate Jesus, then he must do so in every detail, including speaking the same language, dressing the same, and so on. This means, in effect, that the priesthood is eliminated. Others say that if you are a human being you can be a priest because being a human being is an exclusively spiritual identity; the body does not count as part of your definition. This means, in effect, that anyone can be a priest. The extremism here is obvious: either no one can be a priest or everyone can be a priest.

However, what the feminists fail to take into account is the significance of human sexuality. The central fact of Christianity is the Incarnation of the Second Person of the Trinity, complete with body odor, dirty feet, hair under the arms, and male genital organs. The specific role of the priest is to imitate Christ in offering up a sacrifice to the Father. This role can only be filled by a male of the species. This is a perfectly reasonable doctrine. Ordaining a woman as a priest, that is, as another Christ, would be to deny the central belief of Christianity.

In this regard, feminists fail to realize that they are up against much more than cultural inertia. They are up against nature and commonsense. Saying that males and females are both human beings does not mean that men and women are the same in every way. Things can be essentially the same without being accidentally the same. Is not a midget as much of a human being as a giant basketball player? Does your skin color decide your species? It should therefore be plain that there is nothing wrong with using only men to play men and only women to fill female roles. Is there anything wrong with only a male playing the part of Hamlet? And who should play Ophelia: Arnold Schwarzenegger? Was it improper to have only males imitate George Gershwin at the 1984 Olympic Games in Los Angeles?

## God and Fatherhood

The same situation can be seen with respect to the question of God as mother. Is calling God father simply an arbitrary decision, like designating table in French as a feminine word? The answer is no. In Judeo-Christianity, God is a separately existing supreme being, who is in no way a part of the world, a world that he freely creates. This does not mean that God is absent, but it does mean that it is wrong to call God mother, at least insofar as the term has any biological meaning. It does make sense, though, to call nature mother rather than father. This is because whatever limited production does occur in nature must necessarily come from within nature, like a newly developing child within her mother, and so nature is aptly described as Mother Nature. This is confirmed in the Bible, where God is consistently called father. But is not the term mother used or implied in some places? Yes, but it is always in an as-if, metaphorical manner.[13]

Nevertheless, could the use of father still be due solely to the social and political conditions of the times? This might be entertained as a possible reason for the usage, but only if no useful noncultural reason can be found for the title. To find out we must turn to philosophy. Here, though, the split between pantheism and supernatural theism is paramount. If indeed one of the main points of Genesis is to rule out pantheism, then we are left with supernatural theism, in which God, precisely as creator, is entirely separate from his creation. The created world, like a child in her earliest period of formation, is completely outside of the creator, who is therefore aptly called father.[14]

### It's My Body!

Does the feminist separation of body and soul help the cause of equality? Not in the least. Yet we often hear the line, it's my body and I can do what I want with it. Very few, though, realize what is implied by such an assertion. Consider the following. The feminist says: We must go beyond the body to the person. The old person says: I wish I could take my present mind back to a young body. The young person says: I wish I could have a wise old mind in my young body. The selfish businessperson says: Well I don't actually do anything to help the homeless, but I think about them a lot. The man who forgot to get his wife a birthday present says: It is really only the thought that counts. The lazy student on Sunday morning says: My body may be in bed, but my mind is in church. The Hollywood actress says: In my last incarnation I was Cleopatra. The prostitute says: Sell your body not your soul.

What all these statements have in common is the notion that the true self is somehow separated from the body. The true me is really only my soul, consciousness, or mind. In other words, the body does not count as part of my definition as a human being. If and when this belief is actually acted upon, however, it can have strange consequences. It might, for instance, show up in the form of someone's parading around nude on the main street of town, and then feeling very persecuted if she is arrested for doing so. A little thought, though, will show that this feeling is unjustified, even though we might also come to understand why, because of feminist doctrine, she might feel that way.

To test what I am saying, take the "it is my body" doctrine into areas of life other than feminist causes and see what happens. Compare, for instance, the nudity on parade mind-set with someone who claims that it is permissible to violate the speed limit because "it is my car," or to chop down a tree in Central Park because "it is my axe." Why can't I hurl my own body in my own car down the street at twice the community standard? What right do you have telling me what is a safe speed *for me*? Why can't I use my arms, my back, my legs, and my axe in any way and anywhere I want to? Who are you to tell me what to do with my things? Obviously, this attitude has nothing to do with reality.

## DEFINITELY MAYBE

### Morality by Anticipation

In addition to the problems outlined above, there are other serious problems with the third paradigm of virtue. One problem is the fact that, when the morality of an act is judged by its future effects, we will always find ourselves in a position of never knowing, no matter how far we extend our view into the future, whether the action is morally permissible in some absolute sense, and so we are always free to declare it good in some relative sense. As we have already seen with respect to John Stuart Mill, because the future is never finished, attempting to judge the morality of an act by its future consequences never works.

The grain of truth in this futuristic approach is that whatever exists is good insofar as it exists, and as long as we concentrate on the existence of something it is always good. It is obvious that as long as things continue to exist the world has a future, and as long as the world has a future there is the possibility for a better world. Our hope for a better future is based upon the fact of continued existence. The future is always a day away, as Little Orphan Annie sings. This means that no matter what happens, and no matter when it happens, we can always say that, even though things do not appear to be going so well now, tomorrow everything will work out well. Just wait until the future and then you will see just how good the present decision to act in such-and-such a way really is.

Let's take a significant test case. Did Hitler do good or evil? Was he insane? In fact, you do not have to be crazy to be a mass murderer. Lenin, Stalin, Mussolini, Hitler, Idi Amin, Pol Pot, and others were not madmen in any clinical sense. And even if they were, how are we to explain the actions of the many loyal followers who did their bidding? Were they all insane? And what about present-day mass murderers, and those who carry out their dirty deeds? Are they also all insane?

Neither must you be insane to follow the third way. You must, though, be prepared to accept some strange consequences. Going on the basis of hindsight, and taking into account what happened after the war, we could very well argue in the third view that what Hitler did to the Jews in Europe was a good thing for the Jews. In the early part of the twentieth century the Jewish population of Europe was disintegrating culturally, losing its religious character, and in danger of dying out. Intermarriage and international business were very quickly causing the assimilation of the Jews into the surrounding non-Jewish population. Therefore, someone in the third mode of mind could argue that, thanks to Hitler, by means of a Holocaust directed primarily against the Jews, the Jews were saved from extinction. Although it appeared bad at the time, all things considered, given the larger good to be achieved, looking at the greatest good of the greatest number, proportioning the good outcome (preserving Jewish identity) to the bad outcome (killing millions of people), in the long run Hitler did the Jews a favor.

Moreover, in the future, the Holocaust will prove to be an even greater blessing. Following World War II, because of the Holocaust, Jews from all over Europe were encouraged to return to the Holy Land, where they now constitute a large and viable community that is not about to die out. Despite their many problems, both external and internal, highlighted by the assassination of Yitzhak Rabin in November 1995, we can be sure that things will continue to improve for Israel in the future, thus proving beyond any doubt that Hitler was in fact a good friend to Jews all over the world.

The Hitler scenario has an exact parallel today in the area of mercy killing. Suppose that the relief of suffering is a good Christian thing to do. However, if killing the sufferer is justified as a means to relieving the pain of the sufferer, we will soon find ourselves in a ridiculous situation. Assume that someone who engages in mercy killing is regarded as a hero. It follows that the more suffering he relieves, the greater the hero he is. Now, whose suffering would be reduced the most by death, the young child with seventy years left to live or the old person with seven days left to live? Assuming that they are both in pain, the answer must be that the young child has more suffering to lose than the old person. Consequently, killing the youngster would make the mercy killer the greater hero. Moreover, the greater the number of such youngsters killed, the higher the hero he would be.

Now let's extrapolate this to the whole human race. Everyone, sooner or later, is going to suffer, so why not kill off everyone as soon as possible? Thus the abortionist, the person who guns down thirty kids in a schoolroom, and the like are great heroes. Instead of punishing them we should honor them with monuments and statues.

Morality by anticipation also does damage in another way. Standards come in two varieties: the permanent sort and the temporary sort. The temporary kind works well enough for things like citizenship, church membership, entrance to university, voting rights, who is good looking and who is not so good looking, and so forth, but it does not work at all in basic moral matters. Without permanent rules of morality, anyone at anytime can say, yes, I admit that I am not in conformity with moral standard M at the moment, but, since moral standards are changing all the time, M will shortly be different, and so, if you wait, I will be in conformity with the upcoming new moral standard. This can also be called being moral by anticipation, and, in effect, returns us to Absolute Relativism One.

It should be obvious to anyone hearing such arguments that there has to be something very wrong with the third paradigm. As Socrates and Plato figured out a long time ago, when a theory produces absurd results, such as Hitler as a Jewish war hero, we know that there is something terribly amiss with the theory. As reliable philosophical methodology dictates, when a theory fails to match up with the facts of experience, it is the theory that must be changed, not the facts. Being able to deduce the "fact" that Hitler was a great friend to the Jews shows just how faulty the theory really is.

## CREEPING CHAOS

### Rights and Duties

Every right you possess implies a duty placed on someone else. For instance, if I have a legal right to smoke cigarettes then the state has a duty to let me buy them, and other people have a duty to let me smoke them. My right is a relative right if the conditions can be restricted to just certain times and places, say only in my own home or in certain places outside the home. The right is absolute if someone can smoke cigarettes anytime and any place he or she chooses.[15]

The same holds in other cases. If abortion is legal, then you cannot prevent my entering a place where the procedure takes place. If suicide is legal, then you cannot prevent someone (not necessarily a medical doctor) from assisting me in my quest for death. Neither can the method of death be dictated by the state or someone else. Someone might choose, for instance, to die slowly by smoking fifty cigarettes a day or by using hard drugs of questionable quality. Moreover, if I want to leap to my death off the Golden Gate Bridge, it is my body and my business and the police and other do-gooders should keep their noses out of it. On the other hand, if suicide is illegal, then the assistant can be charged with the crime of being an accessory before the fact.

Similarly, if prophylactics are legal, then no one can prevent their manufacture, sale, and use. However, if contraception is not morally permissible, then prophylactics cannot be used in any circumstances connected with sex and reproduction. This is another place where those following the third model step back. Many of them start making distinctions between the use of prophylactics for the purpose of contraception and for the purpose of preventing the transmission of disease. Take the case of a good man, they suggest, who gets AIDS through a tainted blood transfusion. How cruel it would be to now insist, on moral grounds, that the loving husband forever abstain from sexual relations with his loving wife. Surely the use of condoms could be justified in such a case.

However, there is a problem. In the first place, the obvious purpose of sex is reproduction, so obvious in fact that it hardly needs debating. This fact cannot be dismissed because someone suffers an unfortunate accident. It is, of course, possible to challenge anything. Does two plus two really make four? However, there is little point in discussing anything with those who wish to be quarrelsome for the sake of being quarrelsome. The cantankerous and peevish will not agree to anything, and so we can hardly expect them to accept the God-given connection between sex and reproduction.

For another thing, sometimes accidents of birth prevent some people from doing things other people can do. Often there are accidents occurring later in life that change your life in a permanent way. Someone who has had a leg amputated, for example, cannot demand that the whole universe be changed just so he can dance. Because of his condition, he must forgo dancing forever. Why should sex be any different? Asserting that it would be heartless to insist that the husband give up sexual relations with his wife presupposes that we have made sex into God. The claim takes for granted that every male has an absolute right to sex. Yet this cannot possibly be the case. If it were we would get ourselves into actions that even those anxious to support the third theory would not be willing to defend.

Observe what happens when you affirm that males have an absolute right to sex. It means that females have an obligation to gratify the sexual desires of men. The result is that, not only is there no longer any such thing as rape, but it is now the case that the female who fails to comply with the demands of a man can be charged with violating the man's civil rights. And imagine what would happen in the case of one man demanding sexual relations with another man. Likewise with suicide. If I have a right to die, then someone else can be charged with a violation of that right for not helping me die when I demand that he do so. This is a necessary outcome of the third model.

How can we escape this situation (which is comparable to seeing Hitler as a Jewish war hero)? We must say that people do not have an absolute right to sex, and neither do they have an absolute right to children, cigarettes, alcohol, drugs, abortion, suicide, and guns. Sex, even within the bonds of marriage, can only be had under certain conditions. By allowing an exception to a moral principle, those in the third camp are justifying a zany situation in which the victim is charged with a crime, while the villain goes free, something straight out of *Saturday Night Live*. Rather than urging the husband and wife to use their suffering as a way of showing that they love God and each other more than sex, as is done by some unmarried men and women who freely remain celibate for the love of God, the third model is constantly searching for loopholes, so much so that its moral theory looks like a piece of Swiss cheese.[16]

### Risky Business

Another major problem with the third position is the fact that allowing one exception in theory means allowing millions of exceptions in practice. Several examples will illustrate the point. Take, for instance, the case of female genital mutilation. In some cultures it is deemed to be very salutary to surgically remove a girl's clitoris before puberty. The future effect of the removal is thought to be very good with respect to the girl's relationship with her husband. Without a clitoris, the tiny organ allowing the female to experience sexual pleasure, the woman is much less likely to be unfaithful to her husband. This is good for the family life of those in that culture. Having undergone the procedure will therefore make it much easier for her to find a husband, which in turn is good for society.

What objection can the third camp raise against such a practice? Really none. Furthermore, if allowing the procedure in the case of one girl is accepted as moral, then there is no reason to forbid it in the case of any other girl under the same circumstances (if the parents want it, etc.). Likewise in the case of abortion, the torture of prisoners, the abuse of children, euthanasia, genocide, and so forth.

In contrast, according to Relative Absolutism, there is never any good reason for one human being to directly will the harm of another innocent human being. In this sense, Kant, even though his premises could not support it, was right when he insisted that no human being should ever be used as a means to an end for another human being. So, even assuming, let's say, that the male is naturally sterile and free of all contagious diseases, he still cannot go around having sexual intercourse with numerous females just for the fun of it. To do so, even assuming that the females are willing partners in his exploitation, would mean using the females as mere long lumps of meat with holes at each end. The fact that someone cooperates in someone else's desire to use others does not make the action moral. For this reason, you cannot sell yourself into slavery, or, even though she would still love you, you cannot kick your mother down the stairs. Unfortunately for Kant, his approach lacked any foundation outside of his own will. If I can impose a rule upon myself, I can just as well remove it from myself.

Another example of making exceptions is killing a child resulting from a rape. Why should the child be punished for the sin of the father? By all means punish the rapist, and give the mother every possible emotional, physical, and financial help, but do not execute the innocent. The situation is no different from other situations. For instance, if a man, whose identity is known, kills a famous politician and then manages to escape so as to be forever beyond the reach of the police, should the government arrest and execute the assassin's children as a way of balancing the scales of justice?

Many people are disturbed by such a hard saying. Yet, if it is possible to justify the deliberate killing of even one innocent child, it is possible to defend killing an infinite number of them. This is why any law that forbids abortions, but then adds a vague rider, such as, unless the health of the mother is in danger, is the same as having no law at all. Where health is undefined it can mean anything, with the result that anyone can use it as an excuse for killing. Such a law would be like saying that you must stop for red lights, unless, of course, you feel you do not have to.

If the police chief were morally justified in torturing just one prisoner, let's say in order to elicit from her information that would save the lives of some police officers in the future, the police chief could also justify torturing a countless number of other prisoners when doing so would serve some good end. Similarly, it is murder if a battered wife, because he might, tomorrow, abuse her again, shoots her cruel husband in the back as he is going out the door. If one abused woman can kill her abuser anytime between attacks, then any woman who thinks she is going to be abused at some point in the future can do so. By the same token, any nation can mount a preemptive nuclear strike against any other nation that it thinks might attack it at some time in the future.

According to the third view it is moral to intend the death of a human being when the end to be achieved is proportioned to the killing that is carried out. Thus, someone who loves humanity may decide to help nature improve the species by using artificial selection, thereby helping natural selection by some careful pruning and breeding. Someone thinking this way might decide to round up and eliminate all those who are defective in one way or another. In parallel fashion, many people today sincerely believe, because of the great good to be derived from the elimination of unwanted pregnancies and from the elimination of overpopulation, that abortion is perfectly justified.[17]

However, in Martin Rhonheimer's analysis of the situation, this simply will not wash. Regardless of how much those in the third camp try to disguise it, the fact is that they are advocating a theory from which it follows necessarily that the good end justifies the evil means. According to Rhonheimer:

> Proportionalists say that an action is *right* if what one does is justified by commensurate reason. In this view, a person is a *good* person if he or she does not directly intend to realize a premoral evil, but intends to act so as to maximize goods or to minimize evils ("in the long run," Knauer would add), meaning to act responsibly by commensurate reasons. . . . Proportionalists are concerned with the reasons one might have to bring about certain states of affairs as the consequences of one's doings; and only this allows a judgement about "right" and "wrong." This is why consequentialists discuss for example the question of whether it could be right to execute the innocent, instead of simply asserting: to execute an innocent person for whatever reason is *evil by its object*.[18]

In effect, proportionalism allows everything under the sun. Consequently, you can never say never when it comes to killing an innocent human being. Any such universal negative norm is ruled out in advance. Rhonheimer continues:

> Proportionalism is a methodology by which one in fact always can *with good conscience* act according to the principle "let us do evil so that good comes about," because the methodology gives one the conviction that, provided good comes foreseeably about, what you did was not evil at all, but just the morally right thing, so that the ominous principle does not apply in your case. Whoever nevertheless reproaches you for trying to justify, on the grounds of "good reasons," what in reality is morally evil, will be "misrepresenting" your position.[19]

### Secularist Snake Oil

Another contemporary example of Absolute Relativism Three thinking is the policy of giving out free prophylactics in the schools, which is usually touted as the only humanitarian way to protect the students against disease. Such kindheartedness is sometimes compared to teaching youngsters how to swim in order to protect them against drowning. Those who disagree with such a policy are condemned as being heartless. And when the latter respond by saying that abstention is the way to avoid problems, the former call them naive.

Following the same line of thought, though, we could just as well demand that cigarettes, drugs, and drug paraphernalia be freely distributed in the schools. Don't be naive; no matter what you say to them, students are going to smoke and use drugs. So, in order to prevent their doing harm to themselves, the state has an obligation to hand out safe cigarettes, uncontaminated drugs, and clean needles. Furthermore, in some parts of some cities there is a high degree of crime in the schools. Consequently, who would be so heartless as to deny to students and teachers what they require in order to protect themselves? It follows, therefore, that both students and teachers must be supplied with protective vests and small arms. And how should we deal with the unavoidable use of alcohol by students? Should schools have bars so that students of all ages can drink booze under safe, supervised conditions?

Regardless of the example used, however, the basic problem is the same. Before giving away X we have to know whether or not the actions involving X are neutral, moral, or immoral. If the actions are immoral then we cannot use an evil means to achieve a good end. This is why the swimming lessons example is irrelevant to the issue. There is nothing immoral about swimming as a means for achieving the good goal of surviving in water. There is, though, something immoral about contraception.

Yet another contemporary case would be the issue of active euthanasia, whether administered on an involuntary basis or as a case of directly assisted suicide. Very often people propose the voluntary route as a way of showing love for old people, as if, along with abortion, more death is what we need in order to solve most of our personal and social problems. Furthermore, they believe, active euthanasia should be subsidized by the state, or at least sanctioned by the state by granting immunity to those who carry out such charitable work. Those who advocate such a public policy usually think that, since relieving suffering is a good goal, someone's death wish should be fulfilled by the state. Anyone who disagrees with this position is regarded as intolerant and insensitive.

There is a perverse logic here. My sense of symmetry says that, since we have state-sponsored death at one end of life (abortion), let's have it at the other end also. But then my sense of fair play comes into conflict with my sense of symmetry. What about equal treatment for all those in between? Should we discriminate against someone because of age or physical condition? Isn't one's mental condition also very important? Why such a halfhearted humanitarianism? Why are stop signs arbitrarily placed here or there? In a free society, when people wish to die, the state should treat everyone equally. A teenager with pimples, for instance, should be able to take advantage of the same government aid as the old people. Once the teenager's mind is made up, what right does anyone have telling the suffering soul that he or she cannot utilize the state's Ministry for Compassionate Conclusions?

Why not have a specially designed truck, with a crew of caregivers, constantly traveling around the nation, ready and willing to service the suffering. The crew would not be judgmental; it would be forbidden by law to impose its own views, religious or otherwise, on those requesting service. Its job would be to dispatch those who sincerely desire to go. If someone, of any age, and for any reason, decides that life is no longer worth living, the humane-mobile would assist that person in fulfilling his or her wish. If the person desires a slow death, then, regardless of what the insurance companies may say, the state will supply the person with a sufficient supply of fatty foods, cigarettes, liquor, drugs, or even jalapeño peppers, to do the job. If the person desires a quick death, then some quick poison may be in order. If the person wishes to go out in style, then the caregivers might roll out a guillotine.

Moreover, there is no reason why the entertainment industry cannot get in on the act. Why can't legalized suicide be a great boon to TV? Think of the economic impact. Those wishing to kill themselves can volunteer to do so on TV, perhaps on Monday nights, thus giving Monday night football some competition. Using a variety of interesting and creative methods, the volunteers would do their thing in exchange for money that would be passed on to their surviving family members or favorite charities. For their part, the TV stations would increase their ratings, thereby attracting many rich advertizers. How could anyone be opposed to such a thing when everyone would benefit from it so immensely?

Once the state-sponsored death of noncriminals is recognized as the legitimate right of every citizen, there is no reason to hold back the creative impulses of a democratic people. Euthanasia illustrates this point very well. The euthanasia enthusiast is very much concerned about relieving the suffering of the old, terminally ill, person. Therefore, it follows in his or her own mind that whatever the enthusiast wants to do to solve the problem is automatically correct. Since the relief of suffering is a good end, any means for achieving that end must be morally and legally acceptable. What is overlooked, though, is that the reasoning used to justify the one wanted act inevitably leads to the justification of a million other unwanted acts. Instead of proving too little, this loose logic proves too much.

Assuming that the government has the right to issue licenses to kill, the issue becomes the extent of the licensing. Assuming that a Ministry for Compassionate Conclusions is to be established, it is important to know exactly who will be allowed to take advantage of its good offices. This is no problem under a tyranny; the dictator would arbitrarily decide. However, in a liberal democracy the key question becomes: Why should its work be restricted to a privileged few, or just to those to whom the euthanasia enthusiast wants it restricted? Is the enthusiast appointing him- or herself a dictator?

Who has a poor quality of life? In the enthusiast's way of looking at the situation, there are no objective standards for one's quality of life. Each individual is the sole judge of whether he or she is up to snuff. Why, then, in the name of equality, should those who feel themselves to be below par be deprived of government services? Anyone, for whatever reason deemed suitable, should be allowed to use the state's equal opportunity hit men. Anyone who disagrees must be some sort of bigot, unjustly attempting to impose his or her own narrow-minded religious position on other people.[20]

Now if all this sounds bizarre it is because it is, but no more so than giving away prophylactics in the schools. In general, we cannot go around arbitrarily choosing what is right, usually on the basis of what happens to be convenient for us at the moment. Moreover, whenever someone arbitrarily rejects something that is morally correct, it is very difficult to take that person seriously when he or she criticizes someone else for arbitrarily rejecting something else that is morally correct. The end result is the view that nothing is morally correct, which is just another name for Absolute Relativism One.

## POLITICS AND ETHICS

### The Few and the Many

The same holds in the case of the ten prisoners discussed previously, as well as in the case of the overcrowded lifeboat that is about to sink unless its load of human passengers is reduced. According to the fourth view, despite the danger to all, it would be immoral for a self-appointed in-group of the small lifeboat society to gang up on the arbitrarily chosen members of the out-group for the purpose of throwing them overboard. Deliberately killing some so that others might survive would be a case of using an evil means in order to achieve a good end. The only reasonable solution to the problem would be for some people, beginning with the captain, to voluntarily go for a swim.

Deliberately killing the few in order to save the many has a wide area of application. Wolves are attacking a family, so why not throw the beasts a few little kids in order to save the remainder of the family? The Wolf Pack (a street gang) is attacking the people of a city, so why not pay the gang tribute, maybe including some young girls for the pleasure of the gang members, in order to prevent further attacks? A political wolf (Hitler) is attacking a family of nations, so why not throw the beast a few little nations in order to satisfy his hunger and thereby spare other nations? This, of course, was precisely the appeasement policy of Arthur Neville Chamberlain (1869–1940) toward Hitler and Mussolini when he gave away a part of Czechoslovakia and all of Ethiopia in exchange for peace in his time.

Neither can we call upon the political need to secure the common good as a justification for such actions. This is because such actions do not represent instances of the common good, but only of the collective or average good, which is an entirely different sort of thing. Examples of the collective good would be the killing of mentally and physically deformed people so that the average health and beauty of the population will increase, as was done under the nazi policy of race purification, and as is even now being done in China and in other parts of the world; the sacrificing of 10 percent of an army in a rearguard action so that the army on average, as a whole, will be better off than it would be otherwise; the use of abortion, infanticide, and euthanasia as a means for reducing the demand for land and food around the world, thus (maybe) raising on average the standard of living for those allowed to live.

## There Are No Easy Answers Here

Those advocating the third approach in ethics dismiss the charge against them of endorsing evil means to a good end by denying at the outset that there is any such thing as an evil means considered apart from the end to be achieved. To determine the morality of the act (the means) one must look at the balance of the good and evil achieved in the final stage. Hence, because the means cannot be judged in isolation from the overall outcome, those following the third theory cannot be accused of employing an evil means to a good end. The means become good or evil in view of the end; the means are never good or evil in themselves. The moral status of the means is known only through hindsight. Once this neat initial reversal is allowed, saying that the third way justifies an evil means to a good end would indeed be a misrepresentation.

It might even be argued that in some cases doing the deed is necessary in order to prevent some greater evil from taking place. Even assuming, for instance, that the use of contraceptive devices is generally immoral, someone might argue that their use is moral when they are needed in order to prevent AIDS. By thus making an appeal to what is said to be a necessary action, the third position is reinforced.

Nevertheless, even though the members of the third paradigm take great pride in their own theoretical ingenuity, such a scheme of things inevitably leads back to a purely subjective evaluation of right and wrong. The necessary result in political terms is that, in the name of law and order, national security, fighting crime, ending unjust discrimination, forestalling overpopulation, ending the war sooner, relieving suffering, and so forth, the government is justified in doing anything. It can incarcerate American and Canadian Japanese, assassinate the enemies of the state, bomb civilian populations, and distribute condoms in the classroom, and all in the name of the greater good.

There is only one rational way to forestall these consequences, which is to admit that a deed, evil in itself, can never become good. There is no such thing as a necessary evil. Once the door is opened to making an evil deed good because the deed is seen as necessary in order to achieve something good, there is no way to prevent anything and everything, deemed by someone at some time to be necessary, from becoming moral. If condoms are needed to fight AIDS, why not give everyone guns to fight crime? The problem here is that technology alone cannot be used as a substitute for human self-control. A gun is great for fighting off a lion, and an antivirus program is great for fighting off an Internet computer virus or worm, but all the advanced technology in the world will not solve our specifically human problems in morality.

Furthermore, if condoms can be deemed moral by some because their use is necessary in preventing AIDS, then others can just as easily deem it necessary for poor white farmers to keep black slaves, for nazis to shoot hostages, or for men to have their fill of pornography in order to satisfy some inner drive. Was the lynching of blacks necessary as a safety valve release mechanism in order to stave off some even greater social catastrophe? Is the use of dirty tricks in politics necessary to win an election because the other party is so bad? This is the sort of situation we get into when we start making exceptions and looking for loopholes in the relationship of means and ends.

Saying that we must do what we must do, meaning that a necessary evil is justified, is like the robber saying to his victim that he will be forced to shoot if the victim does not hand over all his money. Heaping up one evil on top of another is not the way to succeed in life. Remarks about necessary evils, or the lesser of two evils, do not indicate that one is on the path to a higher morality. Such remarks mean that someone is caught in a downward spiral of depravity, wherein one lower level is worse than the previous one.

Often times this happens when one evil is used to cover up another evil. Claiming that the second, third, fourth, and so on evil act is somehow less evil because it is further down the spiral is at best only an especially deplorable form of self-deception, comparable to the claim made by a porno star that the completely submissive female is really the one who is in complete control of her degrading relationship. The situation should rather be viewed as a case of compounded evil, a situation in which the sum total is a greater evil than all of the individual evil acts taken separately.

There is, nonetheless, a grain of truth in the third theory, namely, that we can never go back to the past. Since going back is impossible, it would be foolish to recommend such a thing to anyone. Moreover, every remembered event is always overlaid with the enriching influence of everything that has happened between then and now. Hindsight is always a different sight from that had at the time of the past event. In a certain sense, then, in the present we do see things, including the past, in a forward-looking way. This psychological fact of human experience, though, in no way justifies trying to wiggle off the moral hook by claiming that we can never know the morality of a present act until we arrive in the future. Quite the contrary, a better future requires rejecting such a theory.

### The True Common Good

Compared to the collective good, the common good is an entirely different thing. Rather than aiming at the greatest good of the greatest number (the overall good, the good of society as a whole, the welfare of people in general), the common good means the universal good in the same way that "All men are mortal" is a universal proposition. In such a sentence the predicate (mortal) applies to each and every man without exception. Similarly, the common good, unlike the collective good, serves everyone equally well. No one is left out. Hence, peace serves everyone in the society equally well; all benefit. Education benefits everyone. So also does the right to life. The availability of adequate health care benefits everyone, even if you personally are not using the services of a doctor or hospital at this time. Also, inalienable rights benefit each and every person taken individually.

Does this mean that everyone must contribute exactly the same amount of money, goods, and services to society as everyone else? No. When community action is required it must be carried out in a way proportioned to what different people expect to gain and lose from it. For example, when the society goes to war to protect itself, the expenses involved must not be placed on only the lower economic classes. Those with more to lose (the rich) must give more. A just law spreads out the burden so that, from those who have more, and who have more to lose if the nation is defeated, more is expected. Similarly, the doors to various professions should open more easily to those with greater talents in those areas. Then, after graduation, it is fair to expect them to use their skills for the greater welfare and benefit of the society that educated them.

Neither does the common good mean egalitarianism, that is, everyone getting exactly the same treatment all the time, such that, if you give a three-hundred-pound football player a large rare steak to eat, then you must also feed a baby a large rare steak. Equal treatment means something much more reasonable. With respect to food, it means that everyone should be well fed as far as possible, but what it means to be well fed will vary from person to person and from time to time. In Relative Absolutism, the principle is absolute, but the application of the principle is relative to different people and their differing circumstances.

Because of its universality, the common good (also called the distributive good), which governs the relationship between the individual and the group, should not be confused with the collective or community good (that sort of good dealing only with aggregates and averages), the individual or private good (that sort of good serving only one person to the exclusion of all others, e.g., if I eat this piece of cake then no one else can eat it), or yet another kind of good, the commutative (that good governing the relationship between two individuals).

In political terms, only the common good can act as the secure foundation for a genuine liberal democracy. This is the meaning of the expression that we must be governed by laws, not the whims of men. Yet the common good is what we cannot get out of the third position. Consequently, Absolute Relativism Three must be rejected in political philosophy. Whether in the life of an individual, or in the life of a nation, the third doctrine inevitably leads back to the first, which is as cruel as anyone can get within the realm of interpersonal human relationships.[21]

## CONCLUSION

When considering the third theory the operative phrase is let the buyer beware. Although presented as being more sympathetic than the fourth paradigm, it is in fact a prescription for cruelty. In other words, the third theory is the same as the first. Everything is permissible. According to the juvenile delinquent attitude of Absolute Relativism One, I am perfectly justified in doing anything I can get away with. Therefore, instead of championing compassion, Absolute Relativism Three turns out to be a sugar-coated poison pill.

We swallow this poison pill when we adopt the attitude that if you do not wish to participate in what I am doing, that is up to you, but do not tell me what to do. If I want to cheat people, push drugs, and view pornography on the Internet, that is my business and none of yours. If you find the band Animals In Serious Pain morally objectionable, then avoid it, but do not take away my fun. What the third view boils down to is that, if you do not like what is going on in Hitler's or Stalin's death camps, turn your attention elsewhere. Good and evil is nothing more than a matter of individual opinion. As a result, the position is, despite its claims, anti-Jewish, anti-Christian, and anti-Muslim.

It is worth repeating that no mature person could possibly accept such a doctrine. Hence the need for some theory of morality capable of providing a basis for truly objective moral judgments. This means that we must know, in terms of the specific kind of act, which sort of act is always proper for a person to freely choose, and which is never proper for a person to freely choose, something we can never know within the third model.

# CHAPTER 4

# *Relative Absolutism: God Is the Measure*

To the fifth [objection] I answer, whereas the theologian considers sin as being primarily an offense against God, the moral philosopher considers sin as something contrary to reason.[1]

Therefore [the rational creature] shares in the Eternal Reason and so has a natural inclination to its proper act and end; and this participation of the eternal law in the rational creature is called the natural law.[2]

There is nothing hindering a [good] act from having [simultaneously] two effects, only one of which is intended, while the other one is not intended.[3]

## INTRODUCTION

There is an old joke about how 1950s England was desperate for money, and so the president of the United States talked the queen into prostituting herself with him in exchange for a huge sum of cash. After she agreed, however, he greatly reduced the sum, whereupon she became highly indignant, retorting: What! You expect me to do that for that piddling amount of money. What do you think I am? Then came the punch line: We have already determined that; now we are just haggling over the price.

The lesson of this rude joke is that, in order to avoid moral nihilism, there must be some acts that are always and everywhere morally wrong and some others that are universally right. This is the way of Relative Absolutism, the water table of our common humanity. Whereas the first three theories find it easy to change moral standards to fit the occasion, the fourth way says you cannot do that. Nevertheless, Relative Absolutism remains the only really compassionate position in ethics.

## CONSERVATIVE CHIC

### Pleasure and Happiness

Virtue is not the enemy of pleasure. As long as eating and sex, for example, are needed for the continuation of human life, there is no reason why such activities should not also give you some personal pleasure. If being clean is good for you, go ahead and enjoy bathing. A car, for example, is meant to provide reliable transportation, so that one that is in constant need of repair, broken down, and the like is of no use to you; it is no good. When it is working right, though, there is no reason why you should not derive pleasure from it. You might enjoy gazing upon it as a thing of beauty, changing the spark plugs yourself, or using it to show off your wealth, good taste, sensible practicality, and so on to your friends.

Also, there is certainly nothing wrong with having emotions in the sense of being affectionate. In fact, unlike Star Trek's Spock, emotion accompanies every act of our will. However, this does not mean that all feelings are of equal value. Pleasures too must be ordered to man's final end. The pleasure of eating is to serve eating, which is to serve bodily life, which is to serve the soul. The pleasure of sex is to serve sex, which is to serve reproduction. The pleasure of honors and awards is to serve the good deed, which is to serve the welfare of others. If things were the other way around, anything giving someone pleasure (e.g., torturing cats, rape) would be right and good.[4]

In contrast to moral nihilism, the fourth view maintains that man's ultimate end is not earthly pleasure (sexual, artistic, mechanical, etc.), but eternal happiness. Every action that a person performs, he does, consciously or unconsciously, in order to be happy. Happiness is the final cause of all specifically human activity. This desire for happiness is imbedded in the very nature of man. Hence, even the masochist acts to bring about gratification. Even those who commit suicide do so in order to end a miserable life. This happiness we all seek can only be satisfied by a jealous God who demands high standards of faithfulness from individual human beings. He is not the maudlin God of the third doctrine who, in the name of soapy love, allows anything with respect to interpersonal relationships.

### The Relativity of Relative Absolutism

The fourth theory is an absolutism because there are no exceptions to the moral obligations placed upon us. And yet, because the moral law is based on the God-given purposes built into human nature, there is room for variation and development. It is not my purpose here to discuss highly unusual cases open to long debates, perhaps lasting forever, like JFK assassination theories. Here, as in every system of law, troublesome cases arise that cannot be easily resolved.

With respect to the natural moral law, for example, imagine a case where a man married to Mary is lost at sea and ends up on a little island. After seven years of waiting for her husband to return, Mary remarries. But then, two years later, the man is rescued and returns home to once again be with his wife and family. The resolution of the case is clear enough from the viewpoint of civil law, to wit, Mary is no longer his wife. Not so, however, from the viewpoint of the natural moral law, in which the question of to whom Mary is married could be debated at great length.

In the vast majority of cases, though, knowing the purpose of a law allows the intelligent person with the power of free choice to apply his or her knowledge to many situations, each with its own peculiarities, and to adjust his or her actions accordingly. If, to cite an example used by Aquinas, a city is besieged, and the king orders that the city gates be closed and locked, woe to him who disobeys the order. However, if some people friendly to the city should manage to get to the city gates, there would be no crime committed if the guards opened the gates to let in the friendly people.

Understanding the reason for the king's order to close and lock the gates means that it is possible to interpret the law in a relative way, even while the law remains fixed. The purpose of sealing the gates is to keep out the enemy. The purpose of the law is not for the sake of having a law, as if the law were an end in itself. If that were the case, the gates could not be opened for anyone.

One of the things we learn from this is that it is wrong to think of the natural moral law as some sort of abstract, deductive way of reaching moral conclusions. We are not dealing with abstract essences that are always fixed and unchanging in every detail. Abstractions cannot be found hanging from skyhooks; in fact, they do not exist at all. Reality is always a case of essence *and* existence. The natural moral law always operates within the concrete situation, avoiding abstract and universal essences that must always dictate one and only one course of action regardless of the concrete circumstances.

Another example of this relativism would be one in which a school board passes a law stating that no one over nineteen is allowed to play on high school football teams. The purpose of the law is to prevent stronger boys from dominating the team. What should be done, though, when a twenty-year-old student with Down's Syndrome wants to play for his high school team? All he would really be able to do is run on to the field at the beginning of the game and then sit on the bench for the rest of the game. The fourth view says let him play.

According to this model, the emphasis must always be kept on virtue, which is always a means to an end. Not only is law not an end in itself, neither is virtue an end in itself. Law is a means to the end of virtue, while virtue is a means to ultimate happiness. This means that there is no such thing as the spirit of the law versus the letter of the law. You are not to open the gates to the enemy. What part of no do you not understand? The purpose of the law must be adhered to by everyone, with no exceptions. Nevertheless, without backsliding into the third view, it is possible to open the gates under certain circumstances. The only way to understand this is by means of the natural moral law.

## The Case of the Traffic Signals Explained

In Relative Absolutism civil law is meant as a framework within which people can pursue their ultimate happiness. Not so in other theories. Hobbes and Kant, for example, make law an end in itself. According to a story in John Stuckenberg's 1882 biography of Kant, Kant was very fond of eating dried fruit, and on one occasion became extremely angry with the crew of a ship that was transporting an order of fruit to him from France. He had invited some friends over for dinner and was looking forward to the special treat. However, due to a storm at sea, the ship was delayed long enough to run out of food, and the crew ate Kant's fruit. This infuriated Kant, who asserted that, if the members of the crew had been truly moral men, they would have starved to death rather than violate their duty to deliver the fruit.

What would the world come to, thought Kant, if each individual did not feel an obligation to honor his or her contracts? There must be an uncompromising law (a categorical imperative) stating that one should not do anything that could not be made into a rule for everyone else to follow. This was his attempt to make a morality based on one's will into something absolute. When a businessman friend of his asked Kant if he was really serious about having the ship's crew die, Kant said yes.[5]

For Kant, there was nothing good in the whole world except a good will. Duty was the great sublime name of morality. He even thought that duty was an adequate substitute for the biblical Golden Rule and the Sermon on the Mount. As far as Kant was concerned, acting morally was the same thing as religion. Morality was a realm entirely within the person's will; ethics was autonomous. Kant expected people to be moral for the sake of being moral. The idea of duty, and the particular maxims that could be derived from it, was Kant's substitute for scripture. As a result, man was a lawgiver unto himself; he had to prescribe to himself his own rules of conduct. Personal conscience, therefore, was everything.

This illustrates the danger of making virtue an end in itself, which is the necessary outcome of making either the individual will or the group will supreme. By doing so we become trapped in a very inhuman condition. When your whole worth depends upon your adherence to a law, you can no longer distinguish between the purpose of the law and the means for implementing that purpose. You end up in a legal straitjacket.

To illustrate, imagine that you are driving home at three in the morning along deserted streets. Would it be moral for you to go through a red stoplight? If Hobbes were with you, he would say that it was, because, according to his reduction of human freedom to merely being able to physically move about unrestrained, you are entitled to do whatever you can get away with, even if the state has forbidden it. If Kant were in the back seat, however, he would say no. What would the world be like if everyone were free to either stop or not stop? Most likely the police, perhaps in the form of a camera, would feel the same way. Kant cops must adhere to the law as an end in itself.

Such inflexibility is a good reason to leave Kant and join Aquinas. As Aquinas would explain the situation at the stoplight, the purpose of a traffic light is to control the flow of traffic so that those using one street have as much opportunity to cross the intersection as those using the other street. When the traffic light fulfills its purpose it is good. However, if there is no traffic on the streets, then there is no need for a traffic light. Now, since it would be highly impractical to keep a crew of city workers sitting on the curb all the time, jumping up to remove the light when there is no traffic, and then replacing the light when traffic returns, we can leave it up to the reasonable driver to remove and replace the light as required. Is this too liberal? Not for Aquinas.

### It Is Wrong to Tell a Lie

Is it legitimate to control speech? Obviously it is, since such control is entrenched in civil law. The wickedness of lying is not just a matter of opinion. It is a serious crime to slander someone, libel an organization, shout fire in a crowded theater when in fact there is no fire, turn in a false fire alarm, make a false claim of a crime to the police, defraud an insurance company, lie on your income tax return, and to lie to a jury. Making a false statement while under oath about something material to the case is perjury. Business contracts demand that you tell the truth. Deceiving investors is a crime. Posting false information about a company on the Internet is a crime. Neither is it legal to advertise unlawful deals. In addition, more and more today the law recognizes the imbalance between the power of the public media and the power of the individual and small businessowner. Along with improved technology goes the growth of irresponsible journalism, malicious harassment, and the careless disparagement of goods and products, all of which must be controlled. Currently, even Internet "chat boards" are censored.

When we examine the foundation of the civil laws against lying we find that it is not in the laws themselves, or even in the need for the government to have accurate information on your income tax form. Neither is it a matter of a Darwinian struggle for survival. If the foundation for the laws against lying were only the need for physical survival in a hostile world, animals as well as humans would have articulate speech. No doubt insects and animals communicate, but they do not speak. This is not because they lack the physical means for doing so; it is because they have nothing to say in terms of concepts. We have the power of conceptual (spiritual) knowledge, while subhumans do not.

This, then, reveals to us the purpose of speech and, by extension, of writing, sign language, computer symbolism, and various other forms of specifically human communication. As a spiritual power, the power of speech must have been divinely instituted, and so the power to convey what is in my mind to another spiritual being like myself is the God-given purpose of speech. Following upon our intellectual life comes our emotional life of feelings, desires, wishes, and so forth. Love also goes along with our ideas. The proper meaning of love is willing goodness to another.

These can all be conveyed, howbeit imperfectly, by talking, and so talking is an ordinary part of our lives. Speech is designed to be used in the ordinary course of daily life in order to facilitate the transmission of ideas between spiritual beings who must work out their destinies by means of their material bodies in a material world. Its survival value is beyond dispute, which is why we can be sure that animals do not possess the power of speech. Since its survival value is so great, animals would surely use it if they had it. Yet we see no evidence for such activity among animals.

Assuming that the other spiritual being has some right to know what is in my mind, I would be lying if I were to deny him or her such information. Lying means that what I say and what I know do not match up. So if someone on the street asks me for the time of day, and I have no reason to suspect that he or she is insincere, joking, or harboring criminal intentions, I am breaking the natural moral law if I deliberately give the incorrect information. Likewise, your doctor is lying to you if you ask him or her about your condition and you are told something that does not correspond to what the doctor knows to be your condition.

In these cases, lying means something prescriptive rather than something only descriptive. This indicates an important difference between Absolute Relativism One and Relative Absolutism. Nietzsche, for instance, can still talk about lying in the descriptive sense (the lack of conformity between word and mind), but in the first paradigm there is nothing morally wrong about such a lack of conformity. The superman can lie any time he wants to.

However, the relativity of the fourth view shows up if some tyrant asks you to reveal the hiding place of someone he wants to murder and you prudently hide the truth by means of an evasive answer. As Aquinas points out (*Summa Theologiae*, II-II, 110, 3, ad4; compare II-II, 40, 3), in such a case there is no violation of the natural moral law. The primary purpose of speech is not to sound beautiful, as in singing or poetry, to tell tall tales and funny stories, or to produce cartoons and works of fiction, but to provide a means for mutual communication among incarnated intellectual beings. This purpose cannot be fulfilled if people do not accurately convey data, feelings, and ideas.

We can see the ideal showing through in our modern computers. All technologies are an extension of our human powers in one way or another, and so it is instructive to look at what we expect from our computers. We are so attached to our handiwork that we often regard them as humanlike, and when they break down we even talk about them as being sick. Why is this? Computers, which are in no way alive or intelligent, are wonderful because of their reliability. Once they are properly programmed they never lie to us. How much more wonderful is the power of spiritual beings to speak to one another in an honest way. We, though, unlike machines, have the power of free choice, which gives us the possibility for lying. Hence the need to examine lying as a moral issue.

### No Comment

Lying is always immoral. This is an absolute rule with no exceptions. Nonetheless, there may be occasions when failing to match up what we know with what we say does not violate the God-given purpose of speech. These occasions occur when the person eliciting information from you is not sincere, is a tyrant intent upon hurting you or someone else, is making a joke, or does not have the right to question you in the way he or she is doing. This would not apply to police officers who are doing their job properly. If a duly constituted officer of the government asks you for information pertinent to a case, you have a moral obligation to answer truthfully.

The situation becomes more complicated when you yourself are the criminal being investigated. True, you have the right to self-defense, but only if you are really innocent. If, for instance, a bank robber, fleeing from the police, shoots a cop, he cannot avoid jail by claiming that he was only defending himself. If in fact you are a criminal and you know it, you have no moral right to lie about your crime. In this context, there is no moral basis for refusing to testify because you might incriminate yourself. The philosophical basis for taking the Fifth is the view of Thomas

Hobbes, who maintained that it is moral for you to do anything you can get away with. Hobbes' view, though, is not the true natural moral law, which is to say that self-preservation is not the foundation for the law.

The materialist Hobbes taught that the natural moral law is nothing other than the order of right reason telling us what must be done to preserve life and health for as long as possible. Now, since this is best achieved in a peaceful setting, it behooves people to reach some agreement on peaceful coexistence, that is, to make a deal in which the basic right to use physical force in order to have your own way with others is totally surrendered to a sovereign who then possesses absolute power.

Later, Nietzsche will claim that society has nothing to do with Hobbes' imagined contract. In his *The Genealogy of Morals* (1887, Second Essay, sec. 17), the German makes it clear that the Englishman got it all wrong concerning the origins of human society. Hobbes was too rational. Nature's noblemen, the born rulers, simply come in like an unannounced storm and take over. They instinctively impose their will on others. They think with their guts. They are the greatest artists because their medium is other men. When they lower their hammers on others, they immediately, without any remorse, forge a new society. This is Nietzsche's development of Hobbes' animal view of the natural moral law.

In real life, however, our basic motivation is happiness. This is embedded in our nature and can never be eliminated. It is impossible for us to will our own unhappiness or to will evil for ourselves, or even to will that evil be done. As far as we can tell, Hitler, Stalin, Mao Tse-tung, Idi Amin, Pol Pot, and many others honestly thought they were doing good. The rapist and child molester thinks he is doing good, at least for himself. Likewise, Charles Manson and Teddy Bundy just wanted happiness and fulfillment for themselves.

In Relative Absolutism, even though we have the ability to speak, we do not have to be talking all the time, and there is no need to tell all we know. Truthfulness should not be confused with candor and frankness. There is a time to be candid and a time not to be. Silence is often the best policy and does not involve any violation of the natural moral law. The situation is parallel to many other aspects of life. Having the power to do something does not mean that the power must be actualized all the time. The nonuse of a power is quite different from its misuse. A comparable case would be that of a heavy glass ashtray that sits around for years unused. Although it was designed by a human mind to provide a safe place to deposit hot ashes, its lack of use in no way violates its purpose.

In a similar vein, unless there is something immoral in the lack of action or in the action itself, such as remaining silent when you have an obligation to speak, or using your abilities to write pornography, there is no violation of the law in using the power of verbal communication to tell jokes or write novels and plays. Although secondary, such activities are perfectly legitimate, comparable to walking on your hands or using your feet to pick up something. For the same reason, the unnatural should not be confused with the artificial, such as video recorders and telephones. To be immoral an act must be an *abuse*, a case of acting *contrary* to the God-given purposes built into my law-abiding nature.

There is nothing inherently evil about the unnatural in the sense of technology. There is no immorality in erecting lightning rods, cutting your hair, and wearing clothes. Following the natural moral law does not mean that you must go around swinging from trees like a hairy monkey. Living in a technological world *is* the natural habitat for a rational animal. Neither is there anything wrong with transplanting organs from an already dead human being or from an animal in order to save a human life. The natural moral law is not against the use of anything; it is all for use, but against misuse. Having spark plugs in your car engine is fine, but violating the natural moral law is like taking the spark plugs out of the engine and attaching them to the gas tank.

In general, all of our powers, if and when they are used, must be used in conformity with their divinely appointed purposes. For this reason, when the authorities are being intrusive, there is no obligation for either youngsters or adults to answer questions about sex. In the same vein, it can be seen that those who lead a celibate life are not practicing contraception in violation of the natural moral law. If he wanted to, say for some medical reason, a truly celibate priest could go around wearing a condom. It might seem strange, but it would not be unnatural in the moral sense.

Neither is the natural moral law violated when a police officer wears a bulletproof vest or a woman wears a covering over her cervix when working in an area where she stands a good chance of being raped. It is also moral to use the underground economy when burdened with oppressive taxes. We are not obliged to cooperate with our oppressors. Neither would wearing earplugs at a noisy teenage concert or chewing sugarless gum (which helps digestion by stimulating saliva production) be immoral.

The important point is that the term "natural," in the sense of the physical, should not be confused with "natural" in the sense of deriving from a particular sort of essence. Only the latter meaning applies to the natural moral law. Natural morality means following one's law-abiding nature, being true to one's self. We are the protectors of nature, in both the environmental sense and in the moral sense.

I realize, of course, that within the fourth camp there will be disagreements. For example, when the disciple of nazism asks you where the Jew is hiding, should you say, I refuse to cooperate with you, and take the consequences, or should you point him in a direction away from the hiding place? Some of those adhering to the fourth theory say that you should openly refuse to cooperate and take the consequences, in a fashion similar to the case of the ten prisoners we looked at when discussing John Stuart Mill.

Others, though, would say that, when the person making the inquiry has evil in mind, you are free to say anything, since, when you are not obliged to speak what you know, anything you might say would be as irrelevant as anything else you might say. Hence you could point the nazi in the wrong direction, sing a song, recite the multiplication table, or doodle on the ground with your finger. In any event, without denying the fact that there are in-house disagreements, it is not my purpose here to argue over details of implementation, but to outline the fourth theory in a general way.[6]

With respect to civil law, the law of our nature is the basis for civil law, not the other way around. This is the meaning of the expression that the law cannot legislate morality. The law referred to here is the kind of law passed by city councils, state assemblies, and the United Nations. Such law cannot legislate morality precisely because it is the fundamental law of morality that must decide civil law. If we are to have the good life in the good society, civil law must do what it can to endorse the moral law. The purpose of civil law is to serve the common good of society. All civil law should be directed toward restraining the vicious and encouraging the virtuous, not merely making jobs for politicians. Unfortunately, we often gets things backward nowadays.

## NO THEOCRACIES PLEASE

### Theology and Politics

Theology presupposes the existence of an authoritative scripture, whereas philosophy and science do not. In the latter, appealing to authority is the weakest of arguments. However, where an authoritative scripture is accepted by all, it is possible to imagine using it as a basis for civil law. As we see in places such as Saudi Arabia, the religious law and the civil law are the same thing as far as possible. However, a theocracy is not something required by someone such as Aquinas. If a society is to survive and prosper, he thought, it is necessary that the natural moral law be enforced on everyone in the society. Nonetheless, it is neither necessary for survival, nor proper from the Judeo-Christian perspective, to demand that everyone adhere to the rules and rites of one religion.

In at least one way, of course, all modern democracies are theocratic, demanding that everyone obey certain religious laws. When the rich young man asked Jesus what he should do to be perfect, Jesus told him to give away all he owned to the poor and take up a celibate life helping others. In ancient times the rich young man went away, unwilling to make the sacrifice. In modern times the state forces everyone, willing or not, to make the sacrifice. Someone, for instance, making 2X a year does not pay twice as much tax as someone making X, but several times more. By means of the graduated income tax more money is available to support various social programs. Incidentally, it also ensures celibacy because, after taxes, no one can afford to raise a family.

Interestingly, from the religious perspective, because it is forced, helping the poor in this manner is not worthy of merit. We must always keep in mind that Aquinas takes human freedom very seriously. He knows that faith cannot be forced. It must be lived freely. A religious faith superficially adhered to at gunpoint is completely worthless from the perspective of one's relationship to God. Neither is it the responsibility of the state to force religion on people. Without being antireligious, though, the task of the state is to see to the earthly needs of people, not to their spiritual needs. This is the meaning of the doctrine of the separation of church and state. It does not mean the separation of religion and state, as if the state must be antagonistic toward religion. It means theocracies are not allowed.[7]

We can see this relationship by way of some examples. Imagine a situation in which the head football coach of a championship team is a very religious man, faithfully following the requirements of his church in terms of moral behavior. Now imagine further that he has on his team a famous quarterback, someone who is married, and who is a member of the same church as the coach, a church that condemns divorce and remarriage. This notwithstanding, one day the quarterback abandons his wife and marries another woman. What is the coach supposed to do?

To fire him would be to think along the lines of a theocracy. In this case, there is really no essential connection between the responsibility of a quarterback and his personal life off the field. Unless it can be shown that his life off the playing field somehow interfered with his responsibility as a quarterback, as sometimes happens in sports with drugs and the like, the coach cannot use his personal religious beliefs as a reason for dismissing the quarterback. As much as the coach may dislike the actions of the quarterback, he cannot fire him precisely for those actions.

Under other circumstances, however, the situation would be different. Imagine that someone is hired to teach religion C, but instead teaches religion P. In such a case it would be perfectly proper for the school to fire the teacher. On the surface it sounds like religious persecution, which is undoubtedly what the fired teacher would call it, but in fact it is not. It is really an issue of workmanship. A carpenter, for instance, who improperly nails together the wood frame of a house deserves to be fired. Likewise in the teaching profession. In such a case, unlike the football situation, the religious dimension is a part of the person's employment contract. The religion teacher's situation is no different from the situation of someone hired to teach mathematics or physics. A mathematics teacher who teaches that two times two makes five, or a physics teacher who teaches that the rate of descent of a body is proportional to the weight of the body (as was taught by Aristotle) deserves to be fired.

The same sort of thing must hold throughout the whole society. It is perfectly proper to put pressure on people to do their work properly. Furthermore, some things, such as properly caring for children, are so important that those who fail to do them at all, or who do them poorly, or who do just the opposite of what they are supposed to do, deserve to be punished. As a result, to the extent the natural moral law is required for the good life in the good society, it can be imposed on everyone in society by the power of the state.

## THE THEORETICAL BASIS OF RELATIVE ABSOLUTISM

### God and Creation

There is no necessity for God to create anything, but when he does he creates beings, not naked essences or mere existences without natures. In each created being there is a real distinction between essence and existence. Although every distinction is a nonidentity, it need not be a separation. All separations are distinctions; some distinctions are separations. What a real distinction is can be understood using analogies, for instance, the height and weight, the direction and speed, or all four, in one and the same body. Even though your height and weight are not the same thing, they exist in one and the same being without conflict or contradiction. They are within one unified thing.

Where does this lead in matters of action and doing, in the way we organize our lives, run our businesses, and govern our countries? It means having a choice in the way things are done, choosing goals, and the means to the goals. Philosophy may not bake any bread but it does decide who owns the bakery, who eats the bread, and who profits from the bread. Ethics is directive. Trying to live without philosophy is like trying to find your way around a city without street signs. For instance, it is not the job of the medical doctor to help people understand when it is time to let go. That is the role of a personal counselor applying moral philosophy to a particular case.

However, making ethical decisions is not done in an intellectual vacuum. In order to make correct moral choices we have to know our philosophy of being; we have to know about God, freedom, and the reality of the spiritual life. Many people, though, do not know about these things, and, as a result, get trapped in various dichotomies, divisions in which they think that in having one part they must reject the other part. For example:

Permanence vs. change; being vs. becoming; stability vs. flux; reality vs. process; reality vs. appearance; uniformity vs. diversity; unity vs. variation; sameness vs. difference; essence vs. existence.

Science vs. theistic existentialism; authority vs. authenticity; outer-directed vs. inner-directed; other-directed vs. autonomous; determinism vs. freedom; responsibility vs. liberty; nature vs. nurture; discipline vs. creativity; dogmatic vs. tolerant; being committed vs. being open-minded.

Classical vs. historical; stagnation vs. development; regression vs. growth; other-worldly vs. this-worldly; transcendent vs. immanent; religious vs. secular; faith vs. reason; mysticism vs. the ordinary; tradition vs. modernity; absolute vs. relative; providence vs. contingency; providence vs. chance; eternity vs. immediacy; supernatural vs. natural; timelessness vs. temporality.

Hierarchy vs. democracy; equality vs. hierarchy; collectivism vs. individuality; altruism vs. self-love; the common good vs. the individual good; society vs. the individual; order vs. disorder; rootedness vs. novelty; security vs. adventure; species vs. differentiation; cosmos vs. chaos.

## Distinctions-R-Us

According to Aquinas' philosophy of being, however, all of these dichotomies are at least unnecessary. All of them can be harmonized within Thomism. This does not mean the denial of the principle of noncontradiction, something that was done by Hegel, and continued by Marx and Nietzsche. Because Hegel could not explain change within being, he tried to identify Something and Nothing, which, he thought, was needed in order to explain becoming. Aquinas, though, has no need for such irrationalism. Potency and act (following Aristotle) explain change within being, thus preserving the proper opposition of being and nonbeing, not merely as a law of thought (Hegel, Marx, Nietzsche, James, Russell), but as a law of reality. For example, there is no such thing as a potential human being. You are either human or you are not. A potential human would be like an idea in Plato's world of pure forms. There is no such world. Real potencies exist only within real concrete beings.

However, although Aristotle solved the problem of change in the natural world, Aquinas must go beyond Aristotle in order to solve the more fundamental problem of being. To solve the problem of being, not only is it necessary to go beyond the physics of yesterday, we must also go beyond the physics of today and tomorrow. Given the real distinction between essence and existence, we can state that matter is to form as essence is to existence.

For Aquinas, essence is on the level of potency, thus allowing human beings to become what they are. Even though in constant change, each human being fulfills a given pattern, dynamically moving toward his or her own goal, and, by using his or her power of free choice, either retarding or advancing his or her own development. Further, by using our senses and intellect and studying the way things act, we gain a knowledge of what things are. This is how science proceeds. The operations of individual natural things (rocks, trees, cats, etc.) are predictable, and their interactions are also largely predictable, thus allowing for physics, chemistry, biology, and so forth. This in turn allows for the wonderful world of technology, which we can then use for either good or ill.

Consequently, essences are real and are the basis for the potencies of beings. There is thus a real distinction between potency and act, such that no created being can be identified (as Nietzsche and Sartre tried to do) with its actions. One such essence is human nature, shared equally by all human beings. Your ability (capacity, power, potency) to know and to choose are essential to you, even though you are not actually knowing and choosing all the time. If this were not the case, it would be possible for someone to wait until you fell into a dreamless sleep or a coma, kill you, and then claim that he had not killed a real human being but only a subhuman lump of matter.[8]

### The Hierarchy of Species

Each being belongs to a species, and each species is endowed with a built-in purpose, a goal to fulfill, that is, a natural way of behaving. Wherever there is a nature (an essence) there is a law. This is what makes physical science and technology possible. Possessing a common nature is also the answer to the problem of justifying going from some cases to all cases (the problem of induction), the problem that materialists find impossible to solve. Moreover, whereas the social scientist defines normal behavior as simply what most people do most of the time, and normal beliefs as simply what most people say they believe most of the time, Aquinas defines normality in terms of the constants of human nature. It is only because there is a stable human nature that morality is possible at all.

Species are always named after their highest stage of development: a tree is a tree, not a sapling; an oak is an oak tree, not an acorn; a Great Dane is a dog, not a puppy; a developing human is a human being, not a fetus. Hence human beings are persons, not merely individual things. Each person is an individual; some individual thing is a person. Our claim to dignity rests on our highest powers, which are intellect and will. These give us our personhood.

In contrast, subhuman creatures do not possess the power of free choice. Human beings do. Humans are responsible beings. The smarter the person, the greater the evil when the person falls from grace (as with angels, Jesuits, and nazi scientists). Animals are nonmoral. A lion that attacks a human being is not punished in the same way as a human attacker. It makes no sense, for instance, to put a pig on trial for murder, and thinkers such as Aquinas never allowed for such a thing. The power of free choice, though, follows upon the possession of intellectual powers.

The distinctively human trait is rationality (man is the rational animal), which means that, beginning with sense knowledge, we can form concepts, make judgments, and carry out reasoning processes. The intellect does not impugn the senses, but transcends the senses. Human reasoning incorporates the senses. Because we can see the difference between what is and what should be, laughter is possible in humans. In contrast, animals cannot laugh. We have a knowledge (by means of concepts) of the nature of things and of the relationship between a means and an end. Animals are restricted to the level of the senses and are in fact often better at sensing things than we are. Rationality, therefore, depends upon a spiritual dimension that gives us the capacity to know ourselves and the world in an intellectual way, and, following upon knowledge, to make decisions freely.

### The Meaning of Good

The good is not a thing, like a rock or a tree, but the fulfilling of a nature. Something is good when it does what it is designed to do. A good law is one that promotes the welfare of the community. The combination of computer hardware and software, even though not computing all the time, is good when it computes the way it is supposed to compute. Hiking shoes that fail to protect your feet are no good. Food that nourishes you is good; food that poisons you is bad. A good definition is one that clearly distinguishes what is being defined from anything else that might be confused with it. A theory that does not fit the facts to be explained and a Jesuit who does not defend the pope are bad.

Also, good is an analogous term (compare tall hat, tall tree, tall building), such as good soldier, good book, good food, good hockey game. Although its core meaning remains fixed, part of its meaning will vary from one context to another. The good of one species, for instance, is not necessarily the good of another species. The good for a flatworm is not the same as the good for a horse or for a man.

Animal rights (all of which are material, e.g., enough to eat, a warm, dry place to sleep, sex in season, and so forth) should not be confused with human rights. Although including many of the rights of animals, human rights must transcend the animal level. Specifically human rights are all spiritual in nature (e.g., love, education, opportunities to be creative). In general, what is good on the animal level is not necessarily what is good on the human level. Animals can be content; only intellectual beings can be happy. Our happiness results from fulfilling our nature, which is that of an incarnated spirit.[9]

### Russell's Dilemma

This relationship between the good of something and its nature is often misunderstood, especially by those who have an absolute commitment to materialism. Bertrand Russell (1872–1970), for example, on the basis of his notion of good, argues against the existence of God in the following way.

With respect to God and goodness, either what it means to be good is due solely to God's will, or to something outside of God. If the former, that is, if God and God alone creates things that are good or evil, then God himself is neither good nor evil. If God points his finger at something and says that is a good thing, then it would be meaningless to say that God is good. Does God point a finger at himself and make himself good? But saying that God is not all-good is something that traditional religion would certainly reject. Such a view would also make God into a tyrant.

If the latter, then good and evil must have some objective status independent of God's will, which would mean that God himself is subject to some higher force, power, or being. Would it then be the case that this higher power is also subject to some yet higher power, and so on forever? In any event, this would be polytheism, the existence of many gods. Or, perhaps, in addition to the good God, there is an evil God who made the material world? If so, then we would once again have polytheism, something that traditional religion would certainly reject. Hence, claims Russell, there cannot be one all-good, all-knowing, all-powerful God.[10]

### An Attempted Compromise

We encounter the same problem in the case of Hannah Arendt (1906–75), who thinks that she can do away with Plato's old dilemma stating that either the law is absolute, thus requiring a divine lawgiver, or that the law is only a demonstration of the state's power. This, however, she thinks, is a mistake. An intermediate position is possible, to wit, that laws are edicts from the community, the rules of the political game. If you decide to play the game, then you must follow the will of the people. You, of course, are part of the democratic consensus and are therefore at least partially responsible for the set of laws under which you live.[11]

Unfortunately for the case against racism, however, Arendt substitutes an arbitrary group will for an arbitrary individual will, claiming that consent and custom are sufficient to solve the problem of determining a suitable social morality. A brief reflection, though, will show that this cannot possibly be the case. If, for instance, the community were in general agreement about a law eliminating all Jews, would she agree? Certainly not. Yet, if there is nothing superior to the will of the people to which we can appeal such a consensus, how could we ever reject such a law?

Once again we return to the basic situation, which is that we must be able to define the good in an objective way in order to be able to know the difference between a good and a bad civil law. Neither Russell nor Arendt understands the meaning of good. Goodness is not a thing, like an individual atom of gold, with an essence of its own. God does not create good or bad things. In the first place, there are no naked essences hanging around from skyhooks. In the second place, whatever God creates is good. God creates beings (essence *and* existence) with built-in natures, some of which (human and angelic persons) possess reason and freedom. All things in themselves, insofar as they exist, are good. Even Satan, insofar as he is a being, is good. With respect to any individual thing, though, the virtue or vice of the being depends upon whether it fulfills its nature. A bird nest that does not hold its eggs, a tennis ball that does not bounce, or a broom that does not sweep clean, is no good.

## The Harmony of Natural Moral Law and Civil Law

In actual practice, even those who appeal to civil law alone cannot avoid taking into account certain principles that are not themselves part of civil law. Examples of such principles would include the thinking that similar cases should be treated in the same way by the courts and according to the same legal standards. In addition, the laws should be applied consistently in all cases, the courts should be impartial, the laws should be made public, the charges against someone should be clearly stated, the accused should have adequate time to examine and answer the charges, and due process should be observed at all times. Most basically, everyone should have the benefit of the doubt; the presumption of innocence is the cornerstone of any fair legal system. All things of this sort are not the result of civil law but are presupposed by it. If there were no natural moral law, civil law could never get started. Assuming it could even get started, there would be no way of judging its rightness. Recall that slavery (regardless of skin color), the attempted extermination of the Jews, Apartheid in South Africa, and the like were all perfectly legal in their day.

Moreover, appeals to the natural moral law were made at the time of the American Revolution, at the Nuremberg Trials after World War II, and in Eastern Europe during 1989–91. In 1990–91, the United Nations used it against Iraq, and Amnesty International applies it everywhere. In 1992 the natural moral law was used to convict several East German soldiers for killing someone attempting to escape over the Berlin Wall. In November 1995 the German government used it to condemn eight East German generals for killing 825 people who tried to escape to the West. In 1999 NATO used the natural moral law to justify its attack on Serbia for Serbia's treatment of the Kosovars.

Since the outbreak of civil war in the former Yugoslavia, the natural moral law has been used by the UN to condemn the Serbs for their treatment of the Bosnians. In March 1998 a Bosnian Serb was convicted of raping four Muslim women in the eastern Bosnian town of Foca in 1992. During the war crimes trials in Tokyo after World War II, the UN included rape as one of the crimes against humanity. However, until the 1998 conviction, no one was ever convicted of the crime by the UN International War Crimes Tribunal in The Hague.

For a long time the UN could only try cases involving whole nations. Convictions of individuals for crimes against humanity were carried out by an international court temporarily set up for that purpose. As of July 1998, however, the situation changed. By an overwhelming vote (120 for, 7 against, 21 abstentions) the UN established a permanent court, which operates according to principles transcending national laws. Its purpose is to put on trial individual cases of genocide, hijacking, terrorism, and hostage taking, all of which are violations of the natural moral law. This would eliminate the argument that such actions are perfectly legal according to the national laws of the perpetrators, and that therefore the perpetrators cannot be convicted of any crime.

As described by Martin Luther King, Jr., in his "Letter from Birmingham City Jail," the natural moral law was used to justify the actions of the freedom marchers, who were acting illegally. When the Japanese prime minister publicly apologizes for the actions of Japanese soldiers during World War II, he is admitting that they violated the natural laws of human decency. When Mrs. Clinton went to a UN conference on women in Beijing in the fall of 1995, she was forced to appeal to the natural moral law in her condemnation of China's perfectly legal policy of forcing mothers to kill their own children. When President Clinton went to China in the summer of 1998 and spoke out on human rights, he had to invoke the natural moral law. Even today lawyers talk about the Nuremberg Defense, meaning that, although some civil law is being broken, a higher law is being honored.

### Morality and Human Nature

Acting morally means being ourselves at our best. It means relying on our personhood, on our intellect and will, and using our powers so as to act in accordance with divine purposes. We are naturally inclined toward what is good for us (physical health, nourishing food, clean water, restful sleep, family life, music, poetry, God, etc.), beginning on the animal level and rising up to the intellectual level, and must use our reason to build upon this foundation in order to lead a prosperous life. The spiritual level does not negate the physical level, but builds upon it. Thus, the norm of morality is innate and the same in everyone. To be yourself at your best you must conform your will to that norm.

Conforming to the innate norm of morality, though, must not be confused with the notion that specific bodily organs have specific functions to perform, and that immorality means the misuse of an organ. If, for instance, the tongue were defined as the organ of truth-telling speech, it would be immoral to use it for licking a stamp or an ice cream cone. Rather than this improper way of looking at the natural moral law, the proper way is to realize that speech depends upon many different spiritual powers and physical parts working together, so that the immorality of lying, for example, resides in the misuse of the whole self rather than in the misuse of just one physical part.

Granted that the above is true, doesn't acting rightly then mean doing what comes easily? Not always. It does no good saying that some actions are easy to do and so no immorality is involved in doing such things. Physically speaking, speeding is easy. In many cases, killing is easy, torturing animals is easy, stealing is easy, and so forth.

Furthermore, vague statements about sex being a part of life fare no better. Eating is a part of life, but that does not justify gluttony; sex is a part of life, but that does not justify rape. Defecation is a part of life, and a big part if we are to judge on the basis of TV ads devoted to laxatives, but that does not justify showing such things on TV. And what are we to make of the woman's monthly cycle?

With respect to what comes easily, no one need engage in sexual activity, but, if and when you do, it must be in conformity with the primary purpose of sex. Masturbation, for example, is immoral because it violates the God-given purpose of sexuality. To deliberately will such an act is to go against one's own nature. Put otherwise, good sex is sex that is directed toward the bringing into existence of new human life within the context of a loving family. Thus, sexual activity must be in a family setting and must not deliberately frustrate new human life. Good sex is moral sex. Kosher sex is sexual activity that is in conformity with God's plan for man. Although there is such a thing as sterile sex, there is no such thing as spiritual sex, meaning sexual activity that deliberately frustrates reproduction. If you want to live on a more spiritual level, you must forgo sex altogether.

In contrast, if there were no divinely instituted purpose for sexual activity, then there would be nothing wrong with contraception and masturbation. However, neither would there be anything wrong with any other form of sexual activity, such as incest, rape, prostitution, oral and anal sex, sex with young children, group sex, bondage, pain and sex, violence and sex, teacher-student sex, minister-congregation sex, boss-secretary sex, and anything else you could imagine.

Yet, someone may argue, isn't it possible to have strict limits on sexual activity without divine guidance, for instance by insisting upon the principle that sexual activity not hurt anyone? Such an assertion is possible, but that is all it would be, a mere assertion. In response, someone, such as Nietzsche, could assert just the reverse, namely, that if we are to progress in the world, using other people is the way to go. Yes, you might say in rebuttal, but people like Nietzsche were antisocial and so should be rejected by those interested in the overall good of mankind. Human happiness requires cooperation, harmony, working together, and mutual love. Agreed—and welcome back to the natural moral law.

In order to be credible, the cooperative approach to human social life cannot allow for arbitrary exceptions to mutual love and respect. If selecting certain subgroups, such as blacks or Jews, as fair game for killing is outlawed, then all forms of selective killing, including abortion, must also be outlawed. If bad things, such as drugs, smoking, alcohol, guns, caffeine, and fatty foods should be controlled or eliminated by the government, then so must we outlaw things such as pornography, violence in the popular media, and divorce because of the bad consequences such things have on the psychological and material welfare of people, especially young people.

In this regard, consider current video games, the vast majority of which are devoted to meaningless killing and pornography. Video games are most often used by the younger generation. At computer fairs, videos depicting violence and pornography are on a par with other software. Knifing somebody is on a par with kissing somebody. From a young age, people are trained to think of violence as exciting. They are also trained to imagine things that have nothing to do with reality. One game is totally disconnected from another, and all games are disconnected from the real world.

Some defenders of video game violence claim that the violence is so fantastic that no one, not even ignorant youngsters, would ever take it seriously. This may have been the case in the Saturday movie serials of the 1930s and 1940s, but the same cannot be said about modern video games. In the old serials the mild violence was at least connected with the real world. Today, though, this is not the case. By removing the violence from the consciousness of the player, the danger to society is greatly increased. Video games teach kids that there is no connection between violence and the real world. Violence is sanitized and glamorized. It has no real consequences. Regardless of how ruthless and deadly you are, no one is really hurt. Soon, everything is back the way it was.

No one should be surprised, then, to hear that some young boy has beat up some young girl. After all, as the young boys learn from the video games, that is what girls are for. Girls are objects; their main reason for existing is to provide sensual pleasure to males. If they appear to be harmed in the process, it is only an illusion. Nothing the young boys do, whether it is gunning down their classmates or sexually attacking young girls in the backyard, really has any lasting consequences. Besides, according to the skin flicks, girls enjoy being grabbed, groped, and treated roughly. They squeal with delight when penetrated anywhere and everywhere by the males.

At the very least, if a society is going to prosper, those aspects of the natural moral law concerned with human life, which necessarily entail matters of sex and reproduction, must be reflected in the civil laws as well. Rational self-control has to be the foundation for any decent society. This means, in more concrete terms, that abortion, euthanasia, contraception, sodomy, and the like must be outlawed. If it is not possible for some reason, perhaps because of advances in modern technology or because of the generally low moral level of the members of society, to enforce laws against such practices, then the full force and financial resources of the government must be thrown into the effort to discourage them, as is done with respect to smoking or driving while intoxicated.

This need to adhere to the best in human nature has a parallel in the way technology follows the laws of nature as studied in physics and biology. Subhuman natural things act without freedom and intelligence; a falling rock, for example, has no knowledge of, or control over, its actions. With respect to human beings, although we can know and use the laws of nature, we cannot violate them in the sense of rewriting them. The best we can do is to discover them and use them, for good or ill, in our lives.

In the physical world, regardless of what is taking place on the microcosmic level, on the macrocosmic level the results are always the same and are summarized in numerous science textbooks. Every day we bet our lives on the fact that the scientists have got it right when they teach us thermodynamics, electrodynamics, aerodynamics, and so forth. Numerous man-made devices, such as clothing, medicines, houses, computers, cars, airplanes, space ships, and so forth, presuppose the fact that the laws of nature are fixed forever, thus making predictions possible. How many people, for instance, would get on an airplane if they believed that the aluminum was going to melt in the freezing temperatures five miles up, or that the principles of aerodynamics were going to change just as they were coming in for a landing? Undoubtedly, science helps satisfy our desire for truth and certainty.

There is, of course, human error. We must also cope with the fact that there are many chance events in the world. Chance, though, depends upon an overwhelming predominance of law and order. Chance is what happens when lawful chains of events cross paths, and it is a normal part of life. This is why, in and of itself, there is nothing immoral (irrational) about taking a chance. If taking a chance were wrong, you would not be allowed to cross the street or drive a car. The problem with wagering arises from the content of the bet. It is not wrong to spend your entertainment money on bingo, but it is to gamble on winning a human slave. It is also immoral to spend money on amusement that is needed for food, medicine, and the like. As always, there is a hierarchy of values that must be honored.

We can, and often do, because of our freedom, act against our own best interests. Thus, a violation of the natural moral law is not unnatural in the sense of technology (eyeglasses, space ships, chairs). It is unnatural in the sense of our being our own worst enemy. In addition, acting to restore nature is not a violation of the natural moral law. Neither are we obliged to always be doing all of the things we are entitled to do under the law; for example, if and when you eat, you should eat to live as a top-notch human being, but you certainly need not be eating everything all the time; you should not be living to eat. Moreover, some fasting can be good for you, making you more energetic and even prolonging your life. Obviously, what you eat is also of great importance.

In addition, eating is a social function. Contra Hobbes, man is an inherently social being. Following the natural moral law means that both the individual and the society are served, which is to say that the common good is achieved by means of mutual action. To be ourselves requires the care, love, respect, and challenge of other people. Living the good life in the good society means that rational behavior must always win out over irrational behavior.

### Summary

The natural moral law does not begin by assuming that the ought can be derived from the is. It is fully aware of the difference between descriptive and prescriptive statements. In ethics the basic principle is a practical one, that is, one founded upon action and doing. In contrast to the basic principle of theoretical knowledge (being), the foundation for a moral judgment is the kind of knowledge that aims at action. It is concerned with doing, with the carrying out of activities.

This does not mean, however, that ethics is an autonomous science. The sort of ethics one maintains will in fact depend upon one's conclusions in the theoretical or speculative branches of philosophy. Does God exist? Does man have an immortal soul? Does man possess freedom? Being dependent upon something, though, does not mean being reduced to it. You may depend upon your bicycle to travel around, but that does not mean that you *are* your bicycle.

The basic axiom of the natural moral law is the most practical one—do good and shun evil—and its basic precepts are found highlighted in the Ten Commandments. All societies, if they are to survive at all, must adhere, more or less, to the Ten Commandments. The closer the adherence the higher the level of civilization. For the really good life in the good society all the rules must be followed simultaneously. This, however, is not so easy. Nevertheless it must be done. Look at Russia today. Under the communists Russia deliberately broke every one of the Ten Commandments, and, as a result, is suffering a great deal, and will continue to suffer for many years to come. Are people in other parts of the world any wiser?

Generally speaking, while they neglect the other aspects, people are prepared to follow only those aspects of the natural moral law that contribute to their own immediate livelihood and welfare. Many fiscal conservatives, for instance, knowing the importance of contracts, heartily endorse laws against lying and stealing, but then ignore other moral rules. Then they wonder why society is experiencing such serious problems.

To repeat, the proximate norm for human behavior is human nature. Immorality is schizophrenia. Wherever there is a nature (essence) there is a law. Every nature is fixed on its proper end, which is the good of that kind of thing. Acting normally (rightly, morally) means living in accord with the purposes of things. Following the natural moral law means self-fulfillment, personal happiness, which is our overall aim in life. Along with this goes the inevitable threat of punishment, ultimately of an eternal nature, for doing wrong. Unlike those who scoff at the natural moral law, and who refuse to outlaw things such as pornography, violent TV shows, or infanticide, God does outlaw such things, and does promise punishment to those who knowingly violate his law.[12]

Hence, murder is an unnatural act, just as are sodomy and masturbation, and for exactly the same reason. They are not unnatural in the sense of something artificial, such as made-made medicines, pencils, digital TV sets, cars, computer programs, and secret codes, but in the sense of an *abuse* of my nature, of going *against* my nature. Remember that "natural" in the sense of the natural world should not be confused with "natural" in the sense of deriving from a particular kind of nature (essence).

## MORAL PROGRESS

### Change and Adaptation

Darwin's theory of evolution is at least partially right. All development involves some form of adaptation. Whatever happens has some effect on other things. When an English pub opens in Italy, it will begin to serve up some Italian dishes and drinks. When an Italian restaurant opens in England, it will certainly begin to look and feel somewhat like an English pub. The same sort of thing happens to people. When people develop they must adapt in some way to the environment in which they live. This environment always includes other people. Human development, though, is never a one-way street. Even while you are being changed by others, you are affecting others.

We must realize that some change is unavoidable, but not to the extent that the natural moral law is obliterated. There is no way we can avoid the natural moral law; it is built into our nature, whether we like it or not. Even the most miserable human being, bogged down in the depths of physical and psychological abuse, both of himself and others, who is wallowing in the mud of alcoholism, drugs, prostitution, business and political corruption, and so forth is still a human being. And he knows it. His experiences on the mental level, his use of concepts and ideas, often to justify his own corruption, will not let him rest in the mud like a contented pig. He knows that he continues to transcend the world even as he continues to be a part of the world. His spiritual dimension cannot be suppressed no matter how hard he tries. Most painfully, the harder he tries to forget, the more he is tormented.

In the moral sphere, our only hope for personal happiness is to cooperate with our nature. We can see this verified throughout the world. To the extent that any world civilization has survived, it has followed the natural moral law. In this way, the best insights of Hinduism, Buddhism, Confucianism, and so on correspond to the basic needs of human nature. Why, then, hasn't the whole world reached perfection by now? Is ten thousand years of human development not enough time?

Some, such as Jacques Maritain (1882–1973), would say that even ten thousand years is still early days for human development. As Maritain looks at it, among primitive people the understanding of the natural moral law is also in a primitive state of development. It is this imperfect state of moral development that defines them as primitive. It is not a matter of more or less science and technology. For this reason we can sympathize with those who censure the first adventurers to arrive in the New World. To the extent that Columbus, for example, used torture and fear in order to extort gold from the native inhabitants, he was acting in a primitive fashion.[13]

As the world goes on and human experience grows, we can and do, with various setbacks, gradually come to realize what we really need in order to be happy. This is especially true now with respect to pollution problems, including moral pollution, which is really at the root of environmental pollution problems. For example, future generations will look back on us today and call us crude and cruel for allowing unborn babies to be tortured to death, just as people today are horrified by the common medieval practice of burning criminals to death at the stake, just as those who resorted to the fiery stake were horrified at the thought of earlier generations condemning a woman as a witch just so she could be roasted and eaten.[14]

Around the year 1500, the Spanish Inquisition routinely used torture to elicit confessions from those suspected of beings traitors, a practice that the Spanish leaders regarded as a moderate way to maintain law and order. Yet, when the Spanish adventurers arrived in the New World, they were shocked beyond words at the sight of Aztec savagery and butchery. In the same way, future generations will wonder incredulously at the complacency with which the general population accepted, and the legal system condoned, the misuse of technology so as to destroy the most weak and helpless members of the human race, just as we today wonder at the more ancient methods of controlling the enemies of society and those who applied the methods.[15]

In Maritain's analysis, if we were not inherently inclined toward the natural moral law, moral behavior could never get started. Ordinary people, if asked why something is right or wrong, usually cannot give a precise answer. This, he claims, confirms his thesis. If ordinary people could, for example, explain why it is wrong for mothers to kill their own children, or why they do not commit suicide, they would be operating on a sophisticated level. This has its parallels in other areas. Is it necessary to be a professor of musicology in order to enjoy music? This also explains why the natural moral law always comes back into prominence when a society suffers serious decay.[16]

For human beings, without law there is no freedom at all. Freedom does not mean lawlessness. Aquinas, followed by Maritain, recognizes four (or six) basic types of law: eternal law (which is God himself), natural law (both physical and moral), man-made law (both civil and church), and divine law (scripture). The proximate norm of human morality is the whole human person acting in conformity with his or her rational nature, while the ultimate norm is the eternal law, which is God himself.

Therefore, despite our urges on the mineral, vegetative, and animal levels, it is God-given reason that must remain in charge of all human activity. As an analogical notion (tall man, tall tree, tall building), law will operate in different ways within different contexts. For us law means rational behavior. The alternative is to follow our noses, like Sigmund Freud sniffing out his irrational pleasures, or like a politician sniffing out votes, resulting in greater misery for everyone.[17]

## ECONOMICS AND ETHICS

### The Conditions for Rational Decisionmaking

In real life the rational decisionmaking process requires at least two factors: the power of free choice; and absolute standards of right and wrong against which personal decisions can be measured. The first factor rules out as irrelevant to human life any ethical theory that does not allow for human free choice, which would include all doctrines that are exclusively materialistic. Among those doctrines that do recognize a spiritual side to man, human liberty cannot mean doing whatever you want simply because you feel like it. It must mean freely doing what you are supposed to do. Freedom does not mean being contrary for the sake of being contrary; it means freely agreeing to do what is right. Freedom is not a license to do whatever you please; it is a foundation on which you can be held responsible for your actions.

Furthermore, contrary to what someone such as Sartre says, the existence of absolute standards in no way insults our freedom. Law and love are not opposed to one another. Neither are law and freedom. In fact, only a free person can responsibly obey a command on the level of the intellect. This can be seen if we imagine the difference between the prime minister ordering citizens to pay more taxes and ordering the rain to stop falling. The citizens can obey; but the downpour of water continues.

### Long-Term Economic Planning

Rejecting the necessary conditions for making wise decisions has consequences, even in economic matters. Capitalistic greed leads to widespread poverty for many. Birth control and abortion lead to depopulation, which then creates serious economic problems. Nonexistent people and piles of corpses make very poor customers. It takes people to fill buildings, buy cars, and eat steaks. Yet, despite the warnings of demographers, few today pay sufficient attention to the linkage between good morals and good economics. Any economic problem a society might have will never be solved by more attacks on the natural moral law. Lowering taxes and increasing trade, since they boost consumption, may help for a while, but they cannot make up for poor morals.

More trade and lower taxes are not a reversal of the destructive effects of rejecting the natural moral law, but only a staving off of the consequences. Unless we have a universal moral code that truly respects the earth and human life and allows for the exercise of human creativity within the bounds of the natural moral law, the economic future of the world is bleak indeed. This is something that should not be taken lightly, and as time goes on all governments will have to admit that they have been backing the wrong horse (depopulation) for too long.[18]

### Super Predators

Speaking of demographics, one of the most destructive aspects of modern society is the abundance of families without fathers at home.

Not only does the fatherless household usually have a reduced standard of living for the mother and children, it also causes social problems. A recent study by the Carnegie Corporation of New York describes the terrible situation among young people today. Exactly at the time when their need for guidance is greatest (10–14 years of age), large numbers of children are left to fend for themselves. Neither in school nor at home do young people get the basic moral education they need in order to lead a good life. In order to develop properly, the child requires loving parents, a compassionate mother and a strong and just father, one of whom is home practically all the time. Where one or both is absent, the youngster begins a desperate search for a substitute, usually leading to harm for both himself and others.[19]

Young boys, especially, need a strong father to help them direct their natural aggressiveness along creative paths. Children deprived of the personal attention they need at home will join street gangs and haunt disreputable hangouts. They turn to the popular media and their peer group for guidance. They end up with spiked hair, tattoos, and rings in their belly buttons. It is no wonder that smoking, drugs, sex, and violence abound among today's youth. Many young people have become what the sociologists are calling super predators, that is, people who actually practice what moral nihilism preaches. They think that torturing and killing other human beings is just good fun. If you want something you just take it, even if someone else has to suffer or die in the process. Violence then becomes second nature to them, unrelated to any economic needs they may have at the time.

As the situation worsens, there is a reaction, not, however, to the true center position in which there are certain unyielding restrictions on one's freedom, such as absolutely no uncontrolled capitalistic greed, no racism, no easy divorces, no pornography, and no abortion, but to the opposite extreme of a centralized dictatorship in which some savior of the people imposes, in the name of law and order, great restrictions on freedom. Instead of helping to preserve liberty, therefore, the extremist libertarians are the ones who actually encourage dictatorships. As Cicero (106–43 B.C.) pointed out a long time ago, excessive liberty leads a nation into slavery.[20]

## THE RIGHT STUFF

### The Head and the Heart

Assuming that we have absolute moral standards, what is the best way to apply them to concrete situations? This procedure has been described for us by Jacques Maritain. In an exchange of letters between himself and the French poet-artist Jean Cocteau (1889–1963), Maritain summarizes his main point on the relationship between strictness and leniency:

> I had to start out with controversy; it bores me more and more. I know the errors that lay waste the modern world, and the fact that it has nothing great but its suffering; but this suffering I respect. Everywhere I see truths made captive. What Order of Mercy shall rise up to redeem them? Our business is to find the positive in all things; to use what is true less to strike than to cure. There is so little love in the world; men's hearts are so cold, so frozen, even in people who are right—the only ones who could help the others. One must have a hard mind and a meek heart. Not counting soft minds with dry hearts, the world is almost entirely made up of hard minds with dry hearts and meek hearts with soft minds.[21]

The fact that there are objective moral standards does not mean that we must lack sympathy for those who violate those moral standards. The reason for the violation will have a lot to do with our attitude toward the criminal. To illustrate, even if it should turn out that certain sexual practices are caused by a brain abnormality or a genetic trait, each and every case of sodomy and masturbation would still be always and everywhere wrong. The same holds true for the murderer, whose deviation from the norm of proper human behavior may be caused by a brain tumor, an extra Y chromosome, or something similar. Can a rapist justify his deed by claiming that drugs or drink made him do it? In all such cases, however, the personal guilt of the person may be lessened or even entirely eliminated, with the result that the person will be treated differently from others not so afflicted.

For example, what are we to do with someone who, in a moment of drunkenness, rapes a young woman? A hard-minded, hard (dry)-hearted person will demand that the rapist be castrated. For his part, the soft-minded, soft (meek)-hearted person will want to let the attacker off the hook completely. He will claim that the rapist was the victim of a poor economic situation, an abused child, possessed bad genes, and the like and that therefore he should not be punished in any serious way.

Maritain, however, strikes a balance. It is true that someone's bad habits, upbringing, and heredity should be taken into account when passing judgment on the person. Such mitigating circumstances, however, with respect to one's guilt, in no way changes a serious sin into something good. Rape is a serious sin, and those guilty of it must be punished. The punishment, though, must not be cruel. The person must be given a chance to repent. It is wrong to cut off someone's hand for stealing a loaf of bread, or to confiscate someone's car because it contains a very small amount of illegal drugs. All policies of zero tolerance imposing punishments that exceed the seriousness of the crime are immoral.

While taking individual responsibility seriously (hard-mindedness), Maritain also insists upon mercy (tender-heartedness) when dealing with the lawbreaker. At all times, the dignity of a person as a person, even when guilty of a serious offense, must be upheld. If possible, the rapist should be rehabilitated. This may require a religious dimension to his education. If this is not possible, then he should be isolated from all women, forever if necessary. In this way, both the intellectually weak position of the soft-minded and the spiritually corrupt position of the hard-hearted are avoided.

### Genuine Democracy

A similar outlook should prevail in politics. According to the natural moral law, it is necessary that each rational, law-abiding adult participate in government, but not necessarily in the same way and to the same extent as someone else. Does giving everyone the right to vote mean that we get better politicians? No. These days, because of Hollywood and TV, it means that we get better looking politicians. Does this mean that we should take away the right to vote? No. It means that taking votes in no way guarantees that right will prevail or that justice will be done. The foundation for genuine democracy as a way of life is not our right to vote; it is our equality before God. This means that all human life is precious, from natural conception to natural death. Despite all the money he left behind, the poorest living peasant is better off than Frank Sinatra.[22]

Saying, for instance, that killing is an acceptable way to solve personal or social problems is the very antithesis of what goes on in a real democracy. Despite the constant endorsing of violence and savagery by "Follywood" and the courts, the good society demands that we reject such a view. Yet many today favor death over life. I recently saw a bumper sticker that read: If you're against abortion, then don't have one. The driver probably thinks of herself as being very open-minded. Nevertheless, as with the notion that God would never condemn someone for acting out of love (that is, soapy love), the idea behind the bumper sticker does not go wrong because it says too little. The problem is that it says too much.

Let's try some other sayings: If you're against slavery, then don't own one; If you're against assassinating presidents, then don't shoot one; If you're against child abuse, then don't abuse one; If you're opposed to burning down synagogues, then don't burn one; If you're against torturing cats, then don't torture one; If you're against terrorism, then don't join in; If you're opposed to racist music, then don't sing it or listen to it.[23]

Is this being broad-minded? As you can see, once you have adopted the idea that the end justifies the means, that something can be a necessary evil, the lesser of two evils, or that your aim is the higher average good of society as a whole in the long run, there is no end to the things about which you can be sincerely prochoice. This is what happens in all three of the Absolute Relativism views. With respect to the third theory, for instance, simply asserting that something is moral because of a proportion between a good effect and a bad effect is both rationally unjustified and devastating to human life.[24]

We also see that offering someone the option of killing or not killing makes no sense, especially in a liberal democracy. Taking seriously such an option means that you have rejected the infinite value of each human being, which means that you have rejected the fourth model in ethics; you have thrown away the compass that keeps the good ship virtue from being wrecked on the rocks of Absolute Relativism One. Along the same lines, appealing to diversity as a good in itself would be worse than useless. Things are not made the same by what is different about them. A nation devoted to diversity for its own sake is suicidal; its fate is disintegration. On the other hand, if a nation tries to balance chaos with a strong central government, as in Absolute Relativism Two, it is bound to become a dictatorship along the lines of Marxism, fascism, or nazism.[25]

In addition, what good is democracy without people? Although an act is not evil because of its consequences, evil acts will in fact have bad results. A contemporary example of this is contraception. Any group that practices contraception on a wide scale is doomed to extinction. If it is combined with abortion, the demise of the group comes about even more rapidly. This is what is now happening in many parts of the world. Overall, those of northern European extraction are rapidly dying out. If present trends continue, different rates of reproduction among different subgroups will bring about a vastly different world in a hundred years. Literally speaking, those who follow God (the meek) by rejecting contraception shall inherit the earth and rule the world—and rightfully so.[26]

### Will the True Moderate Please Stand Up

The critics of Relative Absolutism are constantly overlooking the fact that it is the middle ground between theocracy and man-centered state dictatorship. The natural moral law *is* the via media between the two extremes of theocracy and sheer legalism. Without the natural moral law we would be forced to adopt either some scripture in every detail as the law of the land or take the civil laws of the moment as the final word on right and wrong, as in Absolute Relativism Two. In other words, without a set of principles between the extremes, we would be forever condemned to political extremism in one form or another. Once we realize this we also realize that the natural moral law is the most effective and efficient self-correcting legal system possible, exactly the sort of system someone such as Popper valued so highly.

Yet the notion that having absolute moral principles is the only practical path in real life is often rejected. The scoffer says that whatever principles we need we can hold tentatively, that there can be many exceptions and borderline cases, and that, if we refused to live by principles with exceptions, we would never have enough principles to live by. Maybe, but we still need to know, when overweight do you change your eating habits to suit your ideal weight, or do you change your ideal weight to suit your eating habits? With respect to virtue, should your behavior change to match the best moral principles or should the moral principles change to match your behavior? These days many people, even those teaching religion, see nothing wrong with doing whatever they want to do and then altering the doctrine they teach so as to have it match up with their behavior.[27]

Undoubtedly, if we required a different principle for each and every different concrete case, we would never have enough principles. This, though, is only one side of the coin. The other side is the fact that having principles is precisely what allows us to combine many concrete cases under one heading. Knowing the pythagorean theorem in an explicit way, for instance, provides us with an implicit knowledge of how to work with all right-angle triangles. This is real empowerment, something that would be denied to us if the pythagorean theorem, within its boundary conditions, had exceptions.

In addition, the scoffer's position is irrational. Within its area, a principle with an exception is a contradiction in terms. It would be a principle and not a principle at the same time. This reminds me of some logical paradoxes, that is, statements that appear to be both true and false at the same time, something that should not be the case if we are working with a properly formed proposition. The following are a few examples of logical paradoxes.

I affirm absolutely that everything is relative.

It is an indubitable rule that every rule without exception has an exception.

No proposition is negative.

Absolutely, all statements are culturally conditioned (no proposition is eternally true).

I freely choose to say that there is no such thing as free choice.

My absolutely true religious creed is that all religious creeds are no more than a temporary expression of the current political power structure.

If the statement is taken as true, then the statement is false. Thus it seems that the statement is both true and false at the same time. The solution, though, is not to take the statement as true to begin with. There is certainly no obligation to do. By the same token, there is no need to grant the self-defeating assertion that all moral principles (general rules of behavior) must have exceptions.

Just for the sake of argument, let's take something from mathematics as an example of what happens when we try violating the principle of noncontradiction. The mathematical definition of a set is: A collection of elements, distinguishable from nonmembers of the set, and also from each other. This tells us that all of the members of the set must have something in common with each other, while at the same time there is something about each member that allows us to tell it apart from all of the other members within the set. To illustrate, in the series 2, 4, 6, 8, all the numbers are both the same (even) and different (2 is not 4) simultaneously. There is no exception to the principle that the members of a set (class, species, category) must have something in common.

Moreover, to have a real set, one that exists objectively, requires that the common feature (essence) really exists independently of my thinking about it; that is, it is not sufficient for me to simply imagine it. To say otherwise, for instance, that maybe we can squeeze the odd number 3 into the set of even numbers, is to destroy the original principle, and our little gray cells along with it.

The same holds in the moral arena. For instance, the cop who shoots in self-defense is not violating the law that no human being should ever deliberately will the death of another human being. What the cop wills is the termination of the attack, not the attacker. The defensive action, therefore, cannot exceed the minimum needed to stop the attack. If it does, the officer is using excessive force. Furthermore, as a representative of law and order, the officer is also entitled to protect third parties.

The situation, however, is more murky when an evil, such as cut-throat capitalism, polygamy, slavery, wife abuse, drug use, or abortion is endemic to a society. To what extent can someone, even a representative of the state, interfere with a widely accepted social practice? Could an abolitionist in 1850 rescue a slave from an Alabama plantation? Can a worker shoot a factory owner who throws many people out of work? Can you liberate a woman from the sultan's harem? Can an antiabortionist shoot an abortionist in order to save the life of an unborn baby?

According to the natural moral law, we cannot use an evil means to achieve a good end. We can, though, work very hard to change the minds and hearts of the population at large, and we can also get involved in politics in order to make evil practices illegal. At no time, however, would the moderate person turn soft-minded and begin to justify, for instance, a little bit of infanticide (such as partial birth abortions) here and there. To do so would be like saying that child abuse, child exploitation in factories, slavery, wife beating, or rape is fine as long as there isn't too much of it. Can such a "compromise" be the moderate position? Not to the normal person.

## Taking Liberties with Voltaire

Voltaire said that if God did not exist it would be necessary for mankind to invent him.[28] Today we can say that if the natural moral law did not exist it would be necessary for society to invent it. In theory, the fourth position means that all forms of consequentialist ethics, all ideas about a good end justifying an evil means, and all notions about an act being permissible if it is the lesser of two evils, must be rejected. In both the physical and the moral spheres, sustaining a small amount of chaos requires the existence of a vast amount of orderliness. Violations are constantly occurring, but this should not blind us to the fact that the natural moral law is actually being followed practically all the time. Although his thinking may be constantly off-base, even the meanest terrorist *acts* like an ordinary citizen 99 percent of the time.

Inevitably, regardless of what position he may hold, theoretically speaking, anyone who wishes to lead any kind of social life must recognize the existence of inflexible moral principles that govern, not just his general intentions and attitudes, but whole sets of specific actions. Knowing what these actions are is something truly useful, and thus the natural moral law is practicality itself. The same thing applies to human life as a whole. Either there is one final goal for each and every human being (happiness with God forever) or there is not. If there is not, anything goes. If there is, then we had better follow the straight and narrow path that leads to it. This is the true secret of success in life. The only winners in the game of life are those who get to heaven.[29]

However, having available something useful and actually using it all the time are two different things. In all of the theories other than the fourth one, both the ends to be achieved and the means for achieving the ends are wide open to arbitrary decisions. To some this sounds good because they think it means a much greater freedom of action for the individual, and the quest for greater freedom, which they equate with happiness and democracy, is precisely why they steer clear of Relative Absolutism. Nevertheless, such people are living in a fool's paradise. A theory of ethics that allows any end to be declared a good end, and any means to be declared a good means to that end, does not lead to happiness on earth.

## Absolutism-Phobia

Those claiming to be opposed to absolutes because they think that absolutes produce totalitarian regimes are fooling themselves. They think that being opposed to absolutes is the very definition of liberalism, and that "Liberalism is the philosophical kriptonite of the West meant to keep the barbarian hordes from entering."[30] In fact, though, they are not really opposed to absolutes at all. What they really oppose is an incorrect absolutist position. They don't think there is anything wrong with being absolutely right.

The absolutism-phobics ask: How do we prevent the rise of someone such as Hitler, who was absolutely committed to the truth of his racist theory? The naive answer is to do away with all absolutes. This is like saying that the best way to avoid obeying a bad law is to disobey all laws, or that the best way to avoid being involved in an automobile accident is to never ride in a car. Any true absolutism-phobic is also a risk-phobic.

These days absolutism-phobia is also known as deconstructionism. As the followers of Heidegger and Hans-Georg Gadamer are claiming these days, the best way to prevent someone in the educated class, because he is an expert, from lording it over someone in the uneducated class is to deny that there is any truth at all to be possessed, even in the physical sciences. For these avant-garde thinkers, the lack of truth makes us all free and equal. Deconstructionists are so desperate to find some basis for human equality without God that they assert that all "truths" are socially constructed; none of them is really any better than any other one. Thus, for instance, the origin of a tribe of American Indians as described in its own myths is on a par with the scientific view that the American Indians originally came from Asia via Alaska.[31]

All three versions of Absolute Relativism represent this sort of extremism. In contrast to the first three theories, Relative Absolutism is not an extremism, and neither is the fourth view a case of prejudice. That is to say, its opposition to same-sex marriages and the like is not prejudice. Prejudice means an emotional, unthinking acceptance or rejection of something or someone. Prejudice does not exist where there is a carefully worked-out system of things, where the reasons for accepting or rejecting something are clearly understood and supported by good logic and carefully collected data. It may be that the theory is wrong, but in that case the acceptance or rejection of the theory is still not prejudice; it is a case of bad science, philosophy, or theology.

An example of such a thing today, one founded on bad philosophy, is the widespread acceptance of the separation of sex and reproduction. In the present day, when a judge rules in favor of same-sex marriages, that judge is merely mirroring society. Persuaded by several modern movements, the general consensus is that sex and reproduction are divorced. Indeed, one could argue that the main motivation behind some recent movements, such as feminism, is the desire to permanently destroy the moral link between sex and reproduction. In this regard there is really no difference today between heterosexuals and homosexuals. Against this background the legality of same-sex marriages is a reasonable deduction from the premise that the combination of sex and reproduction is as outdated as the horse and carriage. Such a judgment, therefore, is not the result of prejudice.[32]

The problem is that the initial premise is false. Having intimate relations along with long-term economic concerns is not the basis for marriage. The real basis for marriage is a man and a woman entering a lifelong obligation and sincerely wanting to create and care for new human life. Any bond outside of marriage, such as merely having sex or having a child out of wedlock, is for people to treat each other as mere lumps of matter.

In addition, the absolutism-phobics are self-destructive insofar as they must affirm the truth of the very doctrines they are trying to throw out. The following is a typical debate.

Relativist: "Absolutism is bad. Just look at the way religious people have gone about killing each other in the past. Think about Martin Luther (1483–1546) and the Jews. He recommended that their synagogues be burned down, their houses and prayer books be destroyed, they not be allowed to travel, all gold and silver be taken from them, and that they be driven out of the land. It is no wonder that Hitler praised Luther along with Frederick the Great and Richard Wagner.[33] Now think about what has been going on in the Middle East for many years, and how modern Jews confiscate the property of the Palestinians, and how Jews and Muslims are killing each other practically every day of the week. No theist is blameless. Isn't it obvious that theism causes evil?"

Absolutist: "Yes, such things happen. But tell me, what's evil about them?"

Relativist: "Well, isn't it obvious that the wanton killing of people belonging to a different religion is evil? And so is killing those who don't belong to any religion."

Absolutist: "Okay, but even if I agree with you, the question remains, whence the evil? By assuming that such things are evil you are agreeing with me that there is some absolute standard being violated. If this were not the case, the most you could accuse the religious person of being is inconsistent. Inconsistency, though, should not be confused with immoral behavior. Is it immoral to be inconsistent? If morality is not backed up by God in an objective way, the only thing you would have going for you is civil law. This, however, would be a completely inadequate basis for your case.

"According to your view, if evil is only a matter of not getting one's own way, then everyone is free to define good and evil in any way one wishes. In the relativist's philosophy, the only reason rape, murder, extortion, blackmail, and so on are evil, rather than being just sexual intercourse, taking money from someone in exchange for something, and the like is because the power of the government is greater than the power of the individual. If and when I gain sufficient force to have my way, for instance, if I'm a Hitler, then whatever I do will be by definition right and good. Don't you see that realizing this is what differentiates Nietzsche's superman from the members of the herd?

"Once we say that all standards of good and evil are subjective, we can understand why whatever Big Brother says is right, is right. If, for example, you are arrested in China for committing a crime, you would be at the mercy of the dictators. It does no good claiming that you are innocent, that you really did not kill the woman you are accused of killing, because innocence and guilt are decided by the state, not by matching up your action with some objective standard. If the state says you are guilty, then you really are guilty. Saying otherwise implies the existence of some objective measure of right and wrong. However, once you say there is no such measure, you must accept as right whatever subjective power commands the greatest physical force. I'm sure you see that."

## Perry Mason to the Rescue

That the absolutism-phobic does see it can be proven by subjecting him to a cross-examination. It turns out that the person who insists upon being open-minded about things such as common-law marriages and abortion is very closed-minded when it comes to things such as wife beating and child labor in factories. He has no intention whatsoever of throwing out the good with the bad. Obviously, the only absolutes he is opposed to are those leading to evil results. When faced with an evil he recognizes (and it is significant that he does recognize a difference between good and evil), he no longer talks about the exceptions granted under special circumstances in particular situations, but quickly affirms that all cases of wife beating, child abuse, slavery, and the like are always and everywhere wrong. It is no wonder that Plato labeled such people chameleons.[34]

Paradoxically, if you want to live the life of a free person you must accept rigorous laws protecting inalienable rights. This means that it is realistic to expect people to exercise a high degree of self-control. Absolute freedom is not a basic human right. Freedom is not an end in itself. There is such a thing as the abuse of freedom. When someone, for example, sexually forces himself on a girl and then kills her, someone such as Sartre would say that that is the price we pay for using our freedom. In contrast, someone such as Aquinas would say that that is the price we pay for using our freedom to disobey God, that is, for abusing our freedom, for violating the natural moral law.

By the same token, virtue and sex cannot be ends in themselves; they must be means to an end. There is nothing especially subtle about this. For instance, if a man is lost on a desert island with his young daughter, does he have a right to use her sexually? If a man's wife is sick, can he force himself on her anyway? If men have such a right, why are men punished for using prostitutes? If soldiers are in a foreign land, can they use any women they find there? Consider what Japanese soldiers did to thousands of women in the 1930s and 1940s. Surely the honest person does not have to be hit over the head with a baseball bat to see that such behavior is absolutely wrong.

## CONCLUSION

### Universal Human Rights

In some societies, a man has no value unless he is wanted by the government. If he is not wanted he's no better than a roadside weed, a piece of useless vegetation that can be pruned away with a completely clear conscience. In some places a woman is of no value unless she is wanted by a man, or a developing human being in the womb is worthless unless she is wanted by her mother. Is this what it means to live in a liberal democracy? Certainly not. Any view that either does not recognize divine guidance at all (the first two theories), or that pays only lip service to it (the third theory), must produce a fraudulent democracy.[35]

To appreciate Relative Absolutism, your infinite value as a human being must be taken seriously. Unlike "Follywood," where, as James Cagney once said, you are only as good as the other guy says you are, whether or not one human being is wanted by another human being is beside the point. In a real democracy, the situation must be just the reverse: instead of being wanted making you a human being, the fact that you are a human being means that you should be wanted. Your value depends upon what you are created to be by God, not upon what some other individual or public opinion in general makes of you. Any other approach is a sure prescription for political persecution.

With respect to left- and right-wing politics, Relative Absolutism proposes a truly moderate position, one recognizing the strong points of both positions, but also one that does away with those doctrines that are inconsistent with the needs of a real democracy. In other words, both the extreme of individualism running amok and of togetherness going too far (communism, fascism, nazism, popular consensus) must be rejected.

For example, under an extreme individualism the lone individual decides, while under a tyranny the state decides, who is a full human being with full human rights. At the moment, many places around the world have managed to achieve the worst of both worlds by having a situation in which the government has given certain individuals the power of life and death over other individuals. This is legally validated by the neat device of declaring the intended victims to be nonpersons, unwanted aggressors, or suchlike.

### Justice for All

In contrast, in a genuine democracy God decides who is a human being, and, if there is any doubt about the status of a given individual, the state must give the benefit of the doubt. Only in this moderate way can human equality be taken seriously. This is the only way to have a genuine liberalism, meaning that the range of your swinging arm is maximized without hitting someone else's nose. In other words, in actual human life the natural moral law is the only way to be realistic, practical, and reasonable.

An important part of this reasonable vista is realizing that your value in the cosmos is not dependent upon any other creature in the world. The lowest peasant is as important as the highest king. The smallest baby is as important as the most clever lawyer. From the viewpoint of quality, one human life is worth more than the whole physical universe put together. Or, as Dr. Seuss (T. S. Geisel, 1904–91) says in *Horton Hears a Who*, a who is a who no matter how small. This gives us a hint about why the universe is so vast, a universe in which human beings are mere motes of dust. Could it be a lesson about the superiority of quality over quantity?[36]

# Notes

## PREFACE

1. On prudence see Aquinas, *Summa Theologiae*, I-II, 12–17, 57; II-II, 47–56. Although I do not always use their wording, in general I follow the translation of this work by the Fathers of the English Dominican Province. The Latin edition I am using is *Summa Theologica; Summae Contra Gentiles* (6 vols. Rome: Forzani, 1894). In different editions there are slight variations in the spellings of the titles. As expressed by Etienne Gilson (1884–1978): "This [prudence] is truly an art. How am I to deal with such and such a man in particular circumstances without humiliating or injuring him? This is the kind of problem which the virtue of prudence places before the understanding" (*The Christian Philosophy of St. Thomas Aquinas*, 287). Vernon J. Bourke (1907–98) warns us against confusing ethics as a science with the application of moral rules, perhaps with the help of a counselor, to specific personal cases: "The terminology of Thomas Aquinas is still useful here: dealing with particular acts is the work of *prudentia*, while reasoning to somewhat general conclusions about moral matters is the role of *philosophia moralis*" ("The Real Basis of Ethical Discourse," *Proceedings of the American Catholic Philosophical Association*, 125). Also, consult Westberg, *Right Practical Reason*.

## CHAPTER 1: ABSOLUTE RELATIVISM ONE

1. Protagoras of Abdera. This line is from his *Refutatory Arguments*, as found in Freeman, *Ancilla to the Pre-Socratic Philosophers*, 125.
2. Parmenides' poem is contained in Freeman, *Ancilla*, 41–46.

3. This line has been translated in various ways: For it is the same thing to think and to be; That which can be thought can be; That which it is possible to think is identical with that which can be; The same thing exists for thinking and for being; The rational is the real.

4. According to Joseph Owens, atomism exhibits all the marks of an attempt to counteract the Eleatic argument against change, which is the main point of making nonbeing real. See his *A History of Ancient Western Philosophy*, 133.

5. On Protagoras and Gorgias see Owens, *History*, 157–64.

6. For the few passages we have from Protagoras see Freeman, *Ancilla*, 125–27.

7. All references to Emerson are taken from his first (1841) and second (1844) series of essays.

8. All references to Whitman are taken from his *Leaves of Grass*. In Whitman's day, gras (one "s") were works produced by printers for their own enjoyment during their idle time. Concerning slavery, Whitman opposed the extension of slavery to the new territories. However, he also thought that runaway slaves should be returned to their masters. He was not, in other words, absolutely opposed to slavery. Also, in 1998 Bill Clinton gave a copy of the work to Monica Lewinsky.

9. See Camus, *The Rebel*, 225–26.

10. See Mill, *Autobiography of John Stuart Mill*, 32.

11. Consult the bibliography under Heinz Frederick Peters and Walter K. Stewart. In his *The Genealogy of Morals: An Attack* (1887, Third Essay, sec. 27) Nietzsche said that he was planning a book to be called *The Will to Power: A Study in the Transvaluation of All Values*. On this last point see *The Birth of Tragedy. The Genealogy of Morals*, 296.

12. See Cushman (1865–1944), *A Beginner's History of Philosophy*, vol. 2, 341–52, 375–76.

13. Cushman, *Beginner's History*, vol. 2, 341. Schopenhauer saw no value in identifying God with the world. That is pantheism, and it affords no doctrine whatsoever in ethics. Pantheism is just a polite form of atheism for those who are dishonest. See Schopenhauer, *Essays and Aphorisms*, "On Various Subjects," #2, 217–18. According to Schopenhauer, Hegel's pantheism offered to explain one unknown by another unknown. Copleston asks: "But, though Schopenhauer's criticism of pantheism is telling enough, is his own philosophy in a much better situation?" Copleston says that an atheistic system, because it could appeal to enlightened self-interest, might be better off, but then again maybe not. See Frederick Copleston, *Arthur Schopenhauer: Philosopher of Pessimism*, 145.

14. Cushman, *Beginner's History*, vol. 2, 375. In Thomas I. Cook's 1930s work *History of Political Philosophy*, Nietzsche is allotted one short footnote on page 27. Cook taught at the University of California at Los Angeles. Professor Larry Azar notes that Mussolini, for his sixtieth birthday, while under house arrest on the island of La Maddelena, received from Hitler an expensive edition of Nietzsche's writings, accompanied by a personal letter from field marshal Albert Kesselring and a personal dedication from Hitler himself. Consult Azar's *Twentieth Century in Crisis: Foundations of Totalitarianism*, 146–47.

15. Camus, *The Myth of Sisyphus and Other Essays*, 45.

16. For a study of Dostoevsky and suicide see N. N. Shneidman, *Dostoevsky and Suicide*. With respect to Kirillov in particular (pp. 56–62) Shneidman states: "The suicide of Kirillov has received more critical attention than any other act of self-destruction depicted in the works of Dostoevsky. Kirillov kills himself on principle just to prove a point" (p. 56).

17. See Camus, *The Plague*. Dr. Bernard Rieux says to Tarrou, his dying friend: "No. To become a saint you need to live. So—fight away!"(p. 231). Later: "There can be no peace without hope. . . . Did this explain his [Tarrou's] aspiration toward saintliness, his quest of peace by service in the cause of others?"(p. 237). Still later: "They knew now [after the plague] that if there is one thing one can always yearn for, and sometimes attain, it is human love. But for those others, who aspired beyond and above the human individual toward something they could not even imagine, there had been no answer" (pp. 244–45).

18. Sartre's work is translated as *Anti-Semite and Jew*.

19. See Sartre's *Anti-Semite and Jew*, 55, 59, 117, 135, 144.

20. See Sartre, *Anti-Semite*, 7–8.

21. See Sartre, *Anti-Semite*, 144–45.

22. Sartre, *Anti-Semite*, 148.

23. Sartre, *Anti-Semite*, 148–50.

24. On Sartre as a propaganda agent for Russian communism consult Hollander, *Political Pilgrims*, 61–62, 236–39, 360–61, 445, 500. See also Hollander, *The Many Faces of Socialism*. Others, such as Paul Robeson (1898–1976), were doing the same thing.

25. Sartre, *Anti-Semite*, 150–53.

26. See Sartre, *Existentialism and Humanism*. This work was originally delivered as a lecture to Marxists in Paris in 1945. Without God there is no basis for being honest, not beating one's wife, having children, and so forth. According to Sartre, the death of God "for existentialism, is the starting point. Everything is indeed permitted if God does not exist, and man is in consequence forlorn, for he cannot find anything to depend upon either within or outside himself" (pp. 33–34).

27. For an account of Galileo's problems consult Langford, *Galileo, Science, and the Church*. Galileo (1564–1642) was silenced on 22 June 1633. He quietly lived out the rest of his life on a large estate near Florence on a Church pension. Pope Urban VIII sent him a special blessing while he was on his deathbed, and he was buried within the church of the Holy Cross in Florence, along with other famous Italians.

The dispute between Galileo and the cardinals was more a matter of social stability than a scientific debate. Undoubtedly, the cardinals really believed that the earth was motionless. However, even if the earth moved, letting someone carry on about it was not conducive to public safety. In 1633 endorsing the idea that we are all spinning around at a high speed would have been comparable in its effect on the population to the government of today endorsing the news that hostile aliens from outer space had landed in New Jersey.

It is also noteworthy that even today people are punished for saying something in public that is socially disruptive. The difference between 1633 and now is that in Galileo's time astronomy was the leading science, whereas today biology is the leading science, with the result that today you are likely to be punished for saying disturbing things concerning race or sexual orientation. See the articles listed in the bibliography under Holden.

Also, without too much exaggeration, even today in the United States, government agencies, such as the CIA, DEA, and IRS, have powers comparable to the Spanish Inquisition. The mere suspicion that you are guilty of something makes you eligible for various modern forms of torture—and it is all perfectly legal.

Earlier, Bertrand Russell had noted the same sort of thing. He observed: "While I lived in California, there were two men who set to work to inform the world as to the condition of migrant labor in that state. One, who was a novelist, dealt with the theme in a novel; the other, who was a teacher in a state university, dealt with it in a careful piece of academic research. The novelist made a fortune; the teacher was dismissed from his post, and suffered an imminent risk of destitution" (*Authority and the Individual*, 59–60). The novel was John Steinbeck's *The Grapes of Wrath* (1939), and the teacher was Russell himself, who taught in California from 1938 to 1939.

28. If this seems too outlandish to be taken seriously, look into the life of Frank Lloyd Wright (1869–1959). See Secrest, *Frank Lloyd Wright*.

29. There is even legal precedent for such a move in a liberal democracy. If a woman, for instance, is being physically abused by her mate, the law allows her to counterattack before she suffers the next (anticipated) attack. She can burn him alive in his bed, or shoot him in the back as he goes out the door, and not have to suffer any legal penalties. After all, what difference does it make whether she is actually being attacked at the time she kills him? The reasoning is that the abusive relationship is one long attack, and she is free to defend herself at any point during the attack.

30. Nietzsche, *The Genealogy of Morals: An Attack* (1887), Third Essay, section 24; see *The Birth of Tragedy. The Genealogy of Morals*, 287. According to Nietzsche in his *Genealogy*, any talk of per se right and wrong is nonsense (Second Essay, sec. 11, p. 208). For him, the three greatest evils to afflict Europe to date (1887) are, in descending order, Christian asceticism, alcoholism, and syphilis (Third Essay, sec. 21, p. 280). Very likely he himself suffered from the latter two, even while attempting to replace the Christian ascetic with his own atheistic version, the superman, the new suffering savior.

31. See Adler, "Questions Science Cannot Answer," 4–5.

32. See Ayer, *The Central Questions of Philosophy*, 226–27.

33. Nietzsche, *Genealogy*, First Essay, sec. 13, pp. 178–79. The same idea can be found in Sartre's *Being and Nothingness*, liv-lv: "The duality of potency and act falls by the same stroke. The act is everything. . . . That is why we can equally well reject the dualism of appearance and essence. The appearance does not hide the essence, it reveals it; it *is* the essence." Sartre was opposed to Freud's philosophy: Freud denied free will; psychoanalysis served only the upper crust of society; and Freud insisted upon the existence of a hidden mind (a potency) underlying one's outward actions. In fact, you are not what you do nor what you know.

## CHAPTER 2: ABSOLUTE RELATIVISM TWO

1. G. K. Chesterton (1874–1936), *The Autobiography of G. K. Chesterton*, 350–51.

2. See Hobbes, *Leviathan*, Part II, chapter 21, 204–14. Hobbes states: "For it has been already shown, that nothing the sovereign representative can do to a subject, on what pretence soever, can properly be called injustice, or injury; because every subject is author of every act the sovereign doth; so that he never wanteth right to anything, otherwise, than as he himself is the subject of God, and bound thereby to observe the laws of nature" (p. 206). The chief law is: get away with anything you can.

3. Further to this see Azar, *Twentieth Century in Crisis*, 253–61. By creating human nature with intellect and will, God creates each person to be his own ruler. Nevertheless, accomplishing a social goal requires a group effort, which means that individual efforts must be focused on one goal. Concerted effort demands leadership, which in turn means that the people must elect leaders. All political power, therefore, must come from the people, and the government is entitled to rule only as long as it does so with the best interests of the people in mind. This means that both the individual and the government are subject to a set of divine rules that neither the individual nor the government can change. Hence, God's law forms the foundation for a genuine liberal democracy. Consult Aquinas', *Summa Theologiae*, II-II, 42, 2; 104, 1, and his *On Kingship, to the King of Cyprus*.

4. See Rousseau, *The Social Contract and Discourses*, Book IV, chapters 1–3, 102–9; also chapter 8, 129–41, on the need for a rationalized state religion.

5. Bloom, *Love and Friendship*, 39. Later in the century, in answer to Rousseau, the Anglican priest, Thomas Robert Malthus (1766–1834), said that the root of social problems is not institutions but a situation in which the local population increases faster than the local food supply, thus producing a struggle for survival. In this way he hoped to counteract Rousseau's antichurch view. As it turned out, however, his theory was later turned against religion by Charles Darwin, whose own theory of common descent with modification by means of natural selection used the notion of an incessant struggle for survival as a support for the denial of divine providence.

6. See Rousseau, *Social Contract*, Book IV, chapter 2.

7. See Rousseau, *Social Contract*, Book III, chapter 4.

8. See Rousseau, *Social Contract*, Book III, chapter 9. How do we know that a nation is governed well? According to Rousseau, the government under which people increase in the greatest numbers is the best government.

9. Further to Rousseau consult Babbitt, *Rousseau and Romanticism*, and Horowitz, *Rousseau, Nature, and History*.

10. See Mill, *The Essential Works of John Stuart Mill*, 305, 314.

11. See Mill, *Essential Works*, 329, 340.

12. Mill, *Essential Works*, 295.

13. See Mill, *Essential Works*, 350–53. Who was a conservative in politics in 1850? Someone who believed in Original Sin, such as John Henry Newman. Mill was not a believer. Gilmore remarks that although he lived late enough in time to appreciate the importance of universal education Mill was still naive

enough not to realize that the plowboy, when he had learned to read, would prefer the local newspaper over classical literature. See Gilmore, *The World of Humanism, 1453–1517*, 207.

14. Collingwood says that in rejecting essences in natural things "you are attaching yourself to an empiricism like that of John Stuart Mill, for whom a cause simply is an antecedent, and for whom consequently all knowledge is mere observation of fact, devoid of any apprehension of necessity" (*The Idea of Nature*, 163). Yet Mill could not live as just another segment of nature: "But while naturalists were bringing man into nature, treating him as just another biological species and reducing his intellectual and moral capacities to animal instincts, political economists such as Mill were taking him out. Perhaps, more than at any other point in the modern period, natural and social scientists bid one another adieu" (Schabas, "John Stuart Mill and Concepts of Nature," 458).

15. See Aristotle, *Nicomachean Ethics*, I, 6, as found in Aristotle, *The Basic Works of Aristotle*, 940.

16. See Ayer, *The Central Questions of Philosophy*, 129–30, 183, 226–27, 233–35, for a contemporary affirmation of this same outlook. Lacking a firm grasp of the obvious, Ayer claims not to see the connection between lightning and forest fires or sex and babies. Such a view makes science, which seeks the causes of things, impossible. Also, morally speaking, it is completely inhuman.

17. There is no doubt that Lenin, for instance, really believed that the dictatorship of the proletariat was the salvation of humanity. The problem is that, in loving humanity (an abstraction), you overlook the individual, thus justifying killing large numbers of individual human beings in order to bring about the greater good, on average, of the collective.

18. The classic political rebuttal to socialism is Friedrich Hayek's (1899–1992) *The Road to Serfdom*. The socialist sees that the poor are suffering. He wants to correct the situation by making things *more* equal, which he does by forcing on people a *more* equal distribution of wealth. Yet what could such a more-equal status possibly mean? As Hayek's analysis clearly shows, any greater equality rule is perfectly useless in terms of a liberal democracy. All it does is tell us to take money from those who have more and give it to some other people who have less. Who gets what, though, and how much, is up for grabs.

To be fair, whenever we judge something the judgment should always be based upon the thing at its best. When judging an apple pie, for instance, our judgment must be based on a freshly baked pie made to the exact specifications of the recipe, not on the basis of some moldy old pie. Likewise in science, philosophy, and religion. The question is: What can we expect from socialism at its best? The answer is that it has no way of knowing who should get what and how much. Enter the central planners. The more-equal rule would be as dictatorial as an exactly equal rule. It is a prescription for tyranny, as goods and services are arbitrarily spread around. Tyranny is inherent in all socialistic systems.

True, there is a Marxist saying that goes "from each according to his ability, to each according to his needs" (Marx, *Critique of the Gotha Program*, 1875, I, 3), which Marx borrowed from an earlier French writer, and which goes back to the Bible (Acts 2:42–47; 4:32–37). In Marxism, though, the biblical meaning is completely lost and the idea is twisted into something unworkable. The state decides what your abilities and needs are, and those who disagree end up dying slowly by starvation or quickly in death camps. Even under the milder forms of socialism the results are always bad. This is because the greater equality (greater good) rule leaves everything undecided. Enter the dictator.

Moreover, once the government decides to severely penalize financial success, people in society stop trying to be financially successful. Their attitude then becomes one of let someone else work, with bad results for everyone, including those on the dole. Said otherwise, before wealth can be redistributed it must be created, and socialism is especially deficient in that regard. See Feuer, ed. *Marx and Engels: Basic Writings on Politics and Philosophy*, 119.

19. In order to act intelligently, not only must we know what is good with respect to the basic moral issues of life and death, we must also know what is good in all of the subsidiary areas of ethics. With respect to the philosophy of work (economics), for instance, Azar observes: "Now, inasmuch as only an intelligent agent (a person) can relate means to ends, personality cannot be excluded from economics. In fact, persons generally order their lives according to what they apprehend as *good* . . . to maintain that economics is value-laden is to imply that economics cannot prescind from a *normative* system. Justice, for example, cannot be ignored in economic discourse. . . . It may be noted, historically, that the first economists of the modern era were moral philosophers: Adam Smith, Jeremy Bentham, John Stuart Mill" (Azar, *Twentieth Century in Crisis*, 36).

20. See John Dewey's *Experience and Nature*, his main work in the philosophy of being, written in 1925, with a second edition in 1929. He was working on a third edition when he died of pneumonia at age 93.

21. See Popper, *The Open Society and Its Enemies*, 429. Here I am using the first English edition of his work because of its proximity to the Second World War. It gives us a good sense of the antireligious mentality that was temporarily being held in abeyance by the war. Later editions do not introduce any major changes. For a critique of Popper's views on Plato see Wild, *Plato's Modern Enemies*.

22. See Popper, *Open Society*, 431. Both Whitehead (1861–1947) and Toynbee (1889–1975) insist upon talking about God, saying that mankind has lost God and must once again find him. They also recognize the limitations of science. Whitehead, for instance, says: "Insofar as philosophers have failed, scientists do not know what they are talking about when they pursue their own methods; and insofar as philosophers have succeeded, to that extent scientists can attain an understanding of science. With the success of philosophy, blind habits of scientific thought are transformed into analytic explanation" (*The Function of Reason*, 59). See also his *Science and the Modern World*, 136; *Process and Reality: An Essay in Cosmology*, 17. See also Schilpp, *The Philosophy of A. N. Whitehead*, 700.

Russell, like Popper, needed something to counterbalance the chaos of Absolute Relativism One. See Russell, *Why I Am Not a Christian, and Other Essays on Religion and Related Subjects*: "There are certain matters on which common action is necessary; as to these, the common action should be decided by the majority. There are other matters on which a common decision is neither necessary nor desirable. These matters include the sphere of opinion" (p. 185). He thought that, in order to guard against political tyranny, there should be organizations, including religious ones, that possess a limited independence from the state. If Russell were to speak more accurately, the proper conclusion to be drawn from his own premises is that, in order to avoid both private and public tyranny, there must be absolute moral standards that transcend both the individual and the state, and to which both are bound.

Referring to a public debate he had with Russell in the 1930s, Adler recounts the following: "The negotiations went on and on; it took a little more than six months for Lord Russell to find anything he could affirm. Finally, we found the question on which he was willing to take an affirmative position" ("Questions Science Cannot Answer," *The Logic of Science*, p. 4). The issue was whether or not science alone was sufficient for the good life in the good society. Russell began by saying that science is the only trustworthy knowledge we have. However, it cannot resolve moral issues, because they are entirely within the realm of subjective feelings.

Adler goes on: "Notice at once how Lord Russell had contradicted himself: he started out to affirm that science is enough for the good life in the good society, and in the same breath said that science wasn't enough because it could not answer any questions about good or bad, right or wrong, or how one can conduct the good life in the good society" (p. 4). If ethics is only a matter of subjective feelings, how do I know which feeling to follow? "By this time I really had Mr. Russell on the run, because he had just come out publicly, for the first time, against Hitler" (p. 5). But how could Russell know that he was right and Hitler was wrong? He had to admit he could not. "A recent article on Heidegger in *Encounter* reported that Lord Russell, in an exchange of letters in the London *Observer*, said explicitly that his philosophical position would put his dislike for merciless cruelty and his liking for oysters exactly on a par" (p. 5).

In Adler's estimation, the moral difference between Hitler and Russell was only a matter of degree. Reading between the lines, during the trials after the war Lord Russell should have been in the dock along with the German and Japanese top brass. Both those who do harm and those who sound the trumpet urging that harm be done deserve punishment.

23. See Popper, *Open Society*, 452. One of the best insights into Popper's mind can be gleaned from his attack on historicism. Although he has no objection to studying history, he condemns the notion that there is some purpose in the course of historical events. What's really wrong with historicism is its claim to know what is objectively true about human destiny. In fact, he insists, we have no idea where we are going.

24. See Popper, *Open Society*, 222. Saying that things would have been so much better if it were not for all those old theologians must fall under the heading of idle speculation. Other examples would be: What if everything is an illusion, nothing exists, the world began five minutes ago, everything is only in my mind, everything is really only half (or twice) as big as it really is, all our words were different, the rules of reasoning were different, my parents had never met, God had made murder moral? Isn't it strange that all those who favor abortion are those who were *not* aborted? No, it isn't.

25. Popper, *Open Society*, 409. Earlier, Jeremy Bentham, in his *An Introduction to the Principles of Morals and Legislation* (1780), chap. 16, sec. 3, asserted that a political state is nothing but a collection of individuals, an imaginary compound body, and that, as a result, any act that is detrimental to one of its members is detrimental to the whole. Although it is in keeping with his nominalism, this is obviously untrue. In many cases something detrimental to an individual is beneficial to the state. If, for instance, a soldier dies in defense of his country, the nation benefits while he suffers. Bentham himself must have noticed this, because, at the end of the book, in a long note added in 1789, he lambastes those parts of the American Declaration of Independence and Bill of Rights that promise life, liberty, and the pursuit of happiness to each citizen. How can such clauses possibly be taken seriously? If such things were truly unalienable rights the government could never collect taxes, put someone in jail, or send a soldier into battle. See Bentham's *Introduction*, 205, 330–36.

26. See Popper, *Open Society*, 511. Consult Finnis' *Natural Law and Natural Rights* for a critique of Popper's view.

27. See Popper, *Open Society*, 508–9.

28. See Popper, *Open Society*, 684.

29. Popper, *Open Society*, 509.

30. See Popper, *Open Society*, 407, 557. David Miller, a Popper follower, says that "From the point of view of rationality, science is above all its method—essentially the critical method of searching for errors" ("Being an Absolute Skeptic," 1626). Is there in fact only one scientific method? If being rational is the same thing as being scientific, what's the difference between science and philosophy? Further to this see Centore, *Confusions and Clarifications*, chapter 2.

31. See Popper, *Open Society*, 122, 546.

32. Popper, *Open Society*, 124.

33. Popper, *Open Society*, 726.

34. See Popper, *Open Society*, 422.

35. What Aquinas really said is that love means willing good to another, not trying to force happiness on someone. See for example Aquinas' *Summa Theologiae*, I, 20, 1; 60, 1; II-II, 23, 1. We read in the same work (I, 20, 1, ad3): "The act of love always tends towards two things: to the good that one wills, and to the person for whom one wills it, since to love a person is to will that person good. . . . By the fact that anyone loves another he wills good to the other. Thus he puts the other, as it were, in the place of himself, and regards the good done to the other as done to himself." On loving God because God is good, and loving one's neighbor for the love of God, see in the same work II-II, 23–25.

36. See Hook's review of Bloom's book in *The American Scholar*.

37. See Popper, *Open Society*, 301.

38. Even more extreme than Popper is Joseph Margolis. In his *The Truth about Relativism* he wants to purge the principle of noncontradiction in order to rescue moral relativism. All science and morality are matters of creative manipulation, a sort of fiction writing on a grand scale. Chaos is avoided by having group fictions. In the abstract, all moral positions are compatible.

Think of a fictional character such as Sherlock Holmes. Is it not possible for him to both have and not have a mole on his back at the same time? One person imagines that he does; another that he does not. Who is right? Both. Thus it is possible, without being irrational, to have a series of moral propositions, all correct at the same time, that contradict one another. However, since we cannot have the practice of all private judgments at the same time, group-think must decide public morals.

By way of a brief rebuttal, one observes that different people have different imaginations, so we are not dealing with the same thing. There is thus no violation of the principle of noncontradiction. Also, consider the following: Did Bambi have bunions? Since Bambi exists only in the imagination, you can imagine whatever you wish. Why, though, should we think that what works in a fantasy world will work in the real world? Margolis' answer is that there is no real world. What we call the real world is only the creation of society's collective imagination.

Moreover, Margolis does not explain why anyone would pay any attention to the societal norms. Knowing that it is all a matter of fiction, the individual would do anything he or she pleases, regardless of the civil laws. So we would be right back into Absolute Relativism One. This would also apply to society. Is it possible to correct a society that decides that blacks, whites, Jews, Asians, or handicapped people are inferior beings and thus ripe for abuse? Margolis has no answer.

See also his later work *Life Without Principles: Reconciling Theory and Practice*, 89–92, 189–90. Margolis, theoretically speaking, is absolutely sure that lacking a stable human nature with a fixed goal does not entail chaos. This is because mankind has the power to invent its own goals, which then become ensconced in widely accepted cultures, which in turn give solace and guidance to individuals. Group-think imitates the voice of God, and so all is well. Typically, Camus and Sartre are not mentioned, while Nietzsche is mentioned only a few times in passing.

39. See Aaron, *John Locke*, 292–301.

40. In fact, for Locke, we do not know reality at all. What we know are only our own ideas. See Owens, *Cognition: An Epistemological Inquiry*, 22, 25, 34, 56–57.

41. As quoted in Boekraad and Tristram, *The Argument from Conscience to the Existence of God According to John Henry Newman*, 173. On the possibility of miracles, Newman states: "When the various antecedent objections which ingenious men have urged against Miracles are brought together, they will be found nearly all to arise from forgetfulness of the existence of moral laws. In their zeal to perfect the laws of matter they most unphilosophically overlook a more sublime system, which contains disclosures not only of the Being but of the Will of God." And somewhat later: "Accepting, then, what may be called Hume's canon, that *no work can be reasonably ascribed to the agency of God, which is altogether different from those ordinary works from which our knowledge of Him is originally obtained*, I have shown that the Miracles of Scripture, far from being exceptionable on that account, are strongly recommended by their coincidence with what we know from the nature of His Providence and

Moral Attributes" (Newman, *Two Essays on Biblical and on Ecclesiastical Miracles*, 20, 26).

42. Rorty, "Does Academic Freedom Have Philosophical Presuppositions?" 38.

43. See Rorty and Oliver, "Towards a Liberal Utopia: An Interview with Richard Rorty." See also *Political Liberalism* by John Rawls.

44. In contrast to the philosopher, the theologian must begin with faith in his scripture. The Jewish, Christian, Muslim (or other) theologian begins by accepting the Torah, Bible, Koran (or other) as true, and goes on from there. Not to begin with faith means that you are at most a scientist or philosopher who happens to be interested in some of the same issues as the theologian. See Newman, *Apologia Pro Vita Sua: Being a History of His Religious Opinions*, 238–39: "Many persons are very sensitive of the difficulties of Religion; I am as sensitive of them as any one; but I have never been able to see a connexion between apprehending those difficulties, however keenly, and multiplying them to any extent, and on the other hand doubting the doctrines to which they are attached. Ten thousand difficulties do not make one doubt, as I understand the subject; difficulty and doubt are incommensurate."

45. Narveson, "An Interview with Jan Narveson," 95. See also Narveson's *The Libertarian Idea* and Hobbes' *Leviathan*.

46. See Narveson, "Interview," 98–99.

47. Toleration should not be confused with indifference or apathy. Quite contrary to approving of X, tolerating X means that you strongly disapprove of X. An example of toleration would be Augustine's (354–430) or Aquinas' imagining a situation where, because of the general viciousness of the males in a society, prostitution might be temporarily allowed as an alternative to many rapes and abductions. See Aquinas' *Summa Theologiae*, II-II, 10, 11; 62, 5. In the past, the same thing applied to the entrenched social institution of slavery. Saint Paul, who clearly sees slavery as immoral (see his epistle Philemon in the Bible), does not tell slaves to rise up and kill their masters. Also, Augustine knew that slavery was morally evil, although he did not hold out much hope of eliminating it from society. As he makes quite clear in one of his chief works, *The City of God* (XIX, 25), God created man to have dominion over only nonrational creatures, not over other rational beings. Original Sin, though, makes it hard to live up to the ideal. Later, Justinian I (483–565), even though not the best of Christians, wanted to end slavery, and in his famous law code he did what he could to make the keeping of slaves harder and the freeing of slaves easier. Further to this see Pauzer, *The Popes and Slavery*.

Neither does toleration mean agnosticism. Agnosticism may not start a war, but then neither will it stop a war. The same situation exists today with respect to abortion, a form of racism, and pornography, a form of hate literature. In the 1850s slavery was defended in the name of freedom, as we see in the Dred Scott case of 1857: slave owners must remain free to control their property. In 1850 Stephen Douglas (1813–61) was proud of the fact that America, unlike Spain and England, had not outlawed slavery. This pattern is typical of racism: freedom for some (slaveowners, abortionists, pornographers, settlers, conquerors, Aryans, etc.); humiliation, suffering, and death for others. See Ehrlich, *They Have No Rights*.

48. As Hannah Arendt notes, selfishness is a blinding force. Nothing has been so completely refuted by the school of hard knocks as enlightened self-interest. The whole point of self-interest is to be unenlightened. For example, a slum lord, by not maintaining the property, willingly goes against his own long-term interests in order to obtain a quick profit. This sort of thing, although irrational, is commonplace. See Arendt, *On Violence*, 78.

49. See Arendt's *Eichmann in Jerusalem: A Report on the Banality of Evil*. See also Ewart and Winikoff, "Policy Forum."

## CHAPTER 3: ABSOLUTE RELATIVISM THREE

1. Richard A. McCormick, concluding commentary in McCormick and Ramsey, *Doing Evil to Achieve Good: Moral Choice in Conflict Situations*, 263. James J. Walter, in his article "Proportionalism," *The HarperCollins Encyclopedia of Catholicism*, agrees with McCormick: "Proportionalists argue that no judgment of moral rightness or wrongness of acts can be made without considering all the circumstances of the action. Because the human act is a structural unity, no aspect of the act can be morally appraised apart from all the other components. Consideration of the agent's intention, all foreseeable consequences, institutional obligations, and a proportion between the premoral values and disvalues are necessary before making a moral judgment" (p. 1058). See also Hallett's *Greater Good*.

2. Basically, what situation ethics wants is a church of love without law. For an outline of situation ethics at work see Fletcher, *Moral Responsibility: Situation Ethics at Work*. In a later work, Fletcher (1905–91) declares that modern theistic morality has been reduced to only two requirements: act lovingly and be concerned with human needs and welfare. How we carry out these obligations is entirely up to us. In general, he says, in order for an act to be moral, its consequences must produce the greater good for people. What we do not learn from Fletcher is the meaning of love and good. See Fletcher, *The Ethics of Genetic Control*, 127, 138–39. According to the *OED*, the term "situation ethics" was first used in the early 1950s by Karl Rahner (1904–84) to describe the morality of people he called half-Christian. See "situation ethics, morality," *Oxford English Dictionary*, vol. 15, 570. See also Finnis, *Aquinas: Moral, Political, and Legal Theory*, 138, 154, 160 n.133.

3. On Aristotle see his *Nicomachean Ethics*, I, 4–13; X, 6–9. See also Aquinas' *Summa Theologiae*, I-II, 3, 5. In his *Nicomachean Ethics*, X, 8, Aristotle says: "And it is clear that all of these attributes belong to the philosopher most of all. Therefore he is the dearest to the gods and will presumably also be the happiest; so that in this way too the philosopher will be more happy than any other man" (Aristotle, *Basic Works*, 1108).

4. Further to this see Michel, "The Possibility of a Christian Tragedy."

5. See Owens, *Towards a Christian Philosophy*, 313. Reading the proportionalists is like reading Hegel or Hans Küng. Although the terminology still sounds traditional enough, the content has been so altered that I get the eerie feeling of "no longer being in Kansas." The essential meaning of love, the hard sayings, and the nature of the Church as an absolute monarchy under God, are all gone, replaced by a large number of new antipopes. This is not to say that

third-way disciples lack compassion. What is lacking are the intellectual tools needed to guide their feelings. As Maritain said in his *Three Reformers*: "These reformers preach evil? Nonsense! Their intentions are good; they only leave out reality, divine and human" (p. 161). See also in his same work page 157.

6. On this point see Aquinas, *Summa Theologiae*, I, 79, 12; I-II, 91, 3 and 94, 2; II-II, 47, 6 and 15.

7. See Arnold Lunn (1888–1974), in Coulton and Lunn's 1947 work *Is the Catholic Church Anti-Social?*, 186–89, on the gradual erosion of slavery under Judeo-Christianity. Lunn was a skiing enthusiast who invented, and obtained Olympic recognition for, the modern Slalom ski race. He knew the value of making progress slowly. Third-way disciples would instead most likely demand a quick revolution, one in which Saint Paul would order all slaves to rise up and overpower their masters, similar to the way Liberation Theology, which died out about 1990, justified the use of Marxist military tactics in order to overthrow the landlords in Central and South America. On moral percepts as a form of rhetoric designed to elicit action see Toulmin, *An Examination of the Place of Reason in Ethics*, 195–201. Interestingly, on another topic, in 1947 (Coulton and Lunn, *Catholic Church*) Lunn would write: "Doctrines are rarely defined until they are questioned. Nobody questions the Church's teaching on birth control, and consequently it matters little whether it is defined or not" (p. 244). Lunn lived long enough to see his point confirmed once again in the later 1960s.

8. See Modin, *My Five Cambridge Friends*.

9. For a concise critique of proportionalism see Rhonheimer, "Intentional Actions." The debate is not over intentionality. Everyone agrees that one's intentions are important. The main question is whether there are some actions that are never moral to freely intend. With respect to the question of which is primary in moral decisions, the intellect or the will, the following is part of a letter (22 March 1990) sent to me by Joseph Owens. "Correct affectivity is the ground of moral virtue, and on that ground is based the norm of moral goodness, right reason. An act proceeding from the practical intellect so regulated *has to be* a morally good act, otherwise it would not be elicited in accord with that norm. It is an act of the practical intellect, and its truth has to be gauged according to the norms for an action on the part of the practical intellect. The overall answer is that morality is primarily in the practical intellect, which involved a correct orientation of the will. So the question whether the intellect or the will is primary here becomes vacuous. The question does not arise until after the two are functioning together. . . . It would be like asking, which is prior, theoretical or practical science? The two proceed from radically different starting points. "

10. See Aquinas, *Summa Theologiae*, I-II, 20, 2.

11. See Aquinas, *Summa Theologiae*, II-II, 40 (on war); 64 (on murder), especially article 7; 108 (on vengeance). In Question 64, article 3 ("Whether it's lawful for a private person to kill a criminal?") Aquinas explains that: "The care of the common good is entrusted to the leaders holding public authority, and they alone can lawfully execute criminals, not private citizens. " In other words, antiabortionists cannot abort abortionists. In the answer to objection 2 of article 3, he states that performing a criminal act does not make you subhu-

man; as a human being you retain your human rights. Hating the sin but loving the sinner applies to everyone. Even when the human criminal acts like an animal he should not be treated like an animal. Moreover, brutality will not make converts. Aquinas wants to treat the criminal better than the criminal treated his victim. This is an application of turning the other cheek. For a misunderstanding of double effect see McCormick and Ramsey, *Doing Evil to Achieve Good*, 212, 233–34, 262–65.

12. See Simone de Beauvoir, *The Second Sex*, originally published in two volumes in French in 1949. Certainly feminism is more than addressing women as Ms. All males are called Mister, so we should have a similar title for females. In order to look like an abbreviation, Ms. (as in the magazine) must have a period after it. Back in the early 1970s I was moved to write a limerick on the subject: There once was a young lady named Fizz, who at grammar was a great whiz. But one day she went insane, and demanded that her name, be prefixed by an unpronounceable Ms.

Some of Chesterton's insights, as found in his *What's Wrong With the World* (1910), Part III, "Feminism: Or The Mistake About Woman," are in order here. He says: "I do not deny that women have been wronged and even tortured; but I doubt if they were ever tortured so much as they are tortured now by the absurd modern attempt to make them domestic empresses and competitive clerks at the same time" (p. 97). In this regard, if things were bad for women in 1910, they are much worse today. In addition, the observer of some primitive society who sees the woman digging in the fields while the man is sitting in the shade, sees the same thing happening in the backyards of England. Whether in Hawaii or Hoxton, the situation is the same: "That is, the woman does not work because the man tells her to work and she obeys. On the contrary, the woman works because she has told the man to work, and he hasn't obeyed" (p. 114).

13. Consult Psalm 130; Isaiah 46:3–4; 49:15–16; 66:12–14; Matthew 23:37. See also Numbers 11:12; Deuteronomy 32:11–18; Hosea (Osee) 13:7–8; Luke 13:34; 15:8–10.

14. Hence the beginning of the "Our Father": God is the one supreme being, who is in no way a part of the natural world. In other words, because pantheism and supernatural theism are mutually exclusive, insofar as sex names can be applied to God at all, God is properly called father, and acts as the model for all fatherhood: "With this in mind, then, I fall on my knees to the Father of our Lord Jesus Christ, that Father from whom all fatherhood (every family) in heaven and on earth takes its title" (Ephesians 3:14–15).

15. Having an absolute right to life relative to other people does not mean having such a right relative to God. God's divine right supersedes all human rights.

16. This does not mean that there are no borderline cases. Is it morally permissible, for instance, for a husband with AIDS to use a condom when his wife is sterile anyway, perhaps due to a radical cancer operation resulting in the removal of her ovaries and womb? Or would such an act be only a disguised form of masturbation?

17. Scholars often talk about the existence of ancient myths, forgetting that there are also modern myths, one being that the world is overpopulated

with people. Quite irrationally, many pundits are frightened by the mere sound of a large number. Is the sky too small for all the stars? Others claim that because one place (e. g. , Mexico City) is crowded, the whole world must be crowded. In fact, though, if you work it out mathematically, allowing one square yard for each person, 8 billion people could comfortably sit on the land area (2,808 square miles) of the tiny Canary Islands. Twelve times 8 billion people could sit in Yellowstone National Park in Wyoming. This is a far cry from the usual propaganda. See Cohen, *How Many People Can the Earth Support?* and Eberstadt, *The Tyranny of Numbers.*

18. Rhonheimer, "Intentional Actions," 305–7. The Knauer referred to is the German Jesuit Peter Knauer. As Rhonheimer rightly observes, the inability to declare a whole set of acts morally evil has some strange consequences. For instance, imagine someone who, when asked about his approval of abortion, claims that no one really knows when the soul is infused into the body and that the Bible does not explicitly forbid abortions. This is like a judge saying that, even though he is not sure about the guilt of a prisoner, he is going to hang him anyway; the hunter saying that, although he is uncertain about the creature in the woods, it is permissible to shoot first and ask questions later; or the assassin saying that, since the Bible does not explicitly forbid the assassination of JFK, it is permissible for a Jew or Christian to shoot him. The point is that uncertainty is not an argument for abortion, but rather an argument *against* it. In a true democracy, unless you can prove beyond any reasonable doubt that the being in question *is not* a human being, the being in question deserves the benefit of the doubt.

19. Rhonheimer, "Intentional Actions," 310. There is an important difference between noting an inconsistency and condemning an action as evil. A nonbeliever might observe a Muslim eating pork, or a Christian getting divorced and remarried, and comment on the divergence between what is preached and what is actually done, but it takes a true believer to condemn such actions as immoral. The upshot of this is that, unless we can say that some acts are always and everywhere immoral, we could never know for sure that any particular act is immoral. *Some* acts may be immoral—but which ones?

20. In Part I of his defense of the French Revolution (*The Rights of Man*, 1791–92), Thomas Paine (1737–1809) points out that toleration is the counterfeit of intolerance. The intolerant one assumes the right to withhold freedom of conscience, while the tolerant one assumes the right to grant it. Unfortunately for Paine, no sooner was Part II of his work published (in England) when the Reign of Terror began in France. He condemned it as wrong. Neither did Paine care very much for the American federalist system. What he really wanted was Hobbes modified by Rousseau, such that the people, freed from the chains of all religious and civil institutions, would reign supreme. However, he overlooked the fact that, although the civil authorities might happily eliminate religious organizations, they would never eliminate themselves. What he said about the tolerance-touter, though, holds true. With respect to active euthanasia, those who push for it are more imperious than those who oppose it. Where does the government get the right to issue licenses allowing one portion of the population to kill off another portion of the population, and then doing it in

such a halfhearted way? See Paine, *Common Sense and Other Political Writings*, 92.

21. When speaking of justice (*Summa Theologiae*, II-II, 58, 12) Aquinas states: "When speaking of legal justice, it's evident that it stands foremost among all the moral virtues, inasmuch as the common good transcends the individual good of one person." In general, legal justice means serving the common good, not the individual good or the collective good. Telling these goods apart is the work of nature, not of lawmakers. Does a physical law of nature require the approval of lawmakers in order to be true? Believe it or not, many politicians and judges answer yes. Even the popes never claimed such power. In 1971, for example, the Animal Welfare Act allowed the U.S. Department of Agriculture to make mice, rats, and birds into nonanimals. Legally, they do not even exist. This is parallel to a dictator dictating to the people not to call him a dictator. A short time later, in *Roe vs. Wade*, the U. S. Supreme Court did the same sort of thing for the medical profession that the AWA had done for the barnyard profession. Further to this see Seachrist, "Lab Rats Still Not Animals."

## CHAPTER 4: RELATIVE ABSOLUTISM

1. Aquinas, *Summa Theologiae*, I-II, 71, 6, ad5.
2. Aquinas, *Summa Theologiae*, I-II, 91, 2.
3. Aquinas, *Summa Theologiae*, II-II, 64, 7.
4. In Aquinas, pleasure (*delectatio, gaudium, laetitia*, the opposite of *dolor, tristitia*) is important. See his *Summa Theologiae*, I-II, 11; 31–35; 43; 72; II-II, 118; 123. In Part I, 98, 2, ad3, when discussing whether or not there would have been sexual relations in the Garden of Eden, Aquinas points out that not only would there have been sexual intercourse, but that the pleasure of sex would have been greater in Paradise than it is now. In the state of innocence, "rather indeed would sensual delight [*delectatio sensibilis*] have been the greater in proportion to the greater purity of nature and the greater sensibility of the body." It seems that forbidden fruit is not always sweeter than legitimate fruit. According to Gilson, "All sense pleasure is good or evil according to whether or not it is in accord with the demands of reason. In morals, reason is nature" (*The Christian Philosophy of St. Thomas Aquinas*, 281). See also Drost, "In the Realm of the Senses."
5. See Stuckenberg, *The Life of Immanuel Kant*, 138. Even in his own lifetime Kant came across as a cold fish. On page 324 we learn how Kant showed no mercy when a student, who had failed to appear for an appointment, requested another appointment. Kant flatly refused. The poet Heinrich Heine (1797–1856) compared Kant to Robespierre because of Kant's policy of being hard-hearted even in extreme cases that might call for mercy (p. 458, n. 70). For comments on how one's personal life does not invalidate one's philosophy see Cassirer, *Kant's Life and Thought*, 9–10. On Kant's concealed atheism see Vaihinger, *The Philosophy of "As If,"* 302–18.
6. The same sort of thing occurs within any kind of scientific, philosophical, or theological theory; there are always in-house arguments over details. Those who maintain a philosophical theory that denies human freedom, for instance, will debate the relative proportion of influence to be allotted to nature

and nurture. Are you 30 percent determined by your genetic inheritance and 70 percent by your environment, or vice versa? Despite the in-house arguments, though, thinkers such as Darwin, Freud, Ayer, Skinner, and Wilson all deny the reality of free choice.

7. See Aquinas, *Summa Theologiae*, I-II, 91, 4; II-II, 10 (on unbelief in general), especially articles 8, 11, and 12. Article 8 says that someone who has not received the faith of his own free choice must not be compelled to receive it. In article 11 we are told that civil law must sometimes imitate God's rule by tolerating various practices that are forbidden by scripture. Article 12 says that no child should be baptized against the will of his parents. By nature the child belongs in the care of his parents. "Hence it would be contrary to natural justice [*justitiam naturalem*] if a child, before arriving at the age of reason, were to be taken away from the care of his parents, or anything else done to him against the wishes of his parents." In modern times, forced busing to achieve school integration is thought to be immoral.

8. Paraphrasing Horace: I labor to be brief, I am obscure. For a much fuller treatment of the meaning of *to be* see Gilson's *Being and Some Philosophers* and my *Being and Becoming*.

9. See Aquinas, *Summa Theologiae*, I-II, 92, 1; also II-II, 47, 13. The good of a thing is its purpose. "In this way, good is found even in things that are bad in themselves [*in per se malis*]: thus a man is called a good robber [*latro*], because he works in a way that is adapted to his end." By this extended usage, there can be a good (sexy) prostitute, a good (convincing) liar, and a good (efficient) killer.

10. See Russell, *Why I Am Not a Christian*, 12. The essay was originally a talk given at the Battersea Town Hall on 6 March 1927 under the auspices of the National Secular Society. For a rebuttal to this talk see Wood, *Why Mr. Bertrand Russell Is Not a Christian*. In his preface to the 1957 reprint of his essay, Russell states that his views on religion have not changed over the years. He still thinks that faith means believing something on the basis of nothing.

However, his idea of faith does not match up with ordinary experience. Faith does rest on evidence, namely, believing on the word of another. For example, even though I have personally never been to China, on the basis of testimony given by trustworthy witnesses, I have no doubt that China exists. As even William James realized, without trust even ordinary secular human life would be impossible. The use of paper money, for example, requires a great deal of faith.

Also of note is the fact that Russell's dilemma sounds very much like the theme of Plato's *Euthyphro*, a dialogue in which Socrates debates a reader of signs and omens on the subject of whether something is good, right, and just because the gods say it is, or whether the gods say it is because it is so independently of the existence and nature of the gods. Plato's answer to this conundrum is to appeal to an eternal, unchanging, separate world of ideas that is superior to both men and gods. Indeed, in Plato's system, the ideal man (the philosopher) more or less bypasses the gods altogether as he leaves aside his body and makes contact with the realm of pure forms. In other words, Plato accepts the notion of a standard independent of the gods. There is a lesson here for Jews, Christians, and Muslims, namely, do not get your theology from Plato. It's almost as bad as getting theology from TV.

11. See Arendt, *On Violence*, 97–98. Despite the pain she and her family suffered at the hands of Absolute Relativism Two, Arendt never realized that the only way to counteract nazism and preserve liberal democracy is the fourth model. See Villa, *Arendt and Heidegger*. In this context, examining the views of Martha Nussbaum would be interesting.

12. Earlier, Aquinas thought that God might release someone from the last seven of the Ten Commandments, thus explaining why some Old Testament figures broke the laws. Later he said that there really are no exceptions. This is because what appear to be exceptions cannot really be violations of the laws when God himself authorizes the changes that allow the actions to take place. Accordingly, Moses did not steal from the Egyptians because, by transferring the ownership of property, which God has every right to do, the new owner has a right to take what is now his. On the apparent exceptions to the Ten Commandments see the *Summa Theologiae*, I-II, 94, 5; and especially I-II, 100, 1 and 8. In I-II, 94, 4 ("Whether the natural moral law is the same for everyone?") Aquinas affirms that it is, but says that there can also be variations in its application. So, for instance, if someone entrusts his sword to you for safekeeping, you have an obligation to give it back when asked. However, it may happen that "it would be injurious, and therefore unreasonable, to restore goods held in trust; for instance, if they are claimed for the purpose of fighting against one's country. " In like manner, you are not obliged to give a drunk the keys to his car, or give your daughter her allowance so she can buy drugs.

13. See, for instance, Maritain's work *Man and the State*: "And such knowledge [a rational grasp of the natural moral law] is still progressing, [and] it will progress as long as human history endures. That progress of moral conscience is indeed the most unquestionable instance of progress in humanity" (p. 94). Maritain's whole position was summarized in a lecture series given at the University of Toronto in December 1950.

14. Charlemagne (742–814), who was no saint, in about the year 800, had to pass a law forbidding the Saxons from doing just that. According to Wolfgang Braunfels, "The End of the Dark Ages: December 25, A.D. 800": "There was little to choose between the Europe of that day and the Congo of today—a comparison which immediately comes to mind when one reads of a law, promulgated by Charlemagne, that forbade Saxons to accuse a woman of witchcraft solely to kill and eat her, as had been the current practice previously" (p. 38). See also Einhard and Notker the Stammerer, *Two Lives of Charlemagne*, 61. As late as 1995 in Rwanda a million people were murdered because of tribal warfare. In a few cases, members of the clergy showed more loyalty to their tribe than to their Church, either by not resisting the killers or by helping them do their dirty work more efficiently.

15. On religion as restraining violence see G. G. Coulton and Arnold Lunn, *Is the Catholic Church Anti-Social?*, 155–209; Arnold Lunn and Ronald A. Knox, *Difficulties*, 24–27, 39–43. On the failure of religion to restrain violence see Daniel Goldhagen's *Hitler*'s *Willing Executioners: Ordinary Germans and the Holocaust*. In the 1930s it was unpatriotic for Germans to oppose a certain form of racism. Are things any better nowadays? Is it undemocratic to oppose

newer forms of racism (e.g., abortion)? Let's also keep in mind that technology does not substitute for morality, and in fact often causes more problems than it solves. See Tenner, *Why Things Bite Back*.

16. Is this happening now? Ronald Knox sees a parallel between modern and earlier times. "People talk sometimes about the difference between heathen and Christian morality, and wonder whether perhaps pagan morality wasn't a finer thing. But, of course, in their broad outlines there *is* no difference between Christian and pagan morality at all. The Christian Church didn't suddenly impose on the world a set of moral sentiments of which it had never heard before, a set of moral sentiments with which it violently disagreed. How could Christianity have spread so suddenly and so easily if it had not found a response in the consciences of those to whom it was preached? No, the pagans knew well enough what was right in theory, valued fidelity in married people, continence in young people, even virginity as a form of self-devotion; they knew it was wrong to lie and steal and quarrel and all the rest of it, just as we do" (*University Sermons of Ronald A. Knox*, 131). Nonetheless, many people today don't want to hear this. Indeed, the distaste for theocentrism is now so widespread that a pornographer, for instance, might direct a male to ejaculate on a cross, thus showing his contempt for connecting sex with reproduction, and yet not be hauled into court for hate-mongering.

17. See Freud's *Civilization and Its Discontents*: "Thus we should find that the deepest root of the sexual repression which advances along with civilization is the organic defence of the new form of life achieved with man's erect gait against his earlier animal existence" (p. 53, n. 3).When man began walking upright, his nose was separated from the hindquarters of others, thus depriving man of the sexual stimulation caused by the odors emanating from those parts. Earlier (p. 36, n. 1), Freud presents us with an equally eccentric idea on the origins of human civilization, to wit, that some of the earliest men, by renouncing their primal instinct to urinate on every fire they came across, the flames of which they took to be penises in competition with their own, were able to carry off the fire and subdue it for their own use. For their part, women have always been the keepers of fire because they could not, without harming themselves, urinate on a fire.

18. Every day reports appear in the news media concerning problems connected with demographics. These problems stem from the failure of civil law to enforce the natural moral law. Further to the relationship of the two laws see Finnis, *Aquinas: Moral, Political, and Legal Theory*, 138–86, 266–74.

19. On this see Hamburg, *Great Transitions*, and Hechinger, *Fateful Choices*. Contemporary youth are suffering from a vast disorientation, and are seeking rapid remedies, leading to the destruction of themselves and liberal democracy, the latter because more and more intrusive measures (e.g., zero toleration policies, armed guards in the schools, no gatherings on street corners, cameras in restrooms, curfews, etc.) must be imposed by the state in order to control criminal behavior.

20. See Marcus Tullius Cicero, *On the Commonwealth*, 149–50. As expressed by Gilson in a lecture delivered in 1936: "Was Adam the divinely appointed manager of nature, or only one of its parts? Was Job a tragic figure, or was he merely ridiculous? Prometheus was obviously to be bound again to his

rock; or rather, he was binding himself with the chains which he himself had forged. The forging of them was the only use he had ever made of his liberty" (*The Unity of Philosophical Experience*, 291). Gilson was referring to the way modern thinkers had subjugated themselves to the tyranny of blind will, which is the inevitable outcome of rejecting man's rational nature under God.

21. Jacques Maritain and Jean Cocteau, *Art and Faith: Letters Between Jacques Maritain and Jean Cocteau*, 114–15. Maritain knows whereof he speaks. All too often those who labor in a certain field of scholarship turn a cold shoulder toward others who labor in the same field. In this regard, see Maritain's *Bergsonian Philosophy and Thomism*, 12–13, 344–45, wherein he criticizes modern Thomists, including himself in his younger days, for not being as sympathetic toward Bergson as they should have been. Consult also Maritain's Foreword to John M. Oesterreicher, *Walls Are Crumbling*, vii-ix, in which he recalls his love for many thinkers who were treated badly by others.

22. The most basic human right must be the right to life itself. What good, for instance, is the right to vote, to a job, to a pension if you are dead? Do politicians give their speeches in cemeteries? For human beings the highest form of life is intellectual life. On the relationship between intelligence and immortality see Aquinas, *Summa Theologiae*, I, 75, 6: "The senses, except under the conditions of the here and now, do not know existence. But the intellect apprehends existence absolutely and for all time. Consequently, everything that has an intellect naturally desires to live forever."

The importance of intellect was also recognized by the ancients. As Plato demonstrated in his dialogue *Protagoras*, good and evil are certainly not identifiable with bodily pleasure and pain, as if man's highest function were animal sensation. Do we want pigs deciding our ethics for us?

23. In political systems promoting death, the people in the abstract, the state, some race or other, the culture, and so forth, become God. Only the collective is really real. The powers belonging to God, including the power of life and death, are then turned over to the people, state, race, or culture. The leaders then decide who is or is not a real human being. In the sense that all despotisms depend upon centralized government power, all dictatorships are in fact left-wing dictatorships. Nazi, for instance, is short for national socialism.

24. In general, we cannot simply assert that something is proper and then challenge others to either go along with it or shut up. This sort of thing is called begging the question, that is, merely assuming to be true that which requires proof. If you assume, for example, that there is nothing morally wrong with torturing cats, then whether you do so is entirely up to you. Nowadays this is called being open-minded. Along the same line, it is possible to imagine someone's saying that it is profamily to include all sexual arrangements under the heading of marriage. This, however, is illogical. Including every sort of domestic partnership under marriage would be like including oranges under fruit and human beings under animal. Sometimes a true statement can be misleading. There are fruits that are not oranges; animals that are not human beings. When asked to be specific, it does no good giving some broader definition. Yes, an orange is a fruit and a man is an animal, but that is not the information requested. Likewise, although every marriage (we hope) is a caring relationship, there are caring relationships that are not marriages. Pastoral,

professional, friendship, and family bonds can also be caring. A nurse can care for a patient, a mechanic can care for a car, and one roommate can care for another, without any sexual or marriage relationship. Often, the vagueness entailed by moving from the species to the genus is covered over by the slogan "inclusive language," as if obscurantism were better than clear speech.

25. See Martin Luther King, Jr., "Letter from Birmingham City Jail" (16 April 1963), as contained in *A Testament of Hope: The Essential Writings of Martin Luther King, Jr.*: "A just law is a man-made code that squares with the moral law or the law of God. An unjust law is a code that is out of harmony with the moral law. To put it in the terms of Saint Thomas Aquinas, an unjust law is a human law that is not rooted in eternal and natural law" (p. 293). King (1929–68) goes on to point out that being legal does not mean being morally right; for instance, everything Hitler did was legal according to the laws of Germany at the time. Moreover, the morally right Hungarian Revolution was totally illegal. Apartheid in South Africa was also legal, and so forth. King argues that what he is doing, namely, marching down public streets without a parade permit, is morally right, and that the moral right must supersede the legal right. The editor (J. M. Washington) comments (p. 302) that King's "Letter" is the most widely read of King's many writings.

26. Just as the fear of overpopulation is unfounded, so is the fear of starvation. Our planet is capable of producing many times the current amount of food. Consider the fact that the best fed thing in the world today is the garbage can. Reduce the huge amount of waste and a billion more people could be fed. Ten times more food could be produced simply by using all the edible plants on earth. At present we use only about 300 of the 3,000 edible plants. Moreover, over the years each acre of farmland has yielded more and more crops. Since the 1920s the production of an acre of land in the United States has risen 400 percent. Now, with the advent of genetic engineering, production can rise even more. Consider also the fact that much farmland is now used to produce crops for making alcoholic beverages, smoking products, and harmful drugs. This land could be used for food production. Also, there are vast tracts of land that, with irrigation, could produce much food. Add to this the use of hydroponics and the amount is once again vastly increased. Now consider the vast number of small tracts of land in the backyards of the world. My neighbor, for example, on a 2 by 30 foot plot of land, produced so much rhubarb that he begged me to take it away. Now consider harvesting the oceans for zillions of tons of seaweed, which can be made into a tasty protein food. Also, fish farms can generate millions of pounds of food in small areas.

If it is necessary to limit family size, it can be done using the same method that must be used in all other areas of human life, whether social, political, economic, or environmental (refuse, reduce, reuse, recycle, restore), namely, self-control. Technology alone can never solve our human problems. We must adhere to the natural moral law, which often overlaps with scripture. With respect to contraception, for instance, the immediate death penalty imposed upon Onan (Genesis 38:8–10; see Aquinas, *Summa Contra Gentiles*, III, 122) could not have been for his violation of a Jewish law saying that a living brother must take his dead brother's wife as his own. The penalty for that sin (Deuteronomy 25:5–10) was rather mild. By comparison, the only case in the

New Testament (Acts 5:1–11) where some people were immediately struck dead for their sin was a case in which they attempted to defraud the Church of money needed to help the poor. Also condemned in the New Testament is sorcery, which included the use of drugs for contraception, assassination, and abortion. See Galatians 5:19–26; Revelations 9:21, 21:8.

27. This is a main theme in Margolis, *Life Without Principles*.

28. In a 1769 poem Voltaire enunciates his famous line about the need for mankind to invent God if God didn't already exist. The following translation is by John Finn (1918–95), for many years a professor of French in the University of Waterloo: "If heaven, stripped of its vocation, could ever cease to show forth its function, if God did not exist, it would be necessary to invent him. Let the sage announce him, let kings fear him" (Voltaire, *Complete Works of Voltaire*, vol. 10, p. 403).

29. On the fact that all human beings have the same ultimate goal see Aquinas, *Summa Contra Gentiles*, III, 26–37.

30. Margolis, *Life Without Principles*, 11.

31. See the bibliography under Cartmill, "Oppressed by Evolution," Gross and Levitt, *Higher Superstition*, and Gross et al., *The Flight from Science and Reason*.

32. Because they pervert the purpose of sex, should God blanket the whole area with fire and brimstone the next time there is a gay pride parade? If so, God will also have to destroy the rest of the city. This is because, using the natural moral law as the standard, however deviant homosexuals may be, heterosexuals are just as bad, if not worse.

33. See Azar, *Twentieth Century in Crisis*, 258–59.

34. See Plato's *Gorgias*, 490–91, 499–500. Nevertheless, was Plato himself a moral relativist? With respect, for instance, to the role of homosexuality in Plato's *Symposium* see Gilson, *Choir of Muses*, 166–79.

35. This point is especially important with respect to education. If you will a certain goal, you must also will the means necessary to attain that goal. If you are in a hurry to get to a little lake in northern Ontario, and the only way to get there is by airplane, then you must will to take an airplane. Education is no exception. The fact is that democracy needs religion much more than religion needs democracy, as was proven in Poland during the 1980s. That is to say, if certain doctrines are required to sustain democracy, then it is proper to insist that they be taught in all the public schools. Consequently, public prayer and other observances honoring God should be required in all schools. This is the fourth R (religion), at least insofar as it encompasses the Ten Commandments (the basics of the natural moral law).

Ironically, even those who claim to reject religion in the schools secretly endorse it. Such people have no qualms about instructing kids to follow the law of love, not to harm others, to respect each human being regardless of skin color, physical or mental disabilities, or cultural background, to be honest, and so on, all of which are merged into the fourth R. These days, it seems, you can preach about God as long as you do not refer to God by name. If you pretend that it is some sort of secular doctrine, everything is fine. Incredibly, however, if you practice what you preach about being honest, you are discharged.

However, in the end the deception does not work anyway because sooner or later the smarter kids will want to know why they should do what the teacher says. Why was the Holocaust evil? At some point or other the smarter students will have to be told the truth. They will then wonder why it was kept a secret from them. Are we to say it is because the courts think it best that such information be censored? And why would the judges think that? So that the government not be involved in teaching any particular religion.Yes, but the government does in fact teach a certain religion, and so why not be honest about it?

The situation is not made any better by giving instruction on the beliefs and practices of *all* the various religions of the world. The brighter students will not be satisfied with such descriptions. They will want to know why these practices are there. From the viewpoint of good education, sooner or later the teacher will have to explain *doctrine*. And once this happens it will be seen that contradictory doctrines cannot be true at the same time. See Nord, *Religion and American Education*.

36. Another example of something showing the opposite of what it at first appears to show is the argument against the existence of God on the basis of evil: either evil is real *or* God is real, but not both. In fact the situation is just the reverse, namely, you can have good without evil but not vice versa. Aquinas observes: "This excludes the error of those who declare the nonexistence of God because they observe evil in the world. . . . However, contrary to this, the argument should be, if evil exists then God must exist, for there can be no evil if there is no order of good, the privation of which is evil. And there would be no order of good if there were no God " (*Summa Contra Gentiles*, III, 71). Hence, it is a case of evil *and* God.

To repeat, good can exist without evil but not vice versa. If we assume, for instance, that cancer is eliminated from the world, no one would complain that he or she is deprived of an appreciation of health. We need health in order to determine the meaning of illness, not vice versa. Being healthy does not mean that you must also be sick. Indeed, if health could not exist without sickness, what need would we have for medicines? We might just as well stay sick in order to be healthy. As well, we must know about use in order to speak about abuse. Similarly, life without death is possible, but death without first being alive is not.

So also when talking reasonably about a mistake. Can a carpenter know he has a square edge without applying his T-square? Can the construction of the T-square be arbitrarily changed? Do we know the definition of square from whatever the angle of the cut happens to be at the moment? To any sensible person it is obvious that we must know what is right (2 + 2 = 4) in order to know what is wrong (2 + 2 = 5), not vice versa. There is an infinite number of things two plus two is not, and only one thing that it is. Knowing the one thing empowers us to know, at least implicitly, all that it is not, but not vice versa. Likewise for the asymmetrical relationship between good and evil.

# *Bibliography*


Aaron, Richard. *John Locke*. 2nd ed. New York: Oxford University Press, 1955.

Abelard, Peter. *Peter Abelard: Ethical Writings*. Trans. P. V. Spade. Indianapolis, IN: Hackett, 1995.

Acton, John. *The History of Freedom and Other Essays*. London: Macmillan, 1909.

Adler, Mortimer Jerome. "Questions Science Cannot Answer." *The Logic of Science*. Ed. Vincent Edward Smith. New York: St. John's University Press, 1963, 1–16.

Aird, John. *Slaughter of the Innocents: Coercive Birth Control in China*. Washington, DC: American Enterprise Institute for Public Policy Research, 1990.

Allen, Prudence. *Concept of Woman*. Grand Rapids, MI: Eerdmans, 1997.

Annas, George J., and Michael A. Grodin, eds. *The Nazi Doctors and the Nuremberg Code: Human Rights in Human Experimentation*. New York: Oxford University Press, 1992.

Aquinas, Thomas. *Basic Writings of Saint Thomas Aquinas*. 2 vols. Ed. A. C. Pegis. New York: Random House, 1945.

———. *Commentary on the Nicomachean Ethics*. Trans. C. I. Litzinger. Chicago: Regnery, 1964.

———. *Disputed Questions on Virtue*. Trans. Ralph McInerny. South Bend, IN: St. Augustine's Press, 1998.

———. *On Kingship, to the King of Cyprus*. Ed. I. T. Eschmann. Toronto, ON: Pontifical Institute of Mediaeval Studies, 1949.

———. *On the Truth of the Catholic Faith (Liber de Veritate Catholicae Fidei Contra Errores Infidelium qui dicitur Summa Contra Gentiles)*. 5 vols. Trans. A. C. Pegis et al. Garden City, NY: Image, 1955–57.

———. *Opusculum: De Ente et Essentia*. Rome: Marietti, 1948.

———. *The Political Ideas of St. Thomas Aquinas: Representative Selections*. Ed. Dino Bigongiari. New York: Hafner, 1953.

———. *Summa Theologica*. 3 vols. Trans. English Dominicans. New York: Benziger Brothers, 1947.

———. *Summa Theologica; Summae Contra Gentiles*. 6 vols., Rome: Forzani, 1894.

———. *Truth*. 2 vols. Trans. R. W. Mulligan et al. Chicago: Regnery, 1952–54.

Arendt, Hannah. *Eichmann in Jerusalem: A Report on the Banality of Evil*. New York: Viking, 1963.

———. *The Human Condition*. Chicago: University of Chicago Press, 1958.

———. *The Origins of Totalitarianism*. New York: Meridian, 1958.

———. *On Violence*. San Diego: Harcourt Brace Jovanovich, 1970.

Aries, P., and G. Duby, eds. *A History of Private Life*. 5 vols. Cambridge, MA: Harvard University Press, 1987–91.

Aristotle. *The Basic Works of Aristotle*. Ed. R. McKeon. New York: Random House, 1941.

Augustine. *Basic Writings of Saint Augustine*. 2 vols. Ed. W. J. Oates. New York: Random House, 1948.

Augustine, Norman. "What We Don't Know Does Hurt Us: How Scientific Illiteracy Hobbles Society." *Science* 279 (13 March 1998): 1640–41.

Ayer, Alfred Jules. *The Central Questions of Philosophy*. New York: Penguin, 1978.

———. *Language, Truth and Logic*. 2nd ed. [1946], New York: Dover, n.d.

———. *Philosophy in the Twentieth Century*. New York: Random House, 1982.

Azar, Larry. "The Elusive One." *Philosophical Studies* 16 (1967): 104–15.

———. "*Esse* in the Philosophy of Whitehead." *The New Scholasticism* 37 (1963): 462–71.

———. *Man: Computer, Ape, or Angel?* Hanover, MA: Christopher, 1989.

———. "More of Mayr: Ernst Mayr's Evolutionary Stance." *Aquinas Journal* 10 (1997): 85–104.

———. *Twentieth Century in Crisis: Foundations of Totalitarianism*. Dubuque, IA: Kendall/Hunt, 1990.

———. "Whitehead: Challenging a Challenge." *The Thomist* 30 (1966): 80–87.

Babbitt, Irving. *Rousseau and Romanticism*. Boston: Houghton Mifflin, 1919.

Baker, C.C.T. *Introduction to Mathematics*. London: George Newnes, 1966.

Beam, Craig. "The Clash of Paradigms: Taylor vs. Narveson on the Foundations of Ethics." *Dialogue* 36 (1997): 771–81.

Beauvoir, Simone de. *The Second Sex*. Trans. and ed. H. M. Parshley. New York: Knopf, 1976.

Behe, Michael. *Darwin's Black Box: The Biochemical Challenge to Evolution*. New York: Free Press, 1996.

Benson, Herbert. *Timeless Healing: The Power and Biology of Belief*. New York: Scribner's, 1996.

Bentham, Jeremy. *An Introduction to the Principles of Morals and Legislation*. Buffalo, NY: Prometheus, 1988.

Bergmann, Gustav. *The Metaphysics of Logical Positivism*. London: Longmans Green, 1954.

Berkowitz, Peter. *Nietzsche: The Ethics of an Immoralist*. Cambridge, MA: Harvard University Press, 1995.

Bernstein, Richard J. *Hannah Arendt and the Jewish Question*. Cambridge, MA: MIT University Press, 1996.

Blankenhorn, David. *Fatherless America: Confronting Our Most Urgent Social Problem*. New York: Basic Books, 1995.

Blau, Joseph L. *The Story of Jewish Philosophy*. New York: Random House, 1962.

Bloom, Allan. *The Closing of the American Mind*. New York: Simon and Schuster, 1987.

———. *Love and Friendship*. New York: Simon and Schuster, 1993.

Blum, Deborah. *Sex on the Brain: The Biological Differences Between Men and Women*. New York: Viking, 1997.

Boas, George. *Vox Populi: Essays in the History of an Idea*. Baltimore, MD: Johns Hopkins University Press, 1969.

Bobbio, Norberto. *Left and Right: The Significance of a Political Distinction*. Trans. Allan Cameron. Chicago: University of Chicago Press, 1997.

———. *Thomas Hobbes and the Natural Law Tradition*. Trans. Daniela Gobetti. Chicago: University of Chicago Press, 1993.

Boekraad, A. J. and H. Tristram. *The Argument from Conscience to the Existence of God According to John Henry Newman*. Louvain: Nauwelaerts, 1961.

Bongaarts, John. "Demographic Consequences of Declining Fertility." *Science* 282 (16 October 1998): 419–20.

Boughton, Lynne C. "More than Metaphors: Masculine-Gendered Names and the Knowability of God." *The Thomist* 58 (1994): 283–316.

Bourke, Vernon J. *Aquinas' Search for Wisdom*. Milwaukee, WI: Bruce, 1965.

———. *History of Ethics*. Garden City, NY: Doubleday, 1968.

———. "The Real Basis of Ethical Discourse." *Proceedings of the American Catholic Philosophical Association* 56 (1982): 125–32.

———. *Will in Western Thought: An Historico-Critical Survey*. New York: Sheed and Ward, 1964.

Bowen, Robert. *Universal Ice: Science and Ideology in the Nazi State*. London: Belhaven, 1992.

Brady, Bernard V. "An Analysis of the Use of Rights Language in Pre-Modern Catholic Social Thought." *The Thomist* 57 (1993): 97–121.

Braunfels, Wolfgang. "The End of the Dark Ages: December 25, A.D. 800." *Realites* 181 (December 1965): 38–42, 88.

Brown, Kathryn S. "Grammar's Secret Skeleton." *Science* 283 (2 February 1999): 774–75.

Bullock, Alan. *Hitler and Stalin: Parallel Lives*. New York: Knopf, 1992.

Burleigh, Michael. *Death and Deliverance: Euthanasia in Germany 1900–1945*. New York: Cambridge University Press, 1995.

Cahill, Thomas. *The Gifts of the Jews*. New York: Random House, 1998.

Campbell, Gerard T. "Sartre's Absolute Freedom." *Laval Théologique et Philosophique* 33 (1977): 61–91.

Camus, Albert. *The Myth of Sisyphus and Other Essays*. Trans. J. O'Brien. New York: Vintage, 1955.

———. *The Plague*. Trans. S. Gilbert. Harmondsworth, UK: Penguin, 1960.

———. *The Rebel: An Essay on Man in Revolt*. Trans. A. Bower. New York: Vintage, 1956.

———. *Youthful Writings*. Trans. E.C. Kennedy. New York: Knopf, 1976.

"Carlos claims he is just a family man." *The Kitchener-Waterloo Record* (31 August 1994): E8.

Cartmill, Matt. "Oppressed by Evolution." *Discover* 19 (March 1998): 78–83.

Cassirer, Ernst. *Kant's Life and Thought*. Trans. James Haden. New Haven, CT: Yale University Press, 1981.

Cavanaugh, Thomas A. "Aquinas's Account of Double Effect." *The Thomist* 61 (1997): 107–21.

Caws, Peter. *Ethics from Experience*. Boston: Jones and Bartlett, 1995.

Centore, F. F. *Being and Becoming: A Critique of Post-Modernism*. Westport, CT: Greenwood, 1991.

———. "Classical Christian Philosophy and Temporality: Correcting a Misunderstanding." *The Monist* 75 (1992): 393–405.

———. *Confusions and Clarifications: An Introduction to Philosophy for the Twenty-First Century*. Lanham, MD: University Press of America, 1997.

———. "Faith and Biological Reductionism: Darwin as a Religious Reformer." *Proceedings of the American Fellowship of Catholic Scholars*. (forthcoming)

———. "From Cosmos to Theos: The Compatibility of Natural Science and Natural Theology." (forthcoming)

———. "Is Darwin Dead?" *The Thomist* 47 (1983): 550–71.

———. *Persons: A Comparative Account of the Six Possible Theories*. Westport, CT: Greenwood, 1979.

———. *Robert Hooke's Contributions to Mechanics: A Study in Seventeenth Century Natural Philosophy*. The Hague, Netherlands: Martinus Nijhoff, 1970.

———. "Thomism and the Female Body as Seen in the *Summa Theologiae*." *Angelicum* 67 (1990): 37–56.

Chesterton, Gilbert Keith. *The Autobiography of G. K. Chesterton*. New York: Sheed and Ward, 1936.

———. *Orthodoxy*. New York: Dodd Mead, 1950.

———. *What's Wrong With the World*. New York: Sheed and Ward, 1956.

Cicero, Marcus Tullius. *On the Commonwealth*. Trans. G. H. Sabine and S. B. Smith. Indianapolis, IN: Bobbs-Merrill, 1929.

Cockshut, A.O.J. *The Unbelievers: English Agnostic Thought, 1840–1890*. New York: New York University Press, 1966.

———, ed. *Religious Controversies of the Nineteenth Century: Selected Documents*. Lincoln: Nebraska University Press, 1966.

Cohen, Joel E. *How Many People Can the Earth Support?* New York: Norton, 1995.

Coleman, William. *George Cuvier, Zoologist: A Study in the History of Evolution Theory*. Cambridge, MA: Harvard University Press, 1964.

Collingwood, R. G. *The Idea of Nature*. New York: Oxford University Press, 1960.

Cook, Thomas I. *History of Political Philosophy*. New York: Prentice-Hall, 1936.

Copleston, F. C. *Arthur Schopenhauer: Philosopher of Pessimism*. London: Burns Oates and Washbourne, 1947.

———. *Contemporary Philosophy: Studies of Logical Positivism and Existentialism*. London: Burns and Oates, 1960.

Coulton, G. G., and Arnold Lunn. *Is the Catholic Church Anti-Social?* London: Burns Oates and Washbourne, 1947.

Crittenden, Danielle. *What Our Mothers Didn't Tell Us: Why Happiness Eludes the Modern Woman*. New York: Simon and Schuster, 1999.

Cromer, Alan. *Connected Knowledge: Science, Philosophy, and Education*. New York: Oxford University Press, 1997.

Cunningham, F. A. "Distinction According to St. Thomas." *The New Scholasticism* 36 (1962): 279–312.

Curran, Charles E., and Richard A. McCormick, eds. *Readings in Moral Theology, No. 7: Natural Law and Theology*. Mahwah, NJ: Paulist Press, 1991.

Cushman, Herbert Ernest. *A Beginner's History of Philosophy*. 2 vols., rev. ed. Boston: Houghton Mifflin, 1920.

Darwin, Charles Robert. *Darwin on Man*. Ed. H. E. Gruber and P. H. Barrett. New York: Dutton, 1974.

———. *The Origin of Species and The Descent of Man*. N.Y.: Modern Library, n.d.

———. *The Voyage of the Beagle*. Ed. L. Engel. Garden City, New York: Anchor Books, 1962.

Davidson, Donald. *Essays on Actions and Events*. New York: Oxford University Press, 1980.

Davis, Cyprian. "The First Black [American] Catholics." *Catholic Digest* 57 (August 1993): 98–106.

Davis, David Brion. *The Problem of Slavery in Western Culture*. New York: Oxford University Press, 1988.

Dawson, Christopher. "Christian Freedom." *A Century of the Catholic Essay*. Ed. R. H. Gross. Philadelphia: Lippincott, 1946, 297–306.

Dedek, J. F. "Intrinsically Evil Acts: An Historical Study of the Mind of St. Thomas." *The Thomist* 43 (1979): 385–413.

DeMarco, Donald. *The Heart of Virtue*. San Francisco: Ignatius, 1996.

Dennett, Daniel. *Darwin's Dangerous Idea: Evolution and the Meaning of Life*. New York: Simon and Schuster, 1995.

Descartes, R. *The Method, Meditations, and Philosophy of Descartes*. Trans. J. Veitch. Washington, DC: Dunne, 1901.

———. *Descartes: Philosophical Writings*. Trans. and ed. E. Anscombe and P. T. Geach. London: Nelson, 1966.

Desmond, A. J., and J. R. Moore, *Darwin*. London: Michael Joseph, 1991.

Devine, Philip E. *Natural Law Ethics*. Westport, CT: Greenwood, 1999.

Dewey, John. *Democracy and Education*. New York: Macmillan, 1916.

———. *Dewey on Education: Selections*. Ed. M. S. Dworkin. New York: Columbia University Press, 1959.

———. *Experience and Nature*. 2nd ed. New York: Dover, 1958.

———. *Freedom and Culture*. New York: Putnam, 1939.

———. *Individualism, Old and New*. New York: Minton Balch, 1930.

———. *The Influence of Darwin on Philosophy, and Other Essays in Contemporary Thought*. Bloomington: Indiana University Press, 1965.

Donohue, William A. *Twilight of Liberty: The Legacy of the ACLU*. New Brunswick, NJ: Transaction, 1994.

Dostoevsky, Fyodor. *The Brothers Karamazov*. Trans. C. Garnett. New York: Modern Library, 1950.

———. *The Possessed*. Trans. C. Garnett. New York: Modern Library, 1936.

Dougherty, Jude P. "Edith Stein's Conversion: How a Jewish Philosopher Became a Catholic Saint." *Crisis: A Journal of Lay Catholic Opinion* 10 (1992): 39–43.

Dowbiggin, Ian R. *Suspicious Minds: The Triumph of Paranoia in Everyday Life*. Toronto, ON: Macfarlane, Walter and Ross, 1999.

Drinan, Robert F. *The Fractured Dream: America's Divisive Moral Choices*. New York: Crossroad, 1991.

Drost, Mark P. "In the Realm of the Senses: Aquinas on Sensory Love, Desire, and Delight." *The Thomist* 59 (1995): 47–58.

D'Souza, Jerome. "Christianity and Indian Tradition." *America* 102 (3 October 1959): 13–15.

Dulles, Avery. "Saint Robert Bellarmine: A Moderate in a Disputatious Age." *Crisis: A Journal of Lay Catholic Opinion* 12 (1994): 39–44.

Dzielska, Maria. *Hypatia of Alexandria*. Trans. F. Lyra. Cambridge, MA: Harvard University Press, 1995.

Eberstadt, Nicholas. *The Tyranny of Numbers: Mismeasurement and Misrule*. Washington, DC: American Enterprise Institute for Public Policy Research, 1995.

Edgerton, Robert B. *Sick Societies: Challenging the Myth of Primitive Harmony*. New York: Free Press, 1992.

Efron, John M. *Defenders of the Race: Jewish Doctors and Race Science in Fin-de-Siècle Europe*. New Haven, CT: Yale University Press, 1995.

Ehrlich, Walter. *They Have No Rights: Dred Scott's Struggle for Freedom*. Westport, CT: Greenwood, 1979.

Einhard and Notker the Stammerer. *Two Lives of Charlemagne*. Trans. Lewis Thorpe. Baltimore, MD: Penguin, 1969.

Ekirch, Arthur A. *The Idea of Progress in America, 1815–1860*. New York: Peter Smith, 1951.

Elshtain, Jean B. *Augustine and the Limits of Politics*. Notre Dame, IN: Notre Dame University Press, 1996.

———. *Democracy on Trial*. New York: Basic Books, 1995.

Embree, Robert A. "Attitudes Toward Elective Abortion: Preliminary Evidence of Validity for the Personal Beliefs Scale [using the Centore Paradigm]." *Psychological Reports* 82 (1998): 1267–81.

———. "Personal Beliefs Scale Redux: A Model for Hypothesis Testing [using the Centore Paradigm]." *Psychological Reports* 78 (1996): 195–203.

Embree, Robert A., and Marlowe C. Embree. "The Personal Beliefs Scale as a Measure of Individual Differences in Commitment to the Mind-Body

Beliefs Proposed by F. F. Centore." *Psychological Reports* 73 (1993): 411–28.

Emerson, Ralph Waldo. *Emerson's Antislavery Writings*. Ed. Len Gougeon and Joel Myerson. New Haven, CT: Yale University Press, 1994.

———. *Essays: First and Second Series*. New York: Allison, 1895.

———. *Selected Essays, Lectures, and Poems*. Ed. R. D. Richardson. New York: Bantam, 1995.

Ewart, Wendy R., and Beverly Winikoff. "Policy Forum: Medicine. Toward Safe and Effective Medical Abortion." *Science* 281 (24 July 1998): 520–21.

Ezekiel, Raphael S. *The Racist Mind: Portraits of Neo-Nazis and Klansmen*. New York: Viking Penguin, 1995.

Farrell, Walter. *The Natural Law According to St. Thomas and Suarez*. Ditchling, UK: St. Dominic's Press, 1930.

Finnis, John. *Aquinas: Moral, Political, and Legal Theory*. New York: Oxford University Press, 1998.

———. *Fundamentals of Ethics*. Washington, DC: Georgetown University Press, 1983.

———. *Moral Absolutes: Tradition, Revision, and Truth*. Washington, DC: Catholic University of America Press, 1991.

———. *Natural Law and Natural Rights*. New York: Oxford University Press, 1981.

———, ed. *Natural Law*. New York: New York University Press, 1991.

Fisher, S., and R. P. Greenberg. *Freud Scientifically Reappraised: Testing the Theories and Therapy*. New York: Wiley, 1996.

Fletcher, Joseph Francis. *The Ethics of Genetic Control*. Buffalo, N.Y.: Prometheus, 1988.

———. *Moral Responsibility: Situation Ethics at Work*. Philadelphia: Westminster, 1967.

———. *Situation Ethics: The New Morality*. Philadelphia: Westminster, 1966.

Fogel, R. W., and S. L. Engerman. *Time on the Cross: The Economics of American Negro Slavery*. New York: Norton, 1995.

Forte, David F. *Natural Law and Contemporary Public Policy*. Washington, DC: Georgetown University Press, 1998.

Freeman, Kathleen. *Ancilla to the Pre-Socratic Philosophers*. Oxford, UK: Blackwell, 1962.

———. *Companion to the Pre-Socratic Philosophers*. Oxford, UK: Blackwell, 1946.

Freud, Sigmund. *Civilization and Its Discontents*. Trans. J. Strachey. New York: Norton, 1961.

———. *New Introductory Lectures on Psychoanalysis*. Trans. J. Strachey. New York: Norton, 1965.

Gadamer, Hans-Georg. *The Enigma of Health*. Trans. J. Gaiger and N. Walker. Stanford, CA: Stanford University Press, 1996.

———. *The Philosophy of Hans-Georg Gadamer*. Ed. L. E. Hahn. Chicago: Open Court, 1997.

———. *Truth and Method*. 2nd ed., Trans. J. Weinsheimer and D. G. Marshall. New York: Crossroad, 1989.

Gard, Richard A., ed. *Buddhism*. New York: Washington Square Press, 1963.

Gasman, Daniel. *The Scientific Origins of National Socialism: Social Darwinism in Ernst Haeckel and the German Monist League*. London: MacDonald, 1971.

Gaukroger, Stephen. *Descartes: An Intellectual Biography*. New York: Oxford University Press, 1995.

Gauthier, David P. *Morals by Agreement*. New York: Oxford University Press, 1986.

George, Robert P. *Making Men Moral: Civil Liberties and Public Morality*. Athens: Ohio University Press, 1995.

———. *Natural Law and Moral Inquiry*. Washington, DC: Georgetown University Press, 1998.

———, ed. *Natural Law Theory: Contemporary Essays*. Athens: Ohio University Press, 1994.

George, Robert P., and Christopher Wolfe, eds. *Public Reason*. Washington, DC: Georgetown University Press, 1999.

Geuter, U. *The Professionalization of Psychology in Nazi Germany*. Trans. R. J. Holmes. New York: Cambridge University Press, 1992.

Gibbons, Ann. "A Blow to the Grandmother Theory." *Science* 280 (24 April 1998): 516.

———. "The Species Problem." *Science* 273 (13 September 1996): 1501.

———. "Why Life After Menopause?" *Science* 276 (25 April 1997): 536.

Gilby, Thomas. *Principality and Polity: Aquinas and the Rise of State Theory in the West*. London: Longmans Green, 1958.

Gilman, Sander L. *Freud, Race, and Gender*. Princeton, NJ: Princeton University Press, 1993.

Gilmore, Myron P. *The World of Humanism, 1453–1517*. New York: Harper and Brothers, 1952.

Gilson, Etienne. *Being and Some Philosophers*. 2nd ed. Toronto, ON: Pontifical Institute of Mediaeval Studies, 1952.

———. *The Breakdown of Morals and Christian Education*. Vancouver: British Columbia University Press, 1952.

———. *Choir of Muses*. Trans. Maisie Ward. New York: Sheed and Ward, 1953.

———. *The Christian Philosophy of St. Thomas Aquinas*. Trans. L. K. Shook. New York: Random House, 1956.

———. *The Unity of Philosophical Experience*. New York: Scribner's, 1947.

Goldhagen, Daniel. *Hitler's Willing Executioners: Ordinary Germans and the Holocaust*. New York: Knopf, 1996.

Golomb, Jacob, ed. *Nietzsche and Jewish Culture*. New York: Routledge, 1997.

Goodrick-Clarke, Nicholas. *The Occult Roots of Nazism: Secret Aryan Cults and Their Influence on Nazi Ideology*. New York: New York University Press, 1992.

Gould, Allan, ed. *What Did They Think of the Jews?* Northvale, NJ: Aronson, 1991.

Gould, Stephen Jay. *Full House: The Spread of Excellence from Plato to Darwin*. New York: Harmony Books, 1996.

———. *Rocks of Ages: Science and Religion in the Fullness of Life*. New York: Ballantine, 1999.

Grisez, Germain. *Beyond the New Morality: The Responsibilities of Freedom*. Notre Dame, IN: Notre Dame University Press, 1980.

Grisez, Germain, Joseph M. Boyle, Jr. *Life and Death with Liberty and Justice: A Contribution to the Euthanasia Debate*. Notre Dame, IN: Notre Dame University Press, 1980.

Gross, Jane. "But They Don't Teach Us Any Rules." *The Globe and Mail* (Toronto, ON, 30 March 1993): A12.

Gross, Paul R. et al., eds. *The Flight from Science and Reason*. NY: New York Academy of Sciences, 1996.

Gross, Paul R., and Norman Levitt. *Higher Superstition: The Academic Left and Its Quarrels with Science*. Baltimore, MD: Johns Hopkins University Press, 1994.

Grunberger, Richard. *A Social History of the Third Reich*. London: Weidenfeld and Nicolson, 1971.

Haakonssen, Knud. *Natural Law and Moral Philosophy: From Grotius to the Scottish Enlightenment*. New York: Cambridge University Press, 1995.

Habermas, Juergen. *Justification and Application: Remarks on Discourse Ethics*. Trans. C. P. Cronin. Cambridge, MA: MIT University Press, 1993.

Haller, Jr., John S. *Outcasts from Evolution: Scientific Attitudes of Racial Inferiority, 1859–1900*. Carbondale: Southern Illinois University Press, 1995.

Hallett, Garth L. *Greater Good: The Case for Proportionalism*. Washington, DC: Georgetown University Press, 1995.

———. *Priorities and Christian Ethics*. New York: Cambridge University Press, 1998.

Hamburg, David A. *Great Transitions: Preparing Adolescents for a New Century*. New York: Carnegie Corporation of New York, 1995.

———. *Today's Children: Creating a Future for a Generation in Crisis*. New York: Random House, 1992.

Hanken, J., and M. K. Richardson. Letter to the editor concerning Haeckel's deceptions with respect to embryos. *Science* 279 (27 February 1998): 1288.

Harak, G. Simon, ed. *Aquinas and Empowerment: Classical Ethics for Ordinary Lives*. Washington, DC: Georgetown University Press, 1996.

Hare, Richard Mervyn. *Essays on Religion and Education*. New York: Oxford University Press, 1992.

———. *The Language of Morals*. New York: Oxford University Press, 1961.

Harris, Sheldon H. *Factories of Death: Japanese Biological Warfare 1932–1945 and the American Cover-up*. New York: Routledge, 1994.

Hawkins, M. *Social Darwinism in European and American Thought, 1860–1945: Nature as Model and Nature as Threat*. New York: Cambridge University Press, 1997.

Hayek, Friedrich. *The Constitution of Liberty*. Chicago: University of Chicago Press, 1960.

———. *The Road to Serfdom*. Chicago: University of Chicago Press, 1944.

Hechinger, Fred M. *Fateful Choices: Healthy Youth for the Twenty-First Century*. New York: Hill and Wang, 1992.

Hegel, Georg W. F. *Hegel's Logic*. 3rd ed. Trans. W. Wallace. New York: Oxford University Press, 1975.

———. *Hegel's Philosophy of Right*. Trans. T. M. Knox. New York: Oxford University Press, 1967.

———. *Phenomenology of Spirit*. Trans. A. V. Miller. New York: Oxford University Press, 1977.

Heidegger, Martin. *Being and Time*. Trans. J. Macquarrie and E. Robinson. New York: Harper, 1962.

———. *An Introduction to Metaphysics*. Trans. R. Manheim. Garden City, N.Y.: Doubleday, 1961.

Heisenberg, Werner. *Physics and Philosophy: The Revolution in Modern Science*. New York: Harper, 1962.

Hilberg, Paul. *Perpetrators, Victims, Bystanders: The Jewish Catastrophe, 1933–1945*. New York: HarperCollins, 1992.

Hirsch, David H. *The Deconstruction of Literature: Criticism after Auschwitz*. Hanover, NH: Brown University Press, 1991.

Hitchcock, Alfred (director). *Rope*. Transatlantic Pictures Corporation, 1948.

Hittinger, Russell. *A Critique of the New Natural Law Theory*. Notre Dame, IN: Notre Dame University Press, 1987.

Hobbes, Thomas. *Leviathan*. Ed. J. Plamenatz. London: Collins, 1971.

Hoffman, Paul F. et al. "A Neoproterozoic Snowball Earth." *Science* 281 (28 August 1998): 1342–46.

Holden, Constance. "Controversial Academic Gets the Axe." *Science* 277 (22 August 1997): 1045.

———. "Men Have More Gray Cells." *Science* 277 (15 August 1997): 903, 905.

———. "Wiley Declines to Publish Jensen Book." *Science* 273 (16 August 1996): 877.

Hollander, Paul. *The Many Faces of Socialism*. New Brunswick, NJ: Transaction, 1983.

———. *Political Pilgrims*. New York: Oxford University Press, 1981.

The Holy Bible. Trans. Ronald A. Knox. New York: Sheed & Ward, 1950.

Hook, Sidney. Review of A. Bloom's *The Closing of the American Mind* in *The American Scholar* 58 (1989): 123–35.

Horowitz, Asher. *Rousseau, Nature, and History*. Toronto, ON: Toronto University Press, 1992.

Hume, David. *Dialogues Concerning Natural Religion*. Ed. N. K. Smith. Indianapolis, IN: Bobbs-Merrill, 1947.

———. *An Enquiry Concerning the Principles of Morals*. LaSalle, IL: Open Court, 1938.

———. *A Treatise of Human Nature: Being an Attempt to Introduce the Experimental Method of Reasoning into Moral Subjects*. Garden City, NY: Dolphin Books, 1961.

Igra, Samuel. *Germany's National Vice*. London: Quality Press, 1945.

Inge, William Ralph. *The End of an Age, and Other Essays*. London: Putnam, 1948.

James I (King). *The True Lawe of Free Monarchies: Or, the Reciprock and Mutuall Dutie Betwixt a Free King and His Naturall Subiects*. London: Walde-Graue, 1603.

James, William. *Essays on Faith and Morals*. Ed. R. B. Perry. Toronto, ON: Longmans Green, 1949.

———. *The Will to Believe and Other Essays in Popular Philosophy; Human Immortality*. New York: Dover, 1956.

———. *The Writings of William James: A Comprehensive Edition*. Ed. J. J. McDermott. New York: Modern Library, 1968.

Jefferson, Thomas. *The Essential Jefferson*. Ed. A. Fried. New York: Collier, 1963.

Jenkins, John I. *Knowledge and Faith in Thomas Aquinas*. New York: Cambridge University Press, 1997.

John of St. Thomas. *Outlines of Formal Logic*. Trans. F. C. Wade. Milwaukee, WI: Marquette University Press, 1955.

Johnson, Harold J., ed. *The Medieval Tradition of Natural Law*. Kalamazoo: Western Michigan University Press, 1987.

Johnson, Philip E. *Defeating Darwinism by Opening Minds*. Downers Grove, IL: InterVarsity Press, 1997.

Jones, James H. *Alfred C. Kinsey: A Public / Private Life*. New York: Norton, 1997.

Kaczor, Christopher. "Double-Effect Reasoning from Jean Pierre Gury to Peter Knauer." *Theological Studies* 59 (1998): 297–316.

———. "Proportionalism and the Pill: How Developments in Theory Lead to Contradictions to Practice." *The Thomist* 63 (1999): 269–81.

Kagan, Jerome. *Three Seductive Ideas*. Cambridge, MA: Harvard University Press, 1998.

Kant, Immanuel. *Critique of Practical Reason*. Trans. L. W. Beck. Indianapolis, IN: Bobbs-Merrill, 1956.

———. *Critique of Pure Reason*. Trans. N. K. Smith. New York: St. Martin's Press, 1965.

———. *Foundations of the Metaphysics of Morals and What Is Enlightenment?* Trans. L. W. Beck. Indianapolis, IN: Bobbs-Merrill, 1959.

———. *Groundwork of the Metaphysics of Morals*. Trans. H. J. Paton. New York: Harper, 1956.

———. *Prolegomena to Any Future Metaphysics*. Trans. P. Carus and L. W. Beck. Indianapolis, IN: Bobbs-Merrill, 1950.

———. *Religion Within the Limits of Reason Alone*. Trans. T. M. Greene and H. H. Hudson. New York: Harper, 1960.

Kay, Richard F. et al. "Anthropoid Origins." *Science* 275 (7 February 1997): 797–804.

Kennedy, Sheila Rauch. *Shattered Faith*. New York: Pantheon, 1997.

Ker, Ian. *John Henry Newman: A Biography*. New York: Oxford University Press, 1990.

Kerford, G. B. *The Sophistic Movement*. New York: Cambridge University Press, 1981.

Kerr, R. A. "Biggest Extinction Looks Catastrophic." *Science* 280 (15 May 1998): 1007.

Kevles, Daniel J. *In the Name of Eugenics: Genetics and the Uses of Human Heredity*. New York: Knopf, 1985.

Kimel, Alvin F., Jr., ed. *Speaking the Christian God: The Holy Trinity and the Challenge of Feminism*. Grand Rapids, MI: Eerdmans, 1992.

King, Martin Luther, Jr., *A Testament of Hope: The Essential Writings of Martin Luther King, Jr.* Ed. James Melvin Washington. San Francisco: Harper, 1991.

Kingwell, Mark. "Two Concepts of Pluralism." *Dialogue* 37 (1998): 375–86.

Kneale, William, and Martha Kneale. *The Development of Logic*. New York: Oxford University Press, 1962.

Knox, Ronald A. *Enthusiasm*. New York: Oxford University Press, 1961.

———. *A New Testament Commentary for English Readers*. 3 vols. New York: Sheed and Ward, 1956.

———. *University Sermons of Ronald A. Knox*. Ed. P. Caraman. Montreal: Palm, 1963.

Koertge, Noretta, ed. *A House Built on Sand: Exposing Postmodernist Myths About Science*. New York: Oxford University Press, 1999.

Kretzmann, Norman. *The Metaphysics of Theism*. New York: Oxford University Press, 1997.

Kretzmann, Norman et al., eds. *Aquinas's Moral Theory: Essays in Honor of Norman Kretzmann*. Ithaca, NY: Cornell University Press, 1999.

Kries, Douglas. "On Leo Strauss's Understanding of the Natural Law Theory of Thomas Aquinas." *The Thomist* 57 (1993): 215–32.

Kuehl, Stefan. *The Nazi Connection: Eugenics, American Racism, and German National Socialism*. New York: Oxford University Press, 1994.

Lambert, L. A. *Tactics of Infidels*. Buffalo, NY: Peter Paul, 1887.

Lang, Berel. *Act and Idea in the Nazi Genocide*. Chicago: University of Chicago Press, 1990.

Langan, Thomas. *Being and Truth*. Columbia: Missouri University Press, 1996.

———. *Tradition and Authenticity*. Columbia: Missouri University Press, 1992.

Langford, Jerome J. *Galileo, Science, and the Church*. 3rd ed. Ann Arbor: Michigan University Press, 1992.

Laqueur, Walter. *Fascism: Past, Present, and Future*. New York: Oxford University Press, 1996.

Larson, Edward J. *Sex, Race, and Science: Eugenics in the Deep South*. Baltimore, MD: Johns Hopkins University Press, 1995.

Laursen, John C., and Cary J. Nederman, eds. *Beyond the Persecuting Society: Religious Toleration before the Enlightenment*. Philadelphia: Pennsylvania University Press, 1998.

Leach, Edmund R. "Humanism." *The Oxford Companion to the Mind*. Ed. R. L. Gregory. New York: Oxford University Press, 1987, 317–19.

Lederer, Susan E. *Subjected to Science: Human Experimentation in America before the Second World War*. Baltimore, MD: Johns Hopkins University Press, 1995.

Lee, Patrick. "Is Thomas's Natural Law Theory Naturalist?" *American Catholic Philosophical Quarterly* 71 (1997): 567–87.

Lehman, David. *Signs of the Times: Deconstruction and the Fall of Paul de Man*. New York: Poseidon, 1991.

Lerner, Richard M. *Final Solutions: Biology, Prejudice, and Genocide*. University Park: Pennsylvania State University Press, 1992.

Levin, Nora. *The Holocaust: The Nazi Destruction of European Jewry, 1933–1945*. Malabar, FL: Krieger, 1990.

Lewis, Clive Staples. *The Four Loves*. Glasgow: Collins, 1977.

Lind, Michael. *The Next American Nation: The New Nationalism and the Fourth American Revolution*. New York: Free Press, 1995.

Lipstadt, Deborah E. *Beyond Belief: The American Press and the Coming of the Holocaust, 1933*. New York: Free Press, 1986.

Lisska, Anthony J. *Aquinas's Theory of Natural Law: An Analytic Reconstruction*. New York: Oxford University Press, 1996.

Locke, John. *An Essay Concerning Human Understanding*. 2 vols. Ed. J. W. Yolton. London: Dutton, 1961.

———. *The Reasonableness of Christianity with A Discourse of Miracles and part of A Third Letter Concerning Toleration*. Ed. I. T. Ramsey. Stanford, CA: Stanford University Press, 1958.

———. *Treatise of Civil Government and A Letter Concerning Toleration*. Ed. C. L. Sherman. New York: Appleton-Century, 1937.

Loving, Jerome. *Walt Whitman: The Song of Himself*. Berkeley: California University Press, 1999.

Lunn, Arnold, and Ronald A. Knox. *Difficulties*. 3rd ed. London: Eyre and Spottiswoode, 1958.

Machiavelli, Niccolo. *The Prince*. Trans. L. Ricci. New York: Mentor, 1952.

Macintyre, Ben. *Forgotten Fatherland: The Search for Elisabeth Nietzsche*. New York: Farrar, Straus and Giroux, 1992.

MacPherson, C. B. *The Life and Times of Liberal Democracy*. New York: Oxford University Press, 1979.

Macrakis, Kristie. *Surviving the Swastika: Scientific Research in Nazi Germany*. New York: Oxford University Press, 1993.

Manent, Pierre. *An Intellectual History of Liberalism*. Trans. R. Balinski. Princeton, NJ: Princeton University Press, 1994.

Margenau, Henry, and Roy Abraham Varghese, eds. *Cosmos, Bios, Theos: Scientists Reflect on Science, God, and the Origins of the Universe, Life, and Homo Sapiens*. LaSalle, IL: Open Court, 1992.

Margolis, Joseph Zalman. "Canons for Objectivist Interpretation." *The Monist* 76 (1993): 494–507.

———. *Life Without Principles: Reconciling Theory and Practice*. Cambridge, MA: Blackwell, 1996.

———. *The Truth about Relativism*. Cambridge, MA: Blackwell, 1991.

Maritain, Jacques. *Antisemitism*. London: Centenary Press, 1939.

———. *Bergsonian Philosophy and Thomism*. Trans. M. L. Andison. New York: Philosophical Library, 1955.

———. *God and the Permission of Evil*. Trans. J. W. Evans. Milwaukee, WI: Bruce, 1966.

———. *An Introduction to Philosophy*. Trans. E. I. Watkin. New York: Sheed and Ward, 1962.

———. *Man and the State*. Chicago: University of Chicago Press, 1956.

———. *Moral Philosophy: An Historical and Critical Survey of the Great Systems*. New York: Scribner's, 1964.

———. *The Person and the Common Good*. Trans. J. J. Fitzgerald. Notre Dame, IN: Notre Dame University Press, 1966.

———. *The Rights of Man and Natural Law*. New York: Scribner's, 1943.

———. *Saint Thomas Aquinas*. Trans. J. W. Evans and P. O'Reilly. New York: Meridian, 1958.

———. *True Humanism*. Trans. M. R. Adamson. Westport, CT: Greenwood, 1970.

Maritain, Jacques, and Jean Cocteau. *Art and Faith*. Trans. J. Coleman. New York: Philosophical Library, 1948.

Marshall, Eliot. "Which Jefferson Was the Father?" *Science* 238 (8 January 1999): 153–54.

Marshall, Robert, and Charles Donovan. *Blessed Are the Barren: The Social Policy of Planned Parenthood*. San Francisco: Ignatius, 1991.

Marshner, William H. Review of Hittinger's *A Critique of the New Natural Law Theory* in *Faith and Reason* 16 (1990): 177–199.

Marx, Karl, and Frederick Engels. *Marx and Engels: Basic Writings on Politics and Philosophy*. Ed. L. S. Feuer. Garden City, NY: Doubleday, 1959.

May, William E. "The Teaching of Theologians from St. Thomas Aquinas until Vatican Council II on the Existence of Moral Absolutes." *Faith and Reason* 18 (1992): 139–80.

McBrien, Richard P., ed. *The HarperCollins Encyclopedia of Catholicism*. San Francisco: HarperCollins, 1995.

McCormick, Richard A. *Ambiguity in Moral Choice*. Milwaukee, WI: Marquette University Press, 1977.

———. *The Critical Calling: Reflections on Moral Dilemmas Since Vatican II*. Washington, DC: Georgetown University Press, 1989.

McCormick, Richard A., and Paul Ramsey, eds. *Doing Evil to Achieve Good: Moral Choice in Conflict Situations*. Chicago: Loyola University Press, 1978.

McGary, Howard, Jr., and Bill E. Lawson. *Between Slavery and Freedom: Philosophy and American Slavery*. Bloomington: Indiana University Press, 1992.

McInerny, Ralph. *Aquinas and Analogy*. Washington, DC: Catholic University of America Press, 1996.

———. *Ethica Thomistica: The Moral Philosophy of Thomas Aquinas*. Rev. ed. Washington, DC: Catholic University of America Press, 1997.

McLuhan, Marshall. *The Medium Is the Massage: An Inventory of Effects*. New York: Bantam, 1967.

———. *Understanding Media: The Extensions of Man*. New York: McGraw-Hill, 1964.

Medved, Michael. "Hollywood's Three Big Lies." *Reader's Digest* 147 (November 1995): 25–29.

———. *Hollywood vs. America: Popular Culture and the War Against Traditional Values*. Grand Rapids, MI: Zondervan, 1992.

Melchert, Norman. *Who's to Say? A Dialogue on Relativism*. Indianapolis, IN: Hackett, 1994.

Menard, Louis, ed. *The Future of Academic Freedom*. Chicago: University of Chicago Press, 1996.

Michel, Laurence. "The Possibility of a Christian Tragedy." *Thought* 31 (1956): 403–28.

Mill, John Stuart. *Autobiography of John Stuart Mill*. New York: Columbia University Press, 1924.

———. *The Essential Works of John Stuart Mill*. Ed. M. Lerner. New York: Bantam, 1961.

———. *On Socialism*. Buffalo, NY: Prometheus, 1987.

———. *Three Essays on Religion: Nature, Utility of Religion, Theism*. New York: Holt, 1874.

Miller, David. "Being an Absolute Skeptic." *Science* 284 (4 June 1999): 1625–26.

Miller, John W. *Biblical Faith and Fathering: Why We Call God "Father."* Mahwah, NJ: Paulist Press, 1989.

Mivart, St. George Jackson. *On the Genesis of Species*. New York: Appleton, 1871.

———. *The Origin of Human Reason, Being an Examination of Recent Hypotheses Concerning It*. London: Paul, Trench, 1889.

Modin, Yuri. *My Five Cambridge Friends*. Toronto, ON: Knopf, 1995.

Moller, David W. *On Death without Dignity: The Human Impact of Technological Dying*. Amityville, NY: Baywood, 1990.

Morris, John M. *Descartes Dictionary*. New York: Philosophical Library, 1971.

Murray, John Courtney. *We Hold These Truths: Reflections on the American Proposition*. New York: Sheed and Ward, 1960.

Murray, Warren J. "The Crisis of Evolution and the Absence of Natural Philosophy." *Philosophia Perennis* 2 (1995): 125–59.

Mussolini, Benito. "Fascismo." *Enciclopedia Italiana, Di Scienze, Lettere, ed Arti*. Ed. Giovanni Treccani, 41 vols. Milano-Roma: Bestetti and Tumminelli, 1929–61, vol. 14 (1932): 847–51.

Narveson, Jan. "An Interview with Jan Narveson." *Cogito* 12 (1998): 93–102.

———. *The Libertarian Idea*. Philadelphia: Temple University Press, 1988.

———. *Moral Matters*. Peterborough, ON: Broadview, 1993.

Newman, John Henry. *Apologia Pro Vita Sua: Being a History of His Religious Opinions*. New York: Longmans Green, 1927.

———. *An Essay in Aid of a Grammar of Assent*. Garden City, NY: Image, 1955.

———. *An Essay on the Development of Christian Doctrine*. Garden City, NY: Image, 1960.

———. *Fifteen Sermons, Preached before the University of Oxford, 1826–1843*. London: Longmans Green, 1909.

———. *Letters of John Henry Newman*. Ed. D. Stanford and M. Spark. Westminster, MD: Newman, 1957.

———. *Two Essays on Biblical and on Ecclesiastical Miracles*. 9th ed. London: Longmans Green, 1890.

Nietzsche, Friedrich Wilhelm. *Beyond Good and Evil: Prelude to a Philosophy of the Future*. Trans. R. J. Hollingdale. New York: Penguin, 1987.

———. *The Birth of Tragedy. The Genealogy of Morals*. Trans. Francis Golffing. Garden City, NY: Anchor Books, 1956.

———. *The Gay Science*. Trans. W. Kaufmann. New York: Vintage, 1974.

———. *The Portable Nietzsche*. Trans. and ed. W. Kaufmann. New York: Penguin, 1982.

———. *Thus Spoke Zarathustra: A Book for Everyone and No One*. Trans. R. J. Hollingdale. Baltimore, MD: Penguin, 1961.

———. *The Will to Power*. Trans. W. Kaufmann and R. J. Hollingdale. New York: Vintage, 1968.

Noonan, John T., and Kenneth L. Winston, eds. *The Responsible Judge: Readings in Judicial Ethics*. Westport, CT: Greenwood, 1993.

Nord, Warren A. *Religion and American Education: Rethinking an American Dilemma*. Chapel Hill: North Carolina University Press, 1994.

Novak, David. *Natural Law in Judaism*. New York: Cambridge University Press, 1998.

Novak, Michael. "Maritain and the Jews." *First Things* 29 (January 1993): 30–35.

Nussbaum, Martha. *Cultivating Humanity: A Classical Defense of Reform in Liberal Education*. Cambridge, MA: Harvard University Press, 1997.

Ober, Josiah. *Mass and Elite in Democratic Athens: Rhetoric, Ideology, and the Power of the People*. Princeton, NJ: Princeton University Press, 1991.

Oddie, William. *What Will Happen to God? Feminism and the Reconstruction of Christian Belief*. San Francisco: Ignatius, 1988.

Oesterreicher, John M. *Walls Are Crumbling*. New York: Devin-Adair, 1952.

Olsen, Paul E. "Giant Lava Flows, Mass Extinctions, and Mantle Plumes." *Science* 284 (23 April 1999): 604–5.

Orend, Brian. "Kant on International Law and Armed Conflict." *The Canadian Journal of Law and Jurisprudence* 11 (1998): 329–81.

Ortony, Andrew, ed. *Metaphor and Thought*. 2nd ed. New York: Cambridge University Press, 1993.

Osler, Margaret J. *Divine Will and the Mechanical Philosophy*. New York: Cambridge University Press, 1994.

Ospovat, Dov. *The Development of Darwin*'s *Theory: Natural History, Natural Theology, and Natural Selection, 1838–1859*. New York: Cambridge University Press, 1981.

Ott, Hugo. *Martin Heidegger: A Political Life*. Trans. A. Blunden. New York: HarperCollins, 1994.

Owens, Joseph. *Cognition: An Epistemological Inquiry*. Houston, TX: St. Thomas University Press, 1992.

———. *A History of Ancient Western Philosophy*. New York: Appleton, Century, Crofts, 1959.

———. *Towards a Christian Philosophy*. Washington, DC: Catholic University of America Press, 1990.

*Oxford English Dictionary*. 2nd ed. 20 vols. Ed. J. A. Simpson and E.S.C. Weiner. Oxford, UK: Oxford University Press, 1989.

Paine, Thomas. *Common Sense and Other Political Writings*. Ed. N. F. Adkins. Indianapolis, IN: Bobbs-Merrill, 1953.

Patterson, Orlando. *Freedom: Freedom in the Making of Western Culture and in the Modern World*. 2 vols. New York: Basic Books, 1991–92.

Pauzer, Joel S. *The Popes and Slavery*. New York: Alba House, 1996.

Pekkanen, John. "The Baby Who Was Born Twice." *Reader's Digest* 40 (June 1996): 55–73.

Pennisi, Elizabeth. "Haeckel's Embryos: Fraud Rediscovered." *Science* 277 (5 September 1997): 1435.

Peters, Francis E. *Aristotle and the Arabs: The Aristotelian Tradition in Islam*. New York: New York University Press, 1968.

———. *Greek Philosophical Terms: A Historical Lexicon*. New York: New York University Press, 1967.

Peters, Heinz Frederick. *Zarathustra's Sister: The Case of Elisabeth and Friedrich Nietzsche*. New York: Crown, 1977.

Phelan, Gerald. *Saint Thomas and Analogy*. Milwaukee, WI: Marquette University Press, 1948.

Pick, Daniel. *War Machine: The Rationalization of Slaughter in the Modern Age*. New Haven, CT: Yale University Press, 1993.

Piel, Gerard. "Natural Philosophy in the Constitution." *Science* 233 (5 September 1986): 1056– 60.

Piore, Michael J. *Beyond Individualism*. Cambridge, MA: Harvard University Press, 1995.

Pittenger, Mark. *American Socialists and Evolutionary Thought, 1870–1920*. Madison: Wisconsin University Press, 1993.

Plato. *The Collected Dialogues of Plato, Including the Letters*. Ed. E. Hamilton and H. Cairns. New York: Pantheon, 1963.

Popenoe, David. *Life Without Father*. New York: Free Press, 1996.

Popper, Karl Raimund. *Conjectures and Refutations: The Growth of Scientific Knowledge*. 2nd ed. London: Routledge and Kegan Paul, 1965.

———. *The Logic of Scientific Discovery*. London: Hutchinson, 1972.

———. *The Open Society and Its Enemies*. Princeton, NJ: Princeton University Press, 1950; 3rd ed. London: Routledge and Kegan Paul, 1957.

———. *The Open Universe: An Argument for Indeterminism*. London: Hutchinson, 1982.

———. *Realism and the Aim of Science*. Ed. W. W. Bartley. Totowa, NJ: Rowman and Littlefield, 1983.

———. *In Search of a Better World: Lectures and Essays of Thirty Years*. Trans. L. J. Bennett. New York: Routledge, 1992.

Proctor, Robert N. *Racial Hygiene: Medicine Under the Nazis*. Cambridge, MA: Harvard University Press, 1989.

Rader, Melvin. *Ethics and the Human Community*. New York: Holt, Rinehart and Winston, 1964.

Rasmussen, David, ed. *Universalism vs. Communitarianism*. Cambridge, MA: MIT University Press, 1990.

Rawls, John. *Political Liberalism*. New York: Columbia University Press, 1993.

———. *A Theory of Justice*. Cambridge, MA: Harvard University Press, 1971.

Redpath, Peter A. *Wisdom's Odyssey: From Philosophy to Transcendental Sophistry*. Atlanta, GA: Rodopi, 1997.

Reilly, Philip R. *The Surgical Solution: A History of Involuntary Sterilization in the United States*. Baltimore, MD: Johns Hopkins University Press, 1991.

Reinhardt, Kurt. *The Existentialist Revolt*. New York: Ungar, 1960.

Rhonheimer, Martin. "Intentional Actions and the Meaning of Object: A Reply to Richard McCormick." *The Thomist* 59 (1995): 279–311.

Ricciotti, Giuseppe. *The History of Israel*. 2 vols. Trans. C. D. Penta and R.T.A. Murphy. Milwaukee, WI: Bruce, 1958.

Rice, Charles E. *50 Questions on the Natural Law*. San Francisco: Ignatius, 1993.

Rice, Madeleine H. *American Catholic Opinion in the Slavery Controversy*. Gloucester, MA: Peter Smith, 1964.

Ritvo, Lucille B. *Darwin's Influence on Freud: A Tale of Two Sciences*. New Haven, CT: Yale University Press, 1990.

Rogers, E. F., Jr., "The Narrative of Natural Law in Aquinas's Commentary on Romans I." *Theological Studies* 59 (1998): 254–76.

Rorty, Richard. *Contingency, Irony, and Solidarity*. New York: Cambridge University Press, 1989.

———. "Does Academic Freedom Have Philosophical Presuppositions?" *The Future of Academic Freedom*. Ed. L. Menard. Chicago: University of Chicago Press, 1996, 21–42.

Rorty, Richard, and Martyn Oliver. "Towards a Liberal Utopia: An Interview with Richard Rorty." *New York Times Literary Supplement* (24 June 1994): 14.

Rosenberg, Alfred. *Selected Writings* [1933–1945]. Ed. Robert Pois. London: Cape, 1970.

Rousseau, Jean-Jacques. *The Social Contract and Discourses*. Trans. G.D.H. Cole. New York: Dutton, 1950.

———. *The Social Contract or Principles of Political Right*. 3rd ed. Trans. Henry J. Tozer. London: Allen and Unwin, 1920.

Russell, Bertrand. *Authority and the Individual*. New York: Simon and Schuster, 1949.

———. *Why I Am Not a Christian, and Other Essays on Religion and Related Subjects*. Ed. Paul Edwards. New York: Simon and Schuster, 1957.

Ryan, Alan. *John Dewey and the High Tide of American Liberalism*. New York: Norton, 1995.

Saari, David J. *Too Much Liberty? Perspectives on Freedom and the American Dream*. Westport, CT: Praeger, 1995.

Sanders, Thomas G. *Protestant Concepts of Church and State*. Gloucester, MA: Peter Smith, 1992.

Sargent, Lyman Tower, ed. *Extremism in America: A Reader*. New York: New York University Press, 1995.

Sarton, George. *A History of Science*. 2 vols. Cambridge, MA: Harvard University Press, 1952–59.

Sartre, Jean-Paul. *Anti-Semite and Jew*. Trans. G. J. Becker. New York: Schocken, 1948.

———. *Being and Nothingness*. Trans. H. E. Barnes. New York: Washington Square Press, 1966.

———. *Between Existentialism and Marxism*. Trans. John Mathews. New York: Random House, 1974.

———. *Existentialism and Humanism*. Trans. P. Mairet. London: Methuen, 1982.

———. *Jean-Paul Sartre: Notebooks for an Ethics*. Trans. D. Pellauer. Chicago: University of Chicago Press, 1992.

———. *Nausea*. Trans. L. Alexander. New York: New Directions Press, 1964.

———. *No Exit and Three Other Plays*. New York: Vintage, 1960.

———. *The Words*. Trans. B. Frechtman. New York: Braziller, 1964.

Satinover, Jeffrey B. *Homosexuality and the Politics of Truth*. Ada, MI: Baker Books, 1996.

Schabas, Margaret. "John Stuart Mill and Concepts of Nature." *Dialogue* 36 (1995): 447–65.

Schall, James V. *At the Limits of Political Philosophy: From "Brilliant Errors" to Things of Uncommon Importance*. Washington, DC: Catholic University of America Press, 1996.

———. *Jacques Maritain: The Philosopher in Society*. Lanham, MD: Rowman and Littlefield, 1998.

Schilpp, Paul Arthur, ed. *The Philosophy of Karl Popper*. 2 vols. LaSalle, IL: Open Court, 1974.

———, ed. *The Philosophy of A .N. Whitehead*. New York: Tudor, 1951.

Schmidt, Alvin J. *The Menace of Multiculturalism: Trojan Horse in America*. Westport, CT: Praeger, 1997.

Scholz, Sally J. "Civil Disobedience in the Social Theory of Thomas Aquinas." *The Thomist* 60 (1996): 449–62.

Schopenhauer, Arthur. *Essays and Aphorisms*. Trans. and ed. R. J. Hollingdale. Baltimore, MD: Penguin, 1970.

———. *The World as Will and Presentation*. 2 vols. Trans. E.F.J. Payne. Clinton, MA: Falcon's Wing Press, 1958.

Seachrist, Lisa. "Lab Rats Still Not Animals." *Science* 264 (10 June 1994): 1533.

Secrest, Meryle. *Frank Lloyd Wright*. New York: Harper, 1993.

Sereny, Gitta. *Albert Speer: His Battle with Truth*. New York: Knopf, 1995.

———. *Into That Darkness: From Mercy Killing to Mass Murder*. London: Deutsch, 1974.

Shain, Barry Alan. *The Myth of American Individualism: The Protestant Origins of American Political Thought*. Princeton, NJ: Princeton University Press, 1995.

Shneidman, N. N. *Dostoevsky and Suicide*. Oakville, ON: Mosaic Press, 1984.

Shook, Laurence K. *Etienne Gilson*. Toronto, ON: Pontifical Institute of Mediaeval Studies, 1984.

Simon, Yves R. *Freedom and Community*. Ed. C. P. O'Donnell. New York: Fordham University Press, 1968.

———. *Philosophy of Democratic Government*. Notre Dame, IN: Notre Dame University Press, 1993.

———. *The Tradition of Natural Law: A Philosopher's Reflections*. Ed. V. Kuic. New York: Fordham University Press, 1992.

Simons, Margaret A. *Beauvoir and the Second Sex*. Lanham, MD: Rowman and Littlefield, 1998.

Skinner, Burrhus Frederic. *About Behaviorism*. New York: Knopf, 1974.

Skvorecky, Josef. *Sins for Father Knox*. Trans. K. P. Henley. Toronto, ON: Lester and Orpen Dennys, 1988.

Smith, Adam. *An Inquiry into the Nature and Causes of the Wealth of Nations*. Ed. John Ramsay McCulloch. London: Ward, Lock, n.d.

Smith, Page. *Rediscovering Christianity: Searching for the Roots of Modern Democracy in Our Religious Past and Present*. New York: St. Martin's Press, 1994.

Sober, Elliott, and David Sloan Wilson. *Unto Others: The Evolution and Psychology of Unselfish Behavior*. Cambridge, MA: Harvard University Press, 1998.

Somit, Albert, and Steven A. Peterson. *Darwinism, Dominance, and Democracy: The Biological Bases of Authoritarianism*. Westport, CT: Praeger, 1997.

Spoerl, Joseph S. "Impartiality and the Great Commandment: A Reply to John Cottingham (and Others)." *American Catholic Philosophical Quarterly* 68 (1994): 203–10.

Stack, George J. *Nietzsche and Emerson: An Elective Affinity*. Athens: Ohio University Press, 1992.

Stark, Rodney. *The Rise of Christianity: A Sociologist Reconsiders History*. Princeton, NJ: Princeton University Press, 1996.

Steiner, George. *Martin Heidegger*. New York: Viking, 1979.

Stepan, Nancy. *The Hour of Eugenics: Race, Gender, and Nation in Latin America*. Ithaca, NY: Cornell University Press, 1991.

———. *The Idea of Race in Science: Great Britain, 1800–1960*. London: Macmillan, 1982.

Stern, Karl. *The Third Revolution: A Study of Psychiatry and Religion*. Garden City, NY: Image, 1961.

Stern, Kenneth S. *A Force Upon the Plain: The American Militia Movement and the Politics of Hate*. New York: Simon and Schuster, 1996.

Stewart, Walter K. "My Sister and I: The Disputed Nietzsche." *Thought* 61 (1986): 321–35.

"Stress Unites Women of the World, Study Says." *Kitchener-Waterloo Record* (5 August 1999): A1.

Stuckenberg, John H. W. *The Life of Immanuel Kant*. Lanham, MD: University Press of America, 1986.

Sullivan, Denis. "Intrinsically Evil Acts: Clarifying a Confused Debate." *Proceedings of the American Catholic Philosophical Association* 72 (1999): 329–40.

Tarcov, Nathan. *Locke's Education for Liberty*. Chicago: University of Chicago Press, 1984.

Taylor, Alfred Edward. *Does God Exist?* London: Macmillan, 1945.

———. *Plato: The Man and His Work*. 6th ed. New York: Meridian, 1961.

Taylor, Charles. *Multiculturalism: Examining the Politics of Recognition*. Princeton, NJ: Princeton University Press, 1994.

Tenner, Edward. *Why Things Bite Back: Technology and the Revenge of Unintended Consequences*. New York: Knopf, 1996.

Thiemann, R. F. *Religion in Public Life: A Dilemma for Democracy*. Washington, DC: Georgetown University Press, 1996.

Thomas, Alfred Barnaby. *Latin America: A History*. New York: Macmillan, 1956.

Thomas, Cal, and Ed Dobson. *Blinded by Might*. Grand Rapids, MI: Zondervan, 1999.

Thompson, Paul, ed. *Issues in Evolutionary Ethics*. Albany: State University of New York Press, 1994.

Thompson, William Robin. Review of W. Coleman's *George Cuvier* in *The New Scholasticism* 39 (1965): 390–92.

Tilson, Charles Everett. *Segregation and the Bible*. New York: Abingdon, 1958.

Tocqueville, Alexis de. *Democracy in America*. 2 vols. Trans. Francis Bowen. Cambridge, MA: Sever and Francis, 1863.

Todd, John Murray. *Martin Luther: A Biographical Study*. Westminster, MD: Newman, 1964.

Toulmin, Stephen E. *An Examination of the Place of Reason in Ethics*. New York: Cambridge University Press, 1960.

Turner, Dean. *Commitment to Care*. Old Greenwich, CT: Devin-Adair, 1978.

Unger, Peter K. *Living High and Letting Die: Our Illusion of Innocence*. New York: Oxford University Press, 1996.

———. *Philosophical Relativity*. Minneapolis: Minnesota University Press, 1984.

Vaihinger, Hans. *The Philosophy of "As If": A System of the Theoretical, Practical and Religious Fictions of Mankind*. Trans. C. K. Ogden. London: Routledge and Kegan Paul, 1952.

Varghese, Roy Abraham, ed. *Great Thinkers on Great Questions*. Oxford, UK: Oneworld Press, 1998.

Veatch, Henry B. *Two Logics*. Evanston, IL: Northwestern University Press, 1969.

Villa, Dana R. *Arendt and Heidegger: The Fate of the Political*. Princeton, NJ: Princeton University Press, 1996.

Vitz, Paul. *Psychology as Religion: The Cult of Self-Worship*. Grand Rapids, MI: Eerdmans, 1977.

Vogel, Cornelia J. de. *Rethinking Plato and Platonism*. Leiden, Holland: Brill, 1986.

Voltaire. *Oeuvres Complètes de Voltaire*. 52 vols. Ed. L. Moland. Paris: Garnier, 1877–85.

———. *Philosophical Letters*. Trans. E. Dilworth. Indianapolis, IN: Bobbs-Merrill, 1961.

Walker, Mark. *Nazi Science: Myth, Truth, and the German Atomic Bomb*. New York: Plenum, 1995.

Wallace, James D. *Ethical Norms, Particular Cases*. Ithaca, N.Y.: Cornell University Press, 1996.

Walter, James J. "Proportionalism." *The HarperCollins Encyclopedia of Catholcism*. Ed. R. P. McBrien. San Francisco: HarperCollins, 1995, 1058.

Warnock, Mary. *Existentialist Ethics*. London: Macmillan, 1967.

Weisheipl, James A. *Friar Thomas D'Aquino: His Life, Thought, and Work*. Garden City, NY: Doubleday, 1974.

West, Cornel. *Keeping Faith: Philosophy and Race in America*. New York: Routledge, 1993.

Westberg, Daniel. *Right Practical Reason: Aristotle, Action, and Prudence in Aquinas*. New York: Oxford University Press, 1994.

Wetter, Gustav A. *Dialectical Materialism*. Trans. Peter Heath. New York: Praeger, 1958.

White, Morton Gabriel. *The Philosophy of the American Revolution*. New York: Oxford University Press, 1978.

Whitehead, Alfred North. *The Function of Reason*. Boston: Beacon, 1958.

———. *Process and Reality: An Essay in Cosmology*. New York: Harper, 1960.

———. *Religion in the Making*. Cleveland, OH: Meridian, 1969.

———. *Science and the Modern World*. New York: Mentor, 1964.

Whitman, Walt. *Leaves of Grass*. New York: Barnes and Noble, 1992.

Wild, John Daniel. *Plato's Modern Enemies and the Theory of Natural Law*. Chicago: University of Chicago Press, 1952.

Williams, David. "The Immutability of Natural Law According to Suarez." *The Thomist* 62 (1998): 97–115.

Williams, George C. *The Pony Fish's Glow: And Other Clues to Plan and Purpose in Nature*. New York: Basic Books, 1998.

Williams, Nigel. "Biologists Cut Reductionist Approach Down to Size." *Science* 277 (25 July 1997): 476–77.

Wilson, Edward Osborne. *Sociobiology*. Cambridge, MA: Harvard University Press, 1980.

Wolterstorff, Nicholas. *John Locke and the Ethics of Belief*. New York: Cambridge University Press, 1996.

Wood, Herbert George. *Why Mr. Bertrand Russell Is Not a Christian: An Essay in Controversy*. London: Student Christian Movement, 1928.

Yolton, John W. *Perception and Reality: A History from Descartes to Kant*. Ithaca, NY: Cornell University Press, 1994.

Zaehner, Robert Charles. *Hinduism*. New York: Oxford University Press, 1970.

Zedler, Beatrice H. "Another Look at Avicenna." *The New Scholasticism* 50 (1976): 504–21.

# Index

## About the Author

F. F. CENTORE is Professor of Philosophy at St. Jerome's College, federated with the University of Waterloo, Ontario. A scholar of note, he is the author of several books and numerous articles. His books include *Persons: A Comparative Account of the Six Possible Theories* (Greenwood Press, 1979), *Being and Becoming: A Critique of Post-Modernism* (Greenwood Press, 1991), and *Confusions and Clarifications: An Introduction to Philosophy for the Twenty-First Century* (1997).

CPSIA information can be obtained
at www.ICGtesting.com
Printed in the USA
BVHW072004020419
544426BV00013B/287/P

9 780313 314124